Marino *saw* the rose, as Adam had seen it in Paradise, and he realized that it lay within its own eternity, not within his words, and that we might speak about the rose, allude to it, but never truly express it, and that the tall, haughty volumes that made a golden dimness in the corner of his room were not (as his vanity had dreamed them) a mirror of the world, but just another thing added to the world's contents.

Jorge Luis Borges, "The Yellow Rose"

The Kantzer Lectures in Revealed Theology

Sponsored by the
Carl F. H. Henry Center for Theological Understanding,
Trinity Evangelical Divinity School

SERIES EDITORS

Thomas H. McCall • Douglas A. Sweeney • Kevin J. Vanhoozer

PUBLISHED

The Election of Grace: A Riddle without a Resolution?
Stephen N. Williams

The God We Worship: An Exploration of Liturgical Theology
Nicholas Wolterstorff

The Election of Grace

A Riddle without a Resolution?

Stephen N. Williams

William B. Eerdmans Publishing Company
Grand Rapids, Michigan / Cambridge, U.K.

Published 2015 by
Wm. B. Eerdmans Publishing Co.
2140 Oak Industrial Drive N.E., Grand Rapids, Michigan 49505 /
P.O. Box 163, Cambridge CB3 9PU U.K.

Printed in the United States of America

21 20 19 18 17 16 15 7 6 5 4 3 2 1

Library of Congress Cataloging-in-Publication Data

Williams, Stephen N. (Stephen Nantlais)
The election of grace: a riddle without a resolution? / Stephen N. Williams.
pages cm
Includes index.
ISBN 978-0-8028-3780-6 (pbk.: alk. paper)
1. Election (Theology) I. Title.

BT810.3.W55 2015
234 — dc23
2014041181

www.eerdmans.com

Contents

Series Foreword

The Kantzer Lectures in Revealed Theology are intended to be the evangelical equivalent of the celebrated Gifford Lectures in natural theology.

The Gifford Lectures were established in 1885 by a generous provision in Adam Lord Gifford's will, in which he stipulated that the lectures be held alternately at each of the four universities of Scotland.

Since their inception, the Gifford Lectures have provided a quasi-institutional, university-based framework for seeking knowledge of God on the basis of science, philosophy, and nature. Taken as a whole, the Gifford Lectures constitute a record of the most important intellectual trends of the twentieth century. However, though Lord Gifford expressed a desire that the lecturers be "sincere lovers of and earnest inquirers after truth," he also stipulated that they treat their subject "as a strictly natural science, . . . that of infinite Being, without reference to or reliance upon any supposed special exceptional or so-called miraculous revelation."

While agreeing with Lord Gifford's premise that all people should benefit from the knowledge of God that "lies at the root of well-being," the Kantzer Lectures begin where the Gifford Lectures leave off: with a sustained focus on the knowledge of God located in God's Word, on the self-presentation of the triune God in the history of redemption, and on its scriptural attestation that culminates in the person and history of Jesus Christ.

It is most appropriate that these lectures in revealed theology take their name from the late Kenneth S. Kantzer (1917-2002). Dr. Kantzer's career spanned the course of the resurgence of North American evangelicalism and was one of the factors that spurred it on. Dr. Kantzer served as professor of biblical and systematic theology at Wheaton College for seventeen years, as Dean of Trinity Evangelical Divinity School for fifteen more, and as editor-in-chief of *Christianity Today.* In 1984 he returned to Trinity, where he eventually became the first director of a Ph.D. program in theological studies. In each of these roles, he was motivated by a heart-felt desire that theology be of service to the church: "Scripture was given to the church, and theology is a necessary work of the church, by the church, in the church, and for the church."

Dr. Kantzer's most important legacy was not a monetary bequest but a divinity school: Trinity Evangelical Divinity School. It was his vision to combine centrist evangelical theological convictions with a commitment to academic excellence. His concern was to help evangelicals major in the majors rather than the minors. In this sense, he was the epitome of the "catholic evangelical." ("The role of church tradition," he once wrote, "is like that of an elder brother in the faith.") He was a model of graciousness who would criticize only after listening charitably. ("Differences are not necessarily contradictions.") He was one of the first evangelicals, for example, to go to Basel and learn from Karl Barth. He completed his Ph.D. at Harvard University, where he wrote a dissertation focused on the knowledge of God in the theology of John Calvin. It is therefore fitting that the lectures that bear his name be located at the institution into which he poured not only the best years of his life, but also his passion, energy, and wisdom.

The Kantzer Lectures speak to what the sociologist Alan Wolfe describes in his book *The Transformation of American Religion* as the "strange disappearance of doctrine in the church." All too often, biblical and theological doctrines have been displaced, discarded, or forgotten in favor of therapeutic, relational, or managerial knowledge drawn less from the canonical Scriptures than from the canon of contemporary popular culture.

The Kantzer Lectures address the crisis of theology in the church. In particular, they confront the powerful, and not entirely unwarranted, prejudice that theology is irrelevant and unrelated to real life. They do this by showing how the knowledge of God derived from revealed theology is indeed practical.

The special focus of the Kantzer Lectures is on the development of doctrine from Scripture and on the ways in which doctrine gives rise to the *lived* knowledge of God. Given the increasingly complex world in which the church now lives, there is nothing more practical, yet elusive, than Christian wisdom. Hence the aim of the lectures is not to add to the church's stock of information — who, what, where — but rather to the church's wisdom and understanding, and hence to the church's witness and well-being. Revealed theology deals not with arcane or obsolete knowledge; theology is no trivial pursuit. On the contrary, as both Calvin and Kantzer insist, the knowledge of God is intrinsically linked with self-knowledge and with knowing how to live well to God's glory.

If evangelical theology has a constructive contribution to make to the contemporary church, it is its passion to root Christian thinking and living in the realities of the gospel of Jesus Christ. To focus on revealed theology is not to bury our heads in ancient Palestinian sand, however, but rather to approach our era's most pressing challenges with the resources of Trinitarian faith. The Kantzer Lectures provide a platform for this kind of Christian thinking, featuring prominent theologians committed to the project of faith seeking understanding, and to making this understanding practical. Hence the remit of the Kantzer Lectures in Revealed Theology: get wisdom; get understanding; get the mind of Christ.

Thomas H. McCall
Douglas A. Sweeney
Kevin J. Vanhoozer

Preface

Out of the depths I cry to you, O LORD;
  O Lord, hear my voice.
Let your ears be attentive
  to my cry for mercy.
If you, O LORD, kept a record of sins,
  O Lord, who could stand?
But with you there is forgiveness;
  therefore you are feared.
I wait for the LORD, my soul waits,
  and in his word I put my hope.
My soul waits for the Lord
  more than watchmen wait for the morning,
  more than watchmen wait for the morning.
O Israel, put your hope in the LORD,
  for with the LORD is unfailing love
  and with him is full redemption.
He himself will redeem Israel
  from all their sins.

Psalm 130[1]

My heart is not proud, O LORD,
  my eyes are not haughty;

1. Unless otherwise indicated, quotations from the English Bible are from the New International Version (NIV).

I do not concern myself with great matters
  or things too wonderful for me.
But I have stilled and quieted my soul;
  like a weaned child with its mother,
like a weaned child is my soul within me.
O Israel, put your hope in the LORD
  both now and forevermore.

Psalm 131

These two juxtaposed psalms serve better than any other two juxtaposed psalms to set the tone for the following brief sortie into the doctrine of election. The first instructs the heart, preparing us for inquiry in the mode of sinners who, discerning their sin, crying out from the depths and believing that God answers them in mercy, contemplate election with the eyes of forgiven and undeserving transgressors. The second instructs the mind, preparing us for inquiry in the mode of creatures whose minds' eye should not be trained too high, not because there is darkness above, but because what it seeks to see lies beyond its perceptual field, in the realm of things "too wonderful for me." Psalm 130 bids those who despair of their sin to wait; Psalm 131 bids those who despair of their ignorance to be at peace. Both conduce to hope and both conclude with the thought of a future in the hands of the God whom to know is to trust. In Scripture, the climactic future is a time of definitive *apocalypsis,* "unveiling." We shall find reason to suppose that this applies to the truth about election.

Meanwhile, pending eschatological disclosure, is election a riddle without a resolution? To ask that question at the beginning of an investigation is to risk starting at the wrong end. If we start at the wrong end, we are liable to finish at the wrong end, perhaps finishing more or less where we started; start with a riddle, without justifying the starting point, and you will likely end either with an unproductive riddle or with the wrong answer. "Only he is an artist who can make a riddle out of the solution," observed Karl Kraus, tempting us to echo with rueful cynicism that only he is a theologian who can turn a solution into a riddle.[2] Karl Barth must be permitted an early intervention to voice his claim that election is the

2. Allan Janik and Stephen Toulmin, *Wittgenstein's Vienna* (New York: Simon and Schuster, 1973), p. 193.

sum of the gospel.[3] Hovering somewhere between talk of riddle and of gospel is Gabriel Marcel's distinction between a mystery and a problem.[4] Without prejudice to talk either of riddle or of gospel, we might provisionally admit at the outset that election enshrines mystery of some kind and to some degree.

> Oh, the depth of the riches of the wisdom and knowledge of God!
> How unsearchable his judgments,
> and his paths beyond tracing out!
> "Who has known the mind of the Lord?
> Or who has been his counselor?" (Rom. 11:33-34)

That is how Paul concludes a sustained treatment of election, and we can scarcely be faulted if we treat his rhetorical climax as our theological a priori. Admitting that it is risky to start out on our investigation with a knapsack purpose-woven in the shape of a question mark and suspending decision on election as the sum of the gospel, we submit that Paul's words supply us with prima facie support for the supposition that election may turn out to be a question whose answer, if it is ever attained, will be eschatological, and brook no premature theological anticipation. It remains to be seen whether or not it should be reckoned something of a riddle until then.

In tackling election, it looks as though we are tackling a peculiarly intractable issue amidst the host of other historically divisive and intractable issues in theology. At the beginning of his study, Paul Jewett observed that "there is . . . something uncommonly persistent about the argument over election."[5] An earlier twentieth-century voice, granting that "the treatment of any doctrine harbors its dangers, and caution is always necessary," proposed that warning was especially in order with respect to the doctrine of election.[6] Although it is worth asking why this is so, if it is so, I shall not

3. As Barth's thought is treated in detail in the appendix, detailed citation of his work is often reserved until then.

4. G. Marcel, *Being and Having* (Westminster: Dacre, 1949), pp. 110-16. In this work, Marcel observed that "we have acquired the execrable habit of considering the problems in themselves, i.e., in abstraction from the manner in which their appearance is woven into the very texture of life" (p. 102). Cf. T. Weinandy, *Does God Suffer?* (Edinburgh: T. & T. Clark, 2000), chap. 2.

5. Paul K. Jewett, *Election and Predestination* (Grand Rapids: Eerdmans, 1985), p. 1.

6. G. C. Berkouwer, *Divine Election* (Grand Rapids: Eerdmans, 1960), p. 7.

be doing so directly in this volume. Chaucer would doubtless have concluded that third-millennium determination to pursue our chosen quarry is a sign that theologians are even more hopelessly incorrigible than are philosophers in their search for the stone that turneth all to gold. "Ask any scholar of discerning; / He'll say the Schools are filled with altercation / On this vexed matter of predestination / Long bandied by a hundred thousand men. How can I sift it to the bottom then?"[7] Better not try to sift it nor even to provoke an early quarrel about the casual elision of "election" and "predestination," unless you have nothing else to do on the road to Canterbury.

Given the longevity and perdurability of the debate, what can we reasonably hope to achieve in yet another inquiry? Is there not something bordering on the tragicomical in the supposition that someone should aspire to say something fresh, helpful, and illuminating on this subject, certainly in public? "Ambition is the death of thought."[8] Nonetheless, two associated factors informed the attempt to investigate the doctrine of election which here sees the light of day. The first was the suspicion that the unresolved persistence of the relevant cluster of questions, particularly when Scripture was regularly used as a court of appeal on opposing sides, was due to the fact that there was something wrong with the way the whole problematic was set up. Struggling to come to terms with her theological background, Harriet Beecher Stowe exclaimed: "There must be a dreadful mistake somewhere," and, working through her struggles, her renewed verdict was unchanged: "There must be a dreadful mistake somewhere."[9] Perhaps "dreadful" is too dramatic a descriptor to apply in the present case, but dispassionate scrutiny of the debate on election surely compels the theologian to keep an open mind as to whether Stowe's sentiment has potential for transplantation.

The second factor was a perceived need to consider seriously the diagnosis of and remedy for the deadlocked condition of the Calvinist-Arminian debate which Charles Simeon offered early in the nineteenth century, and to bring this into line with a fundamental and familiar proposal made by Ludwig Wittgenstein. For reasons which emerge at the end of this volume, it turns out that Simeon features more visibly in the following discussion than does Wittgenstein. If, in the course of this volume,

7. Chaucer, "The Nun's Priest's Tale," in *The Canterbury Tales* (Harmondsworth and New York: Penguin, 1977), p. 243.

8. Ludwig Wittgenstein, *Culture and Value,* ed. G. H. von Wright (Oxford: Blackwell, 1980), p. 27.

9. Quoted by Mark Noll, *America's God: From Jonathan Edwards to Abraham Lincoln* (New York and Oxford: Oxford University Press, 2002), p. 327.

I succeed in making Simeon's proposals lively, I (truly!) shall not ask for much more.[10] If reference to the Calvinist-Arminian debate provokes a weary sigh or audible groan in the reader, it is more than understandable; not only can I sympathize, I can join. How can such a (portended) focus be justified in the post-Barthian dogmatic times in which we live? More importantly, even if we decide that Barth has not successfully or satisfactorily advanced the discussion very much, is it right to sail by Christopher Wright's warning in his valuable and detailed study *The Mission of God*? "Between election in the Hebrew Scriptures of Jesus and election in the formulations of theological systems there sometimes seems to be a great gulf fixed. Few and narrow are the bridges from one to the other."[11] Well, our study begins with the Old Testament and ends with an appendix on Barth. I hope that, by the time we are through with a survey of the biblical materials, it will be clear why Simeon's concerns remain ours. In recent conversation, two leading biblical scholars, theologians of fine quality, to boot, who believe in the need for dogmatic reorientation on the question of election, have expressed to me perplexity in connection with New Testament predestination. As a matter of fact, my interest in Simeon lies more in connection with theological method in general than in his specific involvement in the Calvinist-Arminian debate, although these two things are inseparable in his thought and that particular debate was the occasion of his remarks and even contributed causally to his thinking on method.

I prelude the following piece in the key of lament and hereby post the wailing proposition that the systematic theologian is the least secure of all creatures operating within the subject-domain called "theology," or, if not insecure, a creature who has purchased his or her security at the price of avoidance. He — let me keep the masculine pronoun as a concession to those who will wonder if the following is simply self-absorbed and self-referential — cannot give his time to and may lack the competence for the detailed study and exegesis of Old and New Testaments on whose

10. Elements in the argument set out in chapter 3 in connection with Simeon are anticipated in Stephen Williams, "Observations on the Future of System," in *Always Reforming: Explorations in Systematic Theology,* ed. A. T. B. McGowan (Leicester: Apollos, 2006), pp. 41-66. The other figure who occupies a significant place in that essay, G. C. Berkouwer, comes in for no sustained attention in the present volume. This is a bit puzzling; possibly the author of the present volume is taking small-minded revenge on Berkouwer for ending, rather than starting, his book *Divine Election* with the Old Testament.

11. Christopher J. H. Wright, *The Mission of God: Unlocking the Bible's Grand Narrative* (Nottingham: Inter-Varsity Press, 2006), p. 262.

foundation he seeks to build. He cannot give his time to and may lack the competence for the detailed philosophical adumbration of logical argument whose rigor he seeks to incorporate. Historians shake their heads at his lack of learning; missiologists and practical theologians wait skeptically to see if anything relevant will emerge; radicals and postmoderns will not even bother to watch his antics nine-tenths of the time, save with the semicurious gaze of the cultural anthropologist. Has any creature comparable to the dogmatic or systematic theologian ever appeared on planet earth — the only character on the scholarly scene who manifestly lacks the competence to fulfill his or her assigned responsibility, the devil's walking parody on all two-footed things?[12]

The following chapters will give ample cause for readers to conclude that their author is a fully signed-up member of this sorry troupe. On the one hand, Scripture is my authority and exegesis my guide in what follows, but I shall not be able to devote proper attention to any one biblical text. On the other, the rigorous requirements of analytic philosophical argument cannot be met in the space at my disposal. Hence, reasons for reading Scripture in one way rather than another will be indicated without offering a detailed defense, and reasons for adopting one theological position rather than another will be indicated without providing a detailed demonstration. Treatment of historical theology will be amazingly thin, and the distribution of material in practical theology will be gloriously uneven. What, then, remains in the shrunken effort that follows, except evidence that the writer needs to get out a bit more? Perhaps that fine novelist and observer of humanity, Thomas Hardy, will help to preserve authorial dignity: "Limitation, and not comprehensiveness, is needed for striking a blow."[13] Or there is Leibniz: "It is in limitation that the master primarily displays himself."[14] It is better to resist such specious defenses and pretentious descriptions of what follows and simply say that this book constitutes an attempt to limn — and no more than that — a theological approach to election in stark dogmatic outline. As Austin Farrer put it in a volume which covers material relevant to my concerns, but is omitted from

12. Some readers will recognize here an adaptation of G. K. Chesterton's words in his poem "The Donkey."

13. *Far from the Madding Crowd* (London and New York: Penguin, 1994), p. 250.

14. This is admittedly a rather pedantic rendering of "In der Beschränkung zeigt sich erst der Meister," picked up from and quoted without attribution by P. T. Forsyth in *The Person and Place of Jesus Christ* (London: Hodder and Stoughton, 1909), p. 67, but found in Leibniz, *Philosophical Papers and Letters* (Chicago: University of Chicago Press, 1969), p. 10.

my discussion: "I would rather, if I dared to hope it, provide materials for an exercise in understanding, than formalize a chain of argument."[15] Philip Doddridge bequeaths to us a rubric for the whole study: "If I err, I would choose to do it on the side of modesty and caution, as one who is more afraid of doing wrong than of not doing right."[16]

In short, constraints of space mean that no pretense is made of justifying everything for which I contend; what the reader will encounter is often more the description than the adumbration of a particular argument; theological assumptions or disclaimers as to the possibility of pursuing this or that trail powder the ensuing treatment. Were it not for human nature, these assurances should make for a mighty relaxed company of readers. Such a company should settle down tranquilly in the conviction that it need feel not the least pressure to change its position on anything, on the grounds that my essay makes no pretense to producing the arguments needed to secure its conclusions.

However, we should not expect the dove of peace to descend amongst us. If we confine ourselves, for a moment, to self-styled evangelical North American exchanges, we note how sharp the conflict is in relation to the doctrine of election *(inter alia)*. Some years ago, five contributors, adopting different positions, debated election.[17] In the course of reading, one's attention is liable to shift, at an early stage, from the content of the positions argued for to the form the argument takes. One of the contributors rightly identifies the difficulty attending the discussion, which lies not so much in theological disagreement as in the fact that a given protagonist is prone to judge that the other misses the *clear* teaching of Scripture.[18] This contributor himself rejects classical Calvinism and Arminianism alike. He realizes that his interlocutors will take him, too, to be rejecting "clear" teaching, yet he cannot but express his own bewilderment at others' doubt that he is representing "Paul's clear, systematic and all-pervasive teaching" on the heart of the matter at hand.[19] Nevertheless, he knows that others will be bewildered that he should be bewildered.

15. Austin Farrer, *Faith and Speculation: An Essay in Philosophical Theology* (Edinburgh: T. & T. Clark, 1967), p. vi.

16. Quoted in Alan C. Clifford, *The Good Doctor: Philip Doddridge of Northampton; A Tercentenary Tribute* (Norwich: Charenton Reformed Publishing, 2002), p. 133.

17. Chad Brand, ed., *Perspectives on Election: Five Views* (Nashville: Broadman and Holman, 2006).

18. Brand, *Perspectives on Election,* p. 138.

19. Brand, *Perspectives on Election,* p. 142.

A reader's attention may then shift a second time, this time to the tone. Contributors go beyond frequent expressions of astonishment that others cannot see what is clear, to very strong indictments of each other.[20] Not all are guilty of this; one is noticeably more restrained than the others. The upshot is that the North American evangelical scene alone gives pause for thought to anyone who proposes to sidle in coyly with what might be regarded as a sixth view — and, in counting, we have not begun to train our eyes outside this particular constituency. In the preface to his *Treatment concerning the Religious Affections,* Jonathan Edwards observed: "I am sensible it is much more difficult to judge impartially of that which is the subject of this discourse, in the midst of the dust and smoke of such a state of controversy as this land is now in about things of this nature," adding: "As it is more difficult to write impartially, so it is more difficult to read impartially."[21] If that is how it is when discussion is carried out amongst theologians who state unreserved commitment to the full authority of Scripture and make good that commitment by seeking to ground the essentials of their positions in *sola Scriptura,* it is hard to know how one can make effective headway on the wider scene.

Of course, perhaps we just have to be tough-minded and thick-skinned about the whole affair. If you find the kitchen too hot, don't go in. Why is it so hot? How should we interpret the intraevangelical dispute, not only in its own right, but for the benefit of the wider theological scene? Sticking with the volume cited, I think it is no exaggeration to say that, on the authors' own terms, we have three or four rival versions of Christianity here. Is it basically an exegetical dispute? Obviously it is, in part. However, the disagreement cannot be analyzed simply in exegetical terms. The relevant exegetical exchanges remind me of the first football (soccer) match in which our second son proudly took part in an Oxfordshire village at the age of six. What was lacking in the quality of football was more than made good in the quality of entertainment. Apart from the two rival goalkeepers, who were dividing their attention between trying to figure out what exactly was going on in the midfield skirmish and musing absently on the Great Issues of Life, what you saw on the pitch was two groups of ten small

20. Far from regarding all this as a cause of consternation, the editor celebrates the exchange as an exciting theological banquet, a "treat." Brand, *Perspectives on Election,* p. xi. I have deliberately refrained from naming names because that will only stoke up fires unnecessarily, but, of course, they are easily checked.

21. *Works of Jonathan Edwards,* vol. 2, *Religious Affections* (New Haven: Yale University Press, 1959), p. 84.

children crowded around the ball, trying to kick it. As the ball cannoned off unpredictably in all directions, the two combatant formations scuttled around the pitch like a flock of seagulls at the seaside on a summer afternoon, competing for a coveted piece of bread. Just so, in exegetical debate, the battle moves on text by text, skirmish by skirmish. I am not for a moment demeaning or ridiculing the exegetical task or those who participate in it. That would be self-defeating as well as impious because I regard the exegetical task as theologically foundational and should wish to participate in it, along with everybody else, though as one less qualified than many. However, what the lads in that game obviously needed was some order and structure to their play, and what we theologians need to engage in fruitful exegetical debate, particularly when trying to interpret a theme stretching over the whole of Scripture, is obviously some robust rules of engagement.

Are differences better identified and addressed at the level of hermeneutics? It is true that the wider hermeneutical task is foundational to the more narrowly exegetical task it frames. Yet, are differences any less intractable on the hermeneutical level than they are on the exegetical level? We should certainly profit from meticulously examining competing hermeneutical frameworks in both the age-old and the contemporary debates over election. Whether we should end up with a less colorful and more controlled version, on the hermeneutical level, of the exegetical tussle, I am not sure. However, the intraevangelical debate is characterized by a feature that is more striking and more disturbing than hermeneutical differences, and this applies a fortiori to the wider debate. We have in mind divergences in the way in which God is understood and portrayed. This is disturbing even more than it is striking. Picture it: an experienced Christian steeps himself or herself in Scripture; strives for purity of heart and not just clarity of mind; prays, as well as studies, diligently. Then, in a theological essay emanating from the place of prayer and study, she or he depicts the face of God as it appears to be depicted on the Bible's pages. Another theologian, no less experienced, steeped, striving, praying, and studying, does the same. They compare portraits. Not only are they vastly different. Each does not see how on earth the other can get that portrait out of Scripture. Worse: they do not like each other's pictures at all. "It is a frightful child of a comely parent, with just enough family likeness to make one avert the face in dread," said one commentator on the theology of Nathanael Emmons.[22] Multiply the number of theologians beyond two. It is

22. *Princeton Review* 14, no. 4 (October 1842): 69.

not just that others' portraits are deemed lacking in the quality of truthful representation. The flawed artist is deemed lacking in any sense of divine beauty. In a bleak moment, we might first succumb to an older translation of a Pauline text which represents us as seeing "through a glass, darkly" (1 Cor. 13:12) and then wonder whether Paul's "enigma" (as the Greek has it) was ever supposed to license the production of a number of allegedly grotesque alternatives with which we must willingly put up in the church prior to the eschaton.

Keeping in mind Paul's commendation of that charity with which he surrounds his reference to the "enigma," we must surely be haunted by the question of whether we can all be worshiping the same God. If the face of Jesus Christ is the face of God, do we have not only one Jesus and many Christs, as Don Cupitt suggested long ago, but also many Jesuses?[23] Borges wrote: "Diodorus Siculus tells the story of a god that is cut in pieces and scattered over the earth. Which of us, walking through the twilight . . . has never felt that we have lost some infinite thing. . . . Some feature of the crucified face may lurk in every mirror; perhaps the face died, faded away, so that God might be all faces . . . ?"[24] If these words dismay foes of theological or religious pluralism, its defenders will point out that it is better to conjure up a scene of dispersal than a specter of distortion. Is this not a more felicitous prospect than the prospect of mutual recrimination?[25] Does postmodernity meet us at the end of the road, after all?

For myself, I hope and believe not, and accordingly throw my hat in the ring. This volume started life as the Kantzer Lectures given at Trinity Evangelical Divinity School, Trinity International University, Deerfield, Illinois. Six lectures were delivered there in 2009, warts and all, but the material is now presented in a different order. As the lectures have been considerably expanded as well as revised for publication, there is doubtless

23. Don Cupitt, "One Jesus, Many Christs," in *Christ, Faith, and History: Cambridge Studies in Christology,* ed. S. W. Sykes and J. P. Clayton (Cambridge: Cambridge University Press, 1972), pp. 131-44.

24. Jorge Luis Borges, "*Paradiso* XXXI, 108," in *Collected Fictions* (New York: Penguin, 1999), p. 316.

25. In this context, Borges's reference to dismemberment may be compared with Arminius's allusion over four centuries ago to a "young lady, mentioned by Plutarch, who was addressed by a number of suitors; and when each of them found that she could not become entirely his own, they divided her body into parts, and thus not one of them obtained possession of her whole person. This is the nature of discord, to disperse and destroy matters of greatest consequence." "On Reconciling Religious Dissensions among Christians," in Jacobus Arminius, *Works,* vol. 1 (London, 1825), p. 388.

an accumulation of warts, which I can only hope does not amount to a plague. The week spent in Deerfield giving the lectures was most pleasurable, and memories of the occasion, both on and off campus, in academic and nonacademic contexts, flood back in a merry tide, as this volume (finally!) goes to print. I received outstanding and warm hospitality from a number of people, but I want to thank two in particular. Kevin Vanhoozer chaired the lectures with his customary combination of graciousness and vivacity, exercising his ability both to restrain himself patiently and to offer the occasional and well-judged provocative challenge. Doug Sweeney, then director of the Carl Henry Center, gave consistent support and encouragement, keeping himself in the background, as far as he was concerned, but moving swiftly to the foreground, as far as any help to the lecturer was concerned. Thanks, gentlemen, for your patience with the delay in producing this manuscript.

Above all, I must thank my wife, Susan, for her characteristic and unfailing support through the process of writing this book. It is only exegetical conscience which prevents me from dedicating this volume *eklektē kuria kai tois teknois autēs, hous egō agapō en alētheia* (2 John 1).

CHAPTER ONE

Election in the Old Testament

The Story

Walter Brueggemann has complained about Rudolf Bultmann's "unfortunate articulation" of the history of Israel as a "history of failure."[1] If Brueggemann simply meant that the form of articulation was unfortunate, his complaint was in order, but it would be unfortunate if the phrase "history of failure" were regarded as exceptionable. It doubtless has the ring of political incorrectness about it, even if it correctly summarizes Israel's political fortunes, and we may not be persuaded by Bultmann's reasons for arriving at his judgment. Bultmann held that Israel had been seduced into identifying God's eschatological activity with what happened in history.[2] Nevertheless, he got his conclusion right, and others who differ theologically both from Bultmann and from each other — from H. H. Rowley to N. T. Wright — have come up with similar formulations.[3] The most detailed study known to me of election in the Old Testament is that of Horst Dietrich Preuss, who, writing when it looked as though the sun were setting on the day of classic Continental "Old Testament theologies," constructed his whole OT theology specifically on the base of election. Preuss

1. W. Brueggemann, *Theology of the Old Testament: Testimony, Dispute, Advocacy* (Minneapolis: Fortress, 1997), p. 212 n. 110.

2. See Rudolf Bultmann, "Prophecy and Fulfilment," in *Essays on Old Testament Interpretation,* ed. Claus Westermann (London: SCM, 1960), p. 75, and "The Significance of the Old Testament for the Christian Faith," in *The Old Testament and Christian Faith,* ed. B. W. Anderson (London: SCM, 1964), pp. 8-35.

3. These are the two names picked out in this (general) context by Joel Kaminsky, *Yet I Loved Jacob: Reclaiming the Biblical Concept of Election* (Nashville: Abingdon, 2007), p. 174.

approved of Gerstenberger's observation that "the failure of the people of God is a theme of the OT to the same extent that their election is."[4]

Failure is neither a judgment extrapolated from the Old in the light of a normative New Testament nor a judgment on Israel offered from outside Israel. The OT (or Hebrew Bible) is often castigated for its arrogant religious exclusiveness, menacing a world which would have been better off without it, even if not quite bathed in Elysian tranquillity and benign toleration if left to itself.[5] Does any other scripture belonging to any other world religion tell a story so devastatingly against its own people as does the OT? Preuss's words, apropos of Israel's self-description as a slave in the land of Egypt, warrant extended application: "This manner of argumentation is seldom found in the history of religions and is relatively atypical for a nation's perception of its own history, if not actually unique. A nation does not normally describe its early history in negative terms."[6]

> "You only have I chosen
> of all the families of the earth;
> *therefore* I will punish you
> for all your sins,"

announces Amos, declaring the implications of election (3:2; obviously, my italics). Israel's failure was chillingly sealed in 2 Kings 17:18 when the Lord "removed them [the people of Israel] from his presence" into exile. In diachronic coordination that is all too precise, Judah eventually follows, forcing the books of Kings to close with a scene that is none too hopeful or edifying, featuring King Jehoiachin reduced to listening for the dinner gong before getting stuck into his victuals at the table of Evil-Merodach in Babylon (2 Kings 25:30).

Yet, if we follow the order of the OT and not that of the Hebrew Bible and read the narrative on through the books of Chronicles, Ezra, and Nehemiah, we end on a different note. 2 Chronicles concludes as aston-

4. H. D. Preuss, *Old Testament Theology,* vol. 2 (Louisville: Westminster John Knox, 1996), p. 144. Because of the immense detail into which Preuss goes, which exposes the skimpiness and selectivity of my treatment of election in this chapter, I make regular reference to his work.

5. I distinguish between the Hebrew Bible and the OT according to the order of the canonical books. This means that, unless attention is specifically drawn to one order rather than the other, the designations are standardly interchangeable.

6. Preuss, *Old Testament Theology,* 2:297.

ishingly as 2 Kings ends dismally. "This is what Cyrus king of Persia says: 'The LORD, the God of heaven, has given me all the kingdoms of the earth and he has appointed me to build a temple for him at Jerusalem in Judah. Anyone of his people among you — may the LORD his God be with him, and let him go up'" (2 Chron. 36:23). Behind Cyrus was the Lord himself, who moved his heart to make this "proclamation throughout his realm and to put it in writing" (36:22). In Ezra and Nehemiah, there is a resettlement of a Jewish community centered on Jerusalem, one whose prospects, as we come to the end of the narrative, are by no means hopeless, though Ezra's prayer reveals him to be the perfect realist (Ezra 9:6-15). The turn of events at the close of Chronicles in its own way keeps Bultmann's judgment intact, for the manner of the exiles' return and the consequent possibility of rebuilding the temple actually highlight more than mitigate Israel's failure; after all, it is *Cyrus* who is particularly instrumental in God's hand. In case we have not fully grasped this point, it is repeated and even expanded at the beginning of Ezra (1:2-3), and for the benefit of third-millennium punters whose main interest lies in how projects are funded, Ezra also reports Cyrus's declaration that "the costs [of temple rebuilding] are to be paid by the royal treasury" (6:4). The bold thought might cross even the untutored reader's mind that Cyrus has momentarily assumed the Davidic/Solomonic mantle, but a still bolder word is heard from the lips of Isaiah. Cyrus is God's anointed, whose right hand God has taken hold of (Isa. 45:1), a veritable Gentile Messiah, it would seem.[7] Salvation is apparently of the Gentiles.[8]

If we have followed the OT narrative(s) up to this point, what is most surprising in this turn of events is not that the Gentiles have some *interest* in the temple and the salvation of God's people. Rather, it is their *involvement* in the deliverance and flowering of Israel to the point of temple reconstruction. Presumably, the tabernacle in the wilderness was built partly of materials provided by the Egyptians — willingly, but somewhat unwittingly — when Israel fled Egypt. However, the building itself was surely the work of Israelite hands. With Solomon's temple, we have Solomon's

7. Preuss reiterates these points in *Old Testament Theology,* 2:75, 94, 254, though Gerhard von Rad, for example, thought that this interpretation woodenly missed the biblical author's "rousing rhetorical exaggeration." Von Rad, *Old Testament Theology,* vol. 2 (London: SCM, 1975), p. 244. Preuss rightly challenges this in 2:341 n. 200.

8. Although a comparison of the accounts of Chronicles and Kings enables us to see the overall picture from different angles, their variation in presentation and emphasis does not affect my account at this point.

initiative, carried through to execution in collaboration with Hiram, so that the temple is built with Tyre on hire and with Sidonian labor as well. Transethnic collaboration on this scale is one thing, and its significance with regard to Gentile collaboration is somewhat muted by the forced labor conditions under which Hiram's minions apparently worked. Yet, when the building campaign is relaunched later, the temple is rebuilt by kind permission of Cyrus — and that is another thing altogether. Of course, informed that Nebuchadnezzar had seized the articles of the house of God, Cyrus doubtless harbored a prudent and self-preserving anxiety, for which he can hardly be blamed, to see the items restored (Ezra 6:5). However, that does not matter. At this point, what matters is the work of God and not the motives of men, and, in that respect, Cyrus is part of a much bigger scene. When we scan it as far as the eye can reach, the nations are destined to be beneficiaries of Israel's election.[9]

The call of Abraham is in the interest of the nations. Descended from Shem, Abraham was the idolatrous child of God's covenant with Noah, a covenant of extreme breadth, taking in all the earth and restarting a story which had begun with the creation of Adam and ended its first phase in grief and flood, a restart that substituted, though not unreservedly, emphatic blessing for emphatic cursing (Gen. 8:12-17).[10] It was a covenant announced to Noah and meant for Noah and family, but especially meant for the earth. Soon after his introduction into the narrative, Abraham builds an altar, as Noah had done (12:8; cf. 8:20), and calls upon the name of the Lord, as people had done around the time of Enosh, Adam's grandson by Seth (13:4; cf. 4:26). In a further relaunch, Abraham will mediate a unique blessing to the nations (cf. 1:28; 8:17; 9:1-7; 17:6). God's direct, unmediated blessing to his forefathers lay in the background: Canaan, son of Ham, is destined to be a slave of Japheth as well as of Shem, and Japheth is blessed not only with the extension of territory but also with habitation of the tents of Shem (9:27). The language of blessing here precedes its conspicuous use in the case of Abraham (12:2-3).

In his study of election from a Hebrew Bible perspective, Joel Kaminsky proposes that we speak of the elect, the anti-elect, and the non-elect, Japheth occupying the third category.[11] This raises the question of

9. Note too Darius's words in connection with Jerusalem (Ezra 6:12).

10. The command given to humanity in Gen. 1:28, to be fruitful and multiply, is repeated in 9:1. The language of blessing is sustained throughout Genesis, with some variation in its precise form (12:3; 18:18; 22:18; 26:4-5; 28:14).

11. Kaminsky, *Yet I Loved Jacob,* p. 29. Amorites, Moabites, and Amalekites are

whether we should attribute theological weight to the identification of the Japhethites with the Gentiles.[12] Delitzsch's words are still quoted in recent scholarship: "The fulfillment is palpable: the language of the New Testament is the speech of Javan dwelling in the tents of Shem; the gospel is the proclamation of salvation translated from Semitic into Japhetic, and Gentile Christians are for the most part dwelling in the tents of Shem."[13] Whatever we make of this point, Kaminsky's distinction is suggestive and fair, although its significance cannot be fully explored without teasing out (as I shall not be doing) the question of the extent to which membership in the categories is fixed or fluid in the OT. More space is given in Genesis 10 to the Hamites than to either the Japhethites or the Shemites, and this list features the grim presence of Egypt (10:6) and of Babylon (10:10). Grim, indeed; but we recall both the extraordinary passage in Isaiah 19:24-25, where Egypt and Assyria are coupled with Israel, and Jonah's mission to Nineveh, a place specifically mentioned in Genesis 10:11. The "anti-elect" are within reach of God's seeking mercy.[14] Shem, Ham, and Japheth have seventy descendants, while the Septuagint lists seventy-two nations, the number of missionary heralds that Jesus, according to Luke, dispatched (Luke 10:1).[15] The fact that there is surely a strong theological connection here with Joel 3:1-3 and Matthew 25:31-46 may turn out to

---

amongst the anti-elect. Kaminsky holds that "certain postexilic eschatological texts within the Hebrew Bible like Isa 65 begin to move toward a more dualistic idea of the saved and the damned, a move that would eventuate in the loss of the more neutral category of the non-elect" (p. 175).

12. See Victor P. Hamilton, *The Book of Genesis, Chapters 1–17* (Grand Rapids: Eerdmans, 1990), p. 326.

13. F. Delitzsch, *A New Commentary on Genesis,* vol. 1 (Edinburgh: T. & T. Clark, 1888), p. 298. Delitzsch underlined the fact that the Talmud deduces from the Japhetic promise a justification for the use of Greek in public worship. His conclusions continue to draw attention even where they do not carry conviction. See, e.g., Kenneth A. Mathews, *Genesis 1–11:26* (Nashville: Broadman and Holman, 1996), pp. 424-25; C. Westermann, *Genesis 1–11: A Commentary* (London: SPCK, 1984), pp. 493-94. Perhaps there is no theological significance in the fact that the Chronicler selects Javan, along with Gomer, amongst the seven sons of Japheth: Roddy Braun, *1 Chronicles* (Waco, Tex.: Word, 1986), p. 17 on 1 Chron. 1:5-7.

14. This is not to suggest that the lists in Gen. 10 have merely religious and not also sociocultural significance, e.g., in relation to coastal location or city dwelling.

15. Some texts read "seventy" in Luke. For discussion see, e.g., I. Howard Marshall, *The Gospel of Luke: A Commentary on the Greek Text* (Exeter: Paternoster, 1978), pp. 414-15. I agree with John Nolland that Luke "almost certainly uses the number here to anticipate later mission to all the nations of the earth." Nolland, *Luke 9:21–18:34* (Dallas: Word, 1993), p. 549.

have profound eschatological ramifications.[16] Genesis 12:3 flags up three groups of people: first, Abraham's house; second, those who bless him; and third, those who curse him.[17] Nonelect Ishmael is circumcised and blessed and, along with Isaac, buries Abraham, as Esau later joins Jacob in burying Isaac (Gen. 17:20-23; 25:9; 35:29).[18] Indeed, Ishmael, whose own death is also mentioned (25:17), retrospectively looks as though he headed up a shadow Israel before Jacob took Leah and Rachel as his wives, for he fathers twelve sons who are described as "twelve tribal rulers" (17:20; 25:13-16). As God would be "with Samuel" (1 Sam. 3:19), so he was "with" Ishmael (Gen. 21:20).[19] "Ishmael," Kaminsky remarks, "has more markings of election than perhaps any other nonelect person in the whole Hebrew Bible."[20] However, compared to that blessing which Abraham will mediate, we have seen nothing yet. Ishmael is not a child of the Abrahamic covenant.

In light of the first, ninth, and seventeenth chapters of Genesis, the story of Jacob, who subsequently becomes "Israel," stands under the sign of the Abrahamic covenant enfolded within the story of creation and its Noahic relaunching (Gen. 35:11).[21] In time, Israel, the elect, is to be a light to the nations, shining directly or indirectly as far as can be. When Moses provides for the people of Israel a summary account of its own history, purpose, and destiny, he charges Israel to observe carefully the Lord's decrees when it enters the land, "for this will show your wisdom and understanding to the nations, who will hear about all these decrees and say, 'Surely this great nation is a wise and understanding people' " (Deut. 4:6). Centuries on in the life of Israel, we feel the portentous weight of these words. The visit of the Queen of Sheba to King Solomon is actually closer to the peak

16. For Joel and Matthew, see Leslie C. Allen, *The Books of Joel, Obadiah, Jonah, and Micah* (Grand Rapids: Eerdmans, 1978), p. 109.

17. Exceptional and extraordinary as he is, especially after we have reckoned with the letter to the Hebrews, the account of Melchizedek fits into this framework. Cf. Gen. 27:29 and Deut. 7:15.

18. The text also makes a point of saying that Abraham and Ishmael were circumcised at the same time (Gen. 17:26).

19. For the significance of the language of "with," see Douglas K. Stuart, *Exodus* (Nashville: Broadman and Holman, 2006), p. 700 on Exod. 33:12.

20. Kaminsky, *Yet I Loved Jacob,* p. 34. Compare what is said to Hagar (Gen. 16:10) with what is said to Abraham (13:16; 15:5).

21. See Victor P. Hamilton, *The Book of Genesis, Chapters 18–50* (Grand Rapids: Eerdmans, 1995), p. 381, on Gen. 35:11, for a summary of the diversity of people and circumstances to whom and in which the command to be fruitful and multiply is applied.

of the OT narrative than we might immediately suppose.[22] For she is not only bowled over by the external splendor of the court of the king, she responds thus: "Praise be to the LORD your God, who has delighted in you and placed you on the throne of Israel. Because of the LORD's eternal love for Israel, he has made you king, to maintain justice and righteousness" (1 Kings 10:9). Far from being the negative object of the envy of the non-elect, the elect occasion praise from the nonelect to him who elects. The Chronicler allows us to hear Hiram of Sidon utter praise in terms which are in some ways still stronger than those of the queen: "Praise be to the LORD, the God of Israel, who made heaven and earth! He has given King David a wise son, endowed with intelligence and discernment, who will build a temple for the LORD and a palace for himself" (2 Chron. 2:12). We say "in some ways" because the juxtaposition of palace with temple produces a reader's frown. Nevertheless, we remember that "in you," said God to Abraham, "all the families of the earth shall be blessed," or perhaps we should read: "By you all the families of the earth shall bless themselves" (Gen. 12:3 NRSV margin). That God the Creator should act through Israel is a matter of joy to the nations who are open to hear and heed what is happening in Israel. We are surprised only if we have forgotten Jethro and Exodus 18.[23] Indeed, in time, enemies of Israel, like Kedar and Sela, will join in praise for what Yahweh does for Israel in the midst of history; the anti-elect, not just the nonelect, give thanks.[24]

22. I take it that it is appropriate to speak of "*the* OT narrative," although we have not yet moved from Kings to Chronicles. Richard Bauckham rightly warns us against neglecting to think in terms of a plurality of narratives in the OT, but he also allows that "the Bible as a whole tells a story, in some sense a single story, an overall narrative." *Bible and Mission: Christian Witness in a Postmodern World* (Carlisle: Paternoster, 2003), p. 12. At the point at which he issues his warning, he also speaks of an "overall story" (pp. 92-93). This volume is a characteristically excellent brief, "incognito" study of election (p. 84; my word, not his) which engages Lesslie Newbigin's work, as I shall be doing later in this chapter.

23. Observing that the text embodies a degree of tension, Brevard Childs remarks that Jethro, the extra-Israelite priest, "acts throughout the story as a faithful witness to Yahweh. He is not treated as an outsider, nor does he act as one. He rejoices with Moses because of what Yahweh has done for Israel, and offers him praise in the language of Israel's faith. . . . [H]e bears witness to the greatness of the God of Israel by praise, confession and sacrifice." *Exodus: A Commentary* (London: SCM, 1974), p. 329. Doubtless, an element of gladness that Egypt has had its temporary military comeuppance also entered into Jethro's praise, as it did that of Israel. Note that Jethro seems to have been a Kenite (Judg. 4:11), and Kenites will not stand in relation to Israel as did the Amalekites (1 Sam. 15:6).

24. See J. Goldingay and D. Payne, *Isaiah 40–55*, vol. 1 (London and New York: T. & T. Clark, 2006), pp. 238-39. Kedar, it is true, was a son of Ishmael and so included in

Have we bought into a naive and badly untutored reading of the narrative of the queen and Solomon, collapsing the perspectives of Kings and Chronicles and succumbing to an idealism fostered particularly by the latter? I think not. In both accounts, our introduction to the Queen of Sheba lies in narrative proximity to and connection with what is perhaps the high point, certainly *a* high point, of the OT narrative, Solomon's building and dedication of the temple. They provide parallel descriptions. It is in connection with the temple that we learn what it is that elect Israel has to bestow upon the nations. The Queen of Sheba is not introduced to us as a second-class Shemite citizen whose dark-skinned beauty should subserviently pale in comparison with the temple of the Lord God (if such epidermic pallor is possible, and gratuitously assuming her beauty).[25] At first blush, it looks as though she is not simply reduced to receiving the crumbs of wisdom and understanding while the nutritious food is jealously reserved for Israel. Interesting questions surround not only translation but also text and manuscript at this point, but the connection between the dedication of the temple and the arrival of the queen can be made verbally clear in Kings where it is not in Chronicles when Kings mentions, as Chronicles does not, that the queen had heard of Solomon's reputation *in connection with* his allegiance to the Lord God.[26] In both accounts, Solomon's prayer of dedication includes the petition that the "foreigner who does not belong to your people Israel but has come from a distant land because of your name" should be richly blessed "so that all the peoples of the earth may know your name and fear you, as do your own people Israel" (1 Kings 8:41-43). This has been adjudged "possibly the most marvelously universalistic passage in the Old Testament."[27] There is certainly a widespread foreign stirring, if not a universal pilgrimage afoot, where visiting Solomon is concerned (1 Kings 4:21; 10:24). We must presume that the foreigner was to enjoy the richest of introductions to Yahweh, at least as

---

early blessing (Gen. 25:13), but it is surely the geographical, not the familial, significance of Kedar that is to the fore in this context, Kedar marking Israel's far eastern territorial horizon. See John N. Oswalt, *The Book of Isaiah, Chapters 40–66* (Grand Rapids: Eerdmans, 1998), p. 124. Cf. Jer. 2:10; 49:28.

25. On her Shemite roots and problems of identification in Gen. 10:28, see Hamilton, *Genesis 1–17*, p. 345.

26. 1 Kings 10:1; see Martin J. Mulder, *1 Kings 1–11* (Leuven: Peeters, 1998), p. 511. Cf. 2 Chron. 9:1, but see the phrasing in 2 Chron. 9:8-9 alongside 1 Kings 10:9.

27. Simon J. DeVries, *1 Kings* (Waco, Tex.: Word, 1985), p. 126. For God's response, see 1 Kings 9:3.

regards his power, for the "great name," "mighty hand," and "outstretched arm" of 8:42 denote the deliverance from Egypt, and "it is likely that the foreigner's introduction to YHWH was the *Heilsgeschichte,* the liturgical recounting of the deliverance from Egypt, the covenant, and the settlement in Palestine, which had a sacramental significance for Israel."[28] Moses also had juxtaposed to his words about wisdom and understanding, quoted earlier, the hope that the nations would be awed at the prayer life of Israel. If God is exalted in Israel, the exaltation of Israel is the joy of the whole earth. When the refrain which characteristically features in Chronicles — "his love endures forever" — is taken up in Psalm 100, it is preceded by: "Shout for joy to the LORD, *all* the earth" (100:1).

What, then, induces the suggestion of naivete? The answer is: the text itself. Let us stay with the account in Kings. Eschewing relevant and important questions surrounding the textual presence of the phrase that introduces the name of Yahweh in connection with the fame of Solomon as a force that attracted the queen into the heart of his domain (1 Kings 10:1), we must ask: What exactly is it that awes the Queen of Sheba? Material opulence? If so, there are further questions. On what socioeconomic basis and at what human cost was Solomon's wealth acquired? Who exactly are the happy and blessed under his regime (10:8)? No hermeneutic of suspicion is involved in raising these questions; the narrative long before this point has proved to be anything but an unambiguous panegyric to Solomon.[29] The queen's encomium is not, in fact, all sweetness and light (10:9-10).[30]

28. John F. Gray, *1 and 2 Kings* (London: SCM, 1964), p. 209.

29. Amongst commentators that detail a number of points in this connection, see Walter Brueggemann, *1 and 2 Kings* (Macon, Ga.: Smith and Helwys, 2000), and Iain W. Provan, *1 and 2 Kings* (Peabody, Mass.: Hendrickson, 1995). We do not have to invoke, at this point, the supposition that the Queen of Sheba was actually present on Solomon's turf in the cause of a trade mission; we need only stick to the surface of the text. But see Ezekiel's interest in the trading connections between Tyre, Judah, and Sheba (Ezek. 27:17, 22).

30. Volkmar Fritz remarks that this "glorification . . . is not a confession of Yahweh, but only the common acknowledgement of the national deity by the foreign visitor, who realizes the might and good acts of the god in his domain." *1 and 2 Kings* (Minneapolis: Fortress, 2003), p. 118. Whether or not we agree with this, it is certainly true that the queen's reference to Yahweh does not entail a grand obedience on the part of Solomon, which is the means by which the queen comes to understand something of the greatness of the God of Israel. The account of their meeting has to be read alongside the account of Solomon's dedication of the temple with an eye to the fact that he took longer building his palace than building the temple (6:38–7:1). Cf 1 Kings 3:13, expanded in 2 Chron. 1:12. For a different emphasis

The force of these questions and observations can readily be granted; still, the wording of the queen's praise is most eloquent in connection with the nature of God's electing purpose, even if she innocently had no more idea of the full dimensions of the meaning of her words than had the all-but-innocent Caiaphas when he judged it expedient for one man to die for the people (John 11:50). Brueggemann, no fan of Solomon, connects her words with Isaiah 9:7, which speaks of the son on whose shoulder the government will rest and who will establish the Davidic throne with justice and righteousness; they are connected also with the promises of Isaiah 60, when the nations will bring their tribute to Israel, and with the frankincense and gold the Magi brought to Jesus (Matt. 2:11; cf. Isa 60:6).[31] "Thus Jesus, in the wake of Solomon, is the true Jewish king who receives Gentile tribute."[32] Perhaps Brueggemann is right to aver that "we do not know how cunning the narrative is," but surely narrator and narrative encourage us to view the most exalted possibilities in the midst of deeply flawed actualities or deeply flawed actualities in the midst of the most exalted possibilities.[33] Monarchy was fated to be a problem for Israel because the people's faithless clamor was for an institution with a generic problem

---

from mine, see Walter Brueggemann, *Solomon: Israel's Ironic Icon of Human Achievement* (Columbia: University of South Carolina Press, 2005), especially chap. 5 in the context of his whole argument. I grant that the brevity of my account of Solomon means that is not sufficiently nuanced. However, I believe that Brueggemann goes too far in the other direction. It is surely exaggerated to read 1 Kings 10:9 "as though the foreign [i.e., Gentile] queen must instruct the Israelite king in his covenantal obligations" (p. 121). Bruegemann holds that "it is possible to see its [the temple's] construction as an act of royal self-aggrandizement, for it cannot in any case 'contain' YHWH" (p. 121). On that reasoning, anyone's act of temple construction would be judged the product of an unworthy motive. His attempt to interpret the references to Solomon in Mark and Luke in a way that coheres with his thesis is extremely strained (pp. 246-47). In light of the reference to Bultmann at the beginning of this chapter, note Brueggemann's remarks on realized eschatology in Solomon (p. 132).

31. Brueggemann, *1 and 2 Kings,* pp. 134-38. Brueggemann also points out that 4:20-21 echoes, in the form of fulfillment, the promises of Gen. 22:27, 32:17 and 15:18-21 (pp. 57-72). But see Jer. 6:20.

32. Brueggemann, *1 and 2 Kings,* p. 138. In his discussion, Brueggemann also mentions other possibilities for the theological interpretation of the Solomon-Sheba connection.

33. The quoted words are those of Brueggemann again, *1 and 2 Kings,* p. 139. We should add that the final psalm in the second book of Psalms, concluding the prayers of David (72:20), shows us what Solomon might or could have been: an exemplary revealer and herald of the kingdom of God. It is almost unique in its Solomonic reference (the LXX heads it: "To Solomon"), and it is unsurprising that there has been a tradition of messianic reading of this psalm. Sheba appears in the psalm (72:10-15).

attached to it. Samuel knew it (1 Sam. 8:4-18). Even so, Solomon is not portrayed as the hapless or inevitable victim of fate. He could have obeyed Yahweh and, in a measure, redeemed monarchy beyond his own tenure of it by the power of example. By the simple fact that she had heard of him at all, the advent of the Queen of Sheba may well lay bare the truth that Solomon had overreached himself in empire. Nevertheless, once drawn, she should have been in a position to discern something of the true blessing of the people who knew Yahweh. The narrator sets before us both the great promise and eventually — but with the shadow of anticipation early in his reign — the great tragedy of Solomon.[34] In setting forth the promise, the narrative illuminates the purpose of election; in setting forth the tragedy, it strains, in the event, toward what will be the extraordinary dispensation of God when he involves the Gentiles as beneficiaries of Israel's failure.[35] If it is right to say with Berkouwer that the "nature of God's activity is seen uniquely in the establishment of the monarchy in Israel," it may also be true to say that the nature of God's electing activity is seen uniquely in his dealings with the monarchy in Israel.[36]

34. Apart from the clear indications in the text about Solomon's shortcomings, what are we to make of the early description of Solomon as "walking according to the statutes of his father David" rather than according to the statutes of Yahweh (1 Kings 3:3)? The substitution of the human for the divine name elsewhere in the OT portends unrighteousness: see Jerome T. Walsh, *Studies in Hebrew Narrative and Poetry: 1 Kings* (Collegeville, Minn.: Liturgical Press, 1996), p. 73.

35. It seems to me that 2 Chron. 7:20, in its way, actually heightens the tragedy rather than promotes its diminution, precisely because of how Solomon has been portrayed hitherto. His ingratitude now appears all the greater. If the account in Chronicles omits the early warning of God to Solomon recorded in 1 Kings 3:14, the fall of Solomon is equally serious. The stark contrast in 2 Chron. 12:13-14 between Rehoboam and election is a compressed version of the contrast that emerges between Solomon and election. What light is thrown on Solomon when the book ends with the declaration by *Cyrus* (36:23)? What a shadow here falls on Jedidiah, beloved of the Lord (2 Sam. 12:24-25), the one appointed to be a man of rest (1 Chron 22:9)! See Ralph W. Klein, *1 Chronicles* (Minneapolis: Fortress, 2006), pp. 437-39, including his remarks about the echoes of Joshua. Like Isaiah, the Chronicler is not blinded by human idealism in relation to election, but theological realism means grasping the sovereignty of God not just in the midst of it all but at the beginning and end of it all.

36. G. C. Berkouwer, *The Providence of God* (Grand Rapids: Eerdmans, 1952), p. 92. Shortly before giving the specific Kantzer lecture which was the basis of this chapter, I talked with an Ethiopian student who recounted to me the way in which the Queen of Sheba's adoption of monotheism had prepared the ground for the reception of Christianity in Ethiopia. My ignorance of Ethiopian history means that I am in no position to know how exactly the historical evidence stacks up here, but it is a striking indication of the possibilities of blessing for, and not just through, the nonelect in the course of that hidden (from a biblical

Monarchical and Sheban peaks had been long since foreseen from what one (the NIV) translation describes as "rocky peaks" by that most quixotic of extra-Israelite characters, Balaam.

> "From the rocky peaks I see them,
> from the heights I view them.
> I see a people who live apart
> and do not consider themselves one of the nations.
> Who can count the dust of Jacob
> or number the fourth part of Israel?" (Num. 23:9-10)

A threat? Perhaps. But for those in the know, a sign of blessing.[37]

> "Let me die the death of the righteous,
> and may my end be like theirs!" (Num. 23:10)

Such is the personal aspiration of a singular and isolated seer speaking by divine inspiration. When, in a prophecy which is even more dramatic, he beholds the star that will come out of Jacob, Balaam is still operating within the framework of a distinction between Israel and the nations, foreseeing enmity and not blessing. The drama Balaam beholds does not depend on its messianic interpretation: the star Balaam sees is presumably a representation of kingship. At all events, we have two sides of the coin. The elect has arrived on the scene of world history to be a blessing to but also a judgment upon the nations. However, the world is already under judgment, an assumption basically grounding Paul's argument from the outset of his letter to the Romans, so the story of election is the hopeful story of its undoing, even as it brings judgment to expression and to light.[38] Yet

---

point of view) history of the nations ongoing since the days of Solomon. While I have no reason to be historically skeptical about the biblical account of Solomon's kingship, my aim in this chapter is to remark on the theology of election as it emerges in the OT, so my account is relatively unaffected by historical issues which are important enough in their place.

37. The reference to "living apart" may connote the distinctness of election. Cf. Num. 23:11 (and 24:9) with the promise to Abraham.

38. On the universality of judgment, note the especially dramatic imagery in Jer. 4:23-26 and the highly poetic book of Zephaniah (1:3, 18) thematically concentrated on "the day of the Lord." This is not to interpret along these lines all the OT texts which have been taken to indicate an entire world under judgment. E.g., I am not entirely convinced that the "Apocalypse of Isaiah" provides clear evidence of this. See John D. W. Watts, *Isaiah 1–33* (Waco, Tex.: Word, 1985), pp. 315-17.

Israel, too, is judged as well as blessed. Under its sign, the same is true of the nations. The historical dialectic may be complex, but Israel and the nations are distinguished and yet bound together in judgment and salvation.

The Question of Privilege

If both Israel and the nations are subject to God's judgment and salvation within the scope of God's cosmic purposes, and if election is a divine modus operandi that is at the heart of his dealings with his world, why are all the people of the earth not elect? Some may judge the question confused on the ground that "election" is, by definition, selective. That may not be the case, but, anyway, the definition is neither here nor there, for the question is: Why did God not act in relation to all the nations in the way he acted toward Israel? The question is not an idle one. Amos's words are likely to evoke immediate surprise:

> "Are not you Israelites
> the same to me as the Cushites?" declares the LORD.
> "Did I not bring Israel up from Egypt,
> the Philistines from Caphtor
> and the Arameans from Kir?" (9:7)

What is it in the logic of the OT story, if we may put it that way, which makes these words surprising, especially when we read earlier in Amos that "you alone have I chosen of all the families of the earth," and read the dismaying sequel to this statement?[39] Why did God not deal impartially and equally with all the peoples, establishing, from the outset, complete and unequivocal parity between Israel and the nations, if God's election of grace always had the nations in view?

In Christian perspective, the outstanding reason for the election of one nation in the wider purposes of God is foreshadowed in the Old Testament, but manifested only in the New Testament: the deliverance of the human race comes through the incarnate Son of the Lord God himself,

39. This is a good example of a text whose study could take up the whole chapter and whose ramifications must, unfortunately, be ignored. In connection with the citation of Amos 9:7, proper discussion would need to take account of the claim that "[e]lection is not predicated upon exodus." Shalom M. Paul, *Amos* (Minneapolis: Fortress, 1991), p. 283.

necessarily embodied in and inhabitant of one space and time and, therefore, a land and history.

> "The scepter will not depart from Judah,
> nor the ruler's staff from between his feet,
> until tribute comes to him;
> and to him shall be the obedience of the peoples."
>
> (Gen. 49:10 ESV)

This is an extremely difficult text to interpret; " '[u]ntil tribute is brought to him' has been described as the 'most famous *crux interpretum* in the entire OT.' "[40] Jewish interpreters could treat the text messianically via reference to David long before the church applied it to Jesus Christ. At all events, a man must be born of a woman, a woman belonging to one of the peoples of the world; born into a culture, history, ancestry, inheritance. If God's saving way is neither through the universal communication of propositional information nor through theophany, but through the particularity of incarnation, atonement, and resurrection, election can be termed a kind of necessity in order to attain this end. It is a common complaint that election excludes. Actually, however, it is the only means of inclusion, if the goal is the redemptive action of the God-man within history. There is no hope for the world if the Messiah does not grace it with his presence, and no possibility of his coming into it without the prepared and particular connection of nation and of history. This point of view is generally in line with a long tradition picked up by, for example, Aquinas, that the promise of Christ made to the patriarchs was the ground of Israel's election.[41] From this point of view, there is no need to maintain, as Brueggemann does, that "[t]here is a tension between the universal sovereignty (and *providence*) of God, who cares for and presides over all nations . . . and the *election* of God, who focuses on this distinctive people."[42]

40. W. L. Moran, quoted in Gordon Wenham, *Genesis 16–50* (Dallas: Word, 1994), p. 477.

41. In expounding the view that God had bestowed the Law, along with other advantages, on the Jews because he had promised the coming of Christ, Aquinas specifically refers to election: *Summa Theologiae* (1a2ae 98.4), vol. 29 (Oxford: Blackfriars, 1969), pp. 17-21.

42. Brueggemann, *Genesis* (Atlanta: John Knox, 1982), p. 94, picks out particular texts in Gen. 10–11 in this connection. He adds that "proper interpretation requires maintaining the tension, refusing to relax in either direction."

To highlight this divine purpose in election is not to demote what is so plain and central in the OT, namely, the calling of Israel to be holy and to demonstrate holiness, a demonstration of the greatness and even identity of the Lord God himself. Already we read concerning Abraham in Genesis: "I have chosen him," says the Lord, "so that he will direct his children and his household after him to keep the way of the LORD by doing what is right and just" (Gen. 18:19).[43] Nothing is more important for human beings to learn, as the government of the Messiah will show. This point is actually weakened when it is remarked that "[t]he Lord chose Abraham for the purpose of blessing the nations . . . this appointment also included the *intermediary* step of creating a righteous people whose conduct would be a beacon for the nations."[44] Reference to the demonstrative effect of Israel's holiness rather than to Christ's incarnation does not alter the substance of the original question: Why did God not impart his law to many peoples, even bestowing an appropriate, if not uniform, vocation upon many peoples at one and the same time, so that the world should be populated with nomistic theodidacts, people directly taught of God through his law? We appear to be back with our initial christological answer. The concluding portion of Genesis 18:19, not quoted above, indicates that God is carving out the path of promise before prescribing the way of law. Abraham is called "so that the LORD will bring about for Abraham what he has promised him." The promise can be worded in different ways, but the NT refers it to the seed, Jesus Christ (Gal. 3:16). No experience seems religiously higher than theophany until theophany gives way to incarnation and to the possibility of knowing Jesus Christ. Theophany might be universally possible, but it does not save. The particularity of incarnation will.

Election, then, is a kind of necessity to the end of incarnation and reconciliation. However, the language of "necessity" attaching to election has been applied more widely by that most influential of missiologists, Lesslie Newbigin, and it is illuminating to consider this in relation to the

43. The relevant verb here is *yâdaʿ,* a verb occurring with this meaning only here in the stories of the patriarchs. For the wider semantic field germane to "the historical experience of election," extending beyond the prominent *bāchar* range, see Preuss, *Old Testament Theology,* vol. 1 (Louisville: Westminster John Knox, 1995), p. 31. He rightly attends to the event of election, rather than simply to its vocabulary, in order to understand its nature. See also Preuss, 1:181. "Election," as a noun, does not occur in Hebrew, unlike the Akkadian *itûtu;* see W. Zimmerli, *Old Testament Theology in Outline* (Edinburgh: T. & T. Clark, 1978), p. 44.

44. Kenneth A. Mathews, *Genesis 11:27–50:26* (Nashville: Broadman and Holman, 2005), p. 223, my italics.

OT. George Hunsberger has observed that "Newbigin's interpretation of the significance of election stands apart. Rarely, if ever, has anyone else given it the prominence which it has in his mission theology, and for no one else does it hold so foundational a place in the rationale for mission."[45] Newbigin believed that election is "in a sense the fundamental doctrine of the Bible."[46] In no other mission theology does election "appear as the rationale for the mission and the fabric of the forms which missions must take. For Newbigin it is both."[47] I do not know all of Newbigin's writings, but Hunsberger's judgment certainly applies to one of Newbigin's main works, *The Open Secret,* where we read that the doctrine of election "permeates and controls the whole Bible."[48]

Wherein, according to Newbigin, lies the necessity of election, originating with Israel but extending to the church? The necessity is threefold.[49] First, it is required for theanthropological reasons in view of *"the nature and destiny of humanity."* God wants to indicate human destiny in the forms of *anticipation* and *exemplification* within the sociohistorical nexus of interpersonal relationships. The elect must show forth the secret of humanization and lead the way for the world. Second, election is required by the doctrine of God. God is personal and is known in a personal relationship; therefore, he acts in relation to human beings in their particular history, space, and time so that they might respond to his personal activity. This also is revealed through the elect. Third, the way of election is required by soteriology. "Salvation means 'wholeness,' which must include the restoration of social justice and interpersonal relationships. The method of election means that I cannot be made whole apart from my neighbor, on

45. Hunsberger, *Bearing the Witness of the Spirit: Lesslie Newbigin's Theology of Cultural Plurality* (Grand Rapids: Eerdmans, 1998), pp. 82-83. This volume advances the thesis that election is central in Newbigin's thought. In what follows, I draw quite heavily on Hunsberger, although without assuming that his exposition is entirely uncontroversial.

46. Hunsberger, *Bearing the Witness,* here quotes from an essay Newbigin wrote in 1968, "The World Mission of the Church," p. 66. For a comparison of Newbigin with Barth on election, see pp. 85-87.

47. Hunsberger, *Bearing the Witness,* p. 67.

48. L. Newbigin, *The Open Secret* (London: SPCK, 1978), p. 75. Hunsberger remarks of this work: "Among the mission theologies written in this century, Newbigin's *The Open Secret* stands unique in at least this one important respect: it alone weaves a comprehensive purpose around 'election' as the central and dominant thread." *Bearing the Witness,* p. 66. He adds that Darrell Guder's *Be My Witnesses,* itself influenced by Newbigin, may be a partial exception (p. 83 n. 1).

49. For what follows, see Hunsberger, *Bearing the Witness,* p. 103.

whom I have depended for the message of God's reign. . . . The humility required to receive the message from another corresponds to the humility by which the grace of God must be received as a free gift."

If Hunsberger is describing the argument correctly, it is not clear how Newbigin has shown that election is a matter of *necessity.* Sure enough, for God to fulfill his purposes, as Newbigin understands them, it may be necessary for God to *act in history.* Election is obviously one form of historical action. Furthermore, on Newbigin's account, we might even be led to suppose that election is an *appropriate* vehicle for the revelation of God and his ways — "fitting," it might be said.[50] However, the question remains: How do Newbigin's stipulations establish the necessity of the election of one people? It is precisely in order to answer this question that Hunsberger gathers up these three reasons, responding to the question of why there should not be "a pluralism of 'experimental gardens,'" to use Hendrikus Berkhof's language.[51] Yet, the question is not answered. The necessity for particular election is not demonstrated.

The reason Newbigin, on Hunsberger's account, falls short is instructive for our attempt to get to grips with the OT. Newbigin repeatedly states that election is not for privilege but for responsibility and that this applies to the church as well as to Israel. "God chooses men and women for the service of his mission. To be a Christian is to be part of a chosen company — chosen, not for privilege, but for responsibility."[52] The church is in continuity with the people of Israel, who were "bearers — not exclusive beneficiaries" — of a blessing to the nations, and so "again and again it had to be said that election is for responsibility, not for privilege," whether we are speaking of Israel or of the church.[53] "We have to guard against the perversion which regards election as the conferring of a privileged status."[54] Not only, then, is election not for privilege; also, election does not confer privileged status. These citations are all from *The Open Secret,* but the same note is struck in, for example, *The Gospel in a Pluralist Society:* "As the story unfolds [in Scripture], it becomes clear that to be God's chosen people

50. Those who know their Anselm will also know that, when the action of God is in view, the distinction between "fittingness" and "necessity" can get rather subtle: see Michael Root, "Necessity and Fittingness in Anselm's *Cur Deus Homo,*" *Scottish Journal of Theology* 40, no. 2 (1987): 211-30.

51. Hunsberger, *Bearing the Witness,* p. 102.

52. Newbigin, *The Open Secret,* p. 19.

53. Newbigin, *The Open Secret,* p. 34.

54. Newbigin, *The Open Secret,* p. 86.

means not privilege but suffering, reproach, humiliation."[55] Now election is not privilege. Newbigin aims here to close the gap opened up by a putatively unhealthy doctrine of election. This is the gap between Israel and the nations or between the church and extra-ecclesial communities — the gap which positions the elected and nonelected (or rejected) on opposite sides of a gulf. We must definitely avoid favoritism. To stave off this misrepresentation, Newbigin accents the need for a historical demonstration of edifying religious and social relationships in the life of a nation and argues that this is God's purpose in election. He interprets election as necessary in pursuit of that purpose, interpreting it in terms that make it maximally inclusive in its basic intent.

Newbigin certainly believed in and robustly defended the particular christological reason for election too, namely, incarnation and reconciliation.[56] Nevertheless, when he takes the line described above, does not the phrase "responsibility, not privilege," frequently used by others apart from Newbigin, ring rather strangely on the biblically attuned ear? It is certainly true that "privilege" means very different things to different people. We must vigilantly observe the context of its use in order to grasp its meaning. Further, Newbigin himself could speak of "the privileges of those who have been chosen for special responsibility."[57] In Hunsberger's account, there is a steady emphasis on the Indian and Hindu cultural context within which Newbigin characteristically viewed the question of election and its associated themes in Christianity, and there, it is true, the language of "privilege" carries baggage that should certainly make us cautious in using the word.[58]

55. Newbigin, *The Gospel in a Pluralist Society* (London: SPCK, 1989), p. 84.

56. However, Hunsberger distinguishes Newbigin from those who overemphasize this point as the reason for election; *Bearing the Witness,* pp. 97-98. His distinction is between Newbigin and those who do not emphasize Israel's mission in the world, preferring to concentrate on the redemptive-historical line which culminates in Jesus Christ and highlight Israel's place only within that scheme. It seems to me that Hunsberger does not represent the contrasting positions adequately. In particular, I am not persuaded that Oscar Cullmann's treatment of individual faith and election is an example of insensitivity toward "the living relevance for Israel of her election" (p. 98). See Oscar Cullmann's *Christ and Time* (London: SCM, 1962), pp. 217-21.

57. Hunsberger, *Bearing the Witness,* p. 62, words which Hunsberger rather imprecisely glosses as "not so much for privilege as for responsibility." See too Hunsberger's more general remarks on the frame of reference which informs pertinent comparisons and contrasts, on p. 104.

58. Discussion of Christianity with an areligious Japanese acquaintance of mine once stalled because my use of the phrase "the privilege of being a Christian" was misunderstood.

A positive appropriation of the language of divinely bestowed "privilege" easily conduces to its mishandling in thought as well as in action, and it is thoroughly in order to expose unworthy sentiments spawned by what Vriezen called an "infatuation" with privilege.[59] As Spinoza said, opening his treatment of the vocation and election of the Hebrews in the *Tractatus Theologico-Politicus:* "True joy and happiness lie in the simple enjoyment of what is good and not in the kind of false pride that enjoys happiness because others are excluded from it."[60]

Notwithstanding such conscientiously registered warnings, why confine the word "privilege" to its debased or misunderstood sense, contrasting it antithetically with responsibility? It is one thing to say that Israel is not chosen *for privilege,* though we should scrutinize that statement rather carefully, and I neither accede to nor challenge it for a moment. It is another thing to say that the choice *itself* does not bestow privilege. "You are a people holy to the LORD your God," we read in one of the great election manifestos of Scripture, the book of Deuteronomy. "Out of all the peoples on the face of the earth, the LORD has chosen you to be his treasured possession" (Deut. 14:2, amongst other texts). Later: "The LORD has declared this day that you are his people, his treasured possession as he promised, and that you are to keep all his commands. He has declared that he will set you in praise, fame and honor high above all the nations he has made and that you will be a people holy to the LORD your God, as he promised."[61] Do we not banish something valuable if we allow the bad coin of false pride to drive out the precious gold of bestowed privilege?[62]

> Blessed is the nation whose God is the LORD,
> the people he chose for his inheritance. (Ps. 33:12)

59. Hunsberger, *Bearing the Witness,* picks up Vriezen's formulation from Johannes Blauw, p. 91.

60. B. Spinoza, *Theological-Political Treatise,* trans. M. Silverthorne and J. Israel (Cambridge: Cambridge University Press, 2007), p. 43. He continues: "Anyone who thinks that he is happy because his situation is better than other people's or because he is happier and more fortunate than they, knows nothing of true happiness or joy, and the pleasure he derives from his attitude is either plain silly or spiteful and malicious." See pp. 43-44 for election as accommodation and Spinoza's remarks on God's calling all to salvation. On Spinoza's view of OT language generally, see, e.g., pp. 15 and 45.

61. This is a controversial (NIV) translation of 26:18-19 to which we shall return, but my argument here does not depend on this translation.

62. For a passionate "Pauline" defense of his position, see Newbigin, *The Open Secret,* pp. 81-83.

"You delighted in them" (Ps. 44:3 ESV). It is better to be precise about privilege than to purge Israel of it. "Election by God brings no *comfortable* special status."[63]

We have noticed that Newbigin's formulations vary, but I am less interested in probing their variety (I have probably been too pedantic already) than in the substantive questions he introduces. Independent thinker as he was, Newbigin can be positioned here within a wider history of interpretation. His position resonates with that taken in the midcentury study of election by H. H. Rowley, although Rowley and Newbigin understood the relation of election to mission in different ways.[64] Rowley's "election for service" seems to have been something of a slogan for some writers on mission in the second half of the twentieth century, though Rowley himself observed that "[t]his is not to ignore that it carries with it privilege. For in the service of God is man's supreme privilege and honour."[65] We must be careful not to identify automatically Newbigin's "responsibility" with Rowley's "service," but, if there is a difference, it amounts to little, and there is not only significant positive convergence between them here, but also significantly overlapping wariness of privilege.

The election of Israel is most certainly election for service, and this

63. Childs, *Exodus,* p. 383, my italics. Even though it, too, is liable to serious misuse and misunderstanding, the word "status" may also be defensible. See, e.g., Andrew E. Hill on Mal. 3:17, in *Malachi* (New York: Doubleday, 1998), p. 341.

64. So Hunsberger, *Bearing the Witness,* p. 111. For Rowley, mission follows from election; for Newbigin, the rationale for election is mission. (Hunsberger speaks of election as "corollary" to mission. On the face of it, this contradicts Hunsberger's reference, cited earlier, to "election as the rationale for mission," but the statements can presumably be made consistent if it is supposed that, from God's standpoint, his mission to the nations is the reason why he elected Israel and, from Israel's standpoint, her election gives her reason to undertake a form of mission.) Although the reference here is to Rowley's volume *The Biblical Doctrine of Election* (London: Lutterworth, 1950), Rowley was following a hint given in his own 1944 work *The Missionary Message of the Old Testament* (see Hunsberger, *Bearing the Spirit,* p. 90, who gives the date as 1945). In his magisterial study, which integrates a treatment of election into his discussion of mission, Christopher Wright's very first footnote references Rowley's 1944 volume, which he warmly commends in his text: Christopher J. H. Wright, *The Mission of God: Unlocking the Bible's Grand Narrative* (Nottingham: Inter-Varsity Press, 2006), p. 24.

65. Rowley, *Biblical Doctrine of Election,* p. 45. He proceeds: "The measure of the privilege varies widely according to the glory of the service. Some are chosen for involuntary service, and there is little honour or privilege for them. . . . Yet it is never primarily for the privilege but for the service that the elect are chosen." It is hard to exaggerate the degree to which Rowley, in this volume, drums in the claim that election is for service.

most certainly lies at the heart of the OT understanding of election. Precisely what is involved in that service is a question which opens out into an area too vast to chart, let alone to reconnoitre, and one not patient of exploration in this volume, save in the most general terms. It seems that the desire to remove the perceived scandal in the doctrine of election, generated by its misuse, has led to that intellectually and humanly ubiquitous phenomenon — overreaction. Reactive thinking either creates false antitheses or sees only two possibilities, eliminating any others. It sometimes seems as though we — possibly "we" should read "males in the dominant Western intellectual tradition" — are constitutionally enslaved by it. Behind his unassuming verbiage, Leibniz was making a solid point: "Most philosophical schools are largely right in what they assert, but not so much in what they deny. . . . The commonest failing is the sectarian spirit in which people diminish themselves by rejecting others."[66] (Out of the corner of my foreseeing eye, I observe Simeon nod and remind us that this is what went wrong with Calvinists and Arminians — they "are right in all they affirm, and wrong in all they deny.")[67]

The perceived scandal in the doctrine of election is, of course, the scandal of exclusivism. There is an exclusivist interpretation of election which, it is alleged, fosters a blinkered outlook focused solely on the transcendent eschatological destiny of the church, the privileged community foreshadowed by and rooted in the privileged community of Israel.[68] There is no need to deny the truth in this charge. Corporate election to the task of ministry to the nations is certainly at the heart of Old Testament election. More specifically, Christopher Wright has compellingly defended a social mandate in connection with election, which, as we noted earlier, he treats in the context of mission.[69] There is a striking passage by Stuhlmueller which clamors for our appreciation: "Israel's election is to be considered

66. G. McDonald Ross, *Leibniz* (Oxford: Oxford University Press, 1984), p. 75. I am certainly not accusing Newbigin in these terms.

67. A. W. Brown, *Recollections of the Conversation Parties of the Reverend Charles Simeon, M.A.* (London: Hamilton, Adams and Co., 1863), p. 267.

68. We recall Newbigin's missiological and broadly apologetic motive. He sought to look at the question of election from an outsider's standpoint (especially in India, in his case) and not just the insider's. To quote Hunsberger again: "This patently missionary and cross-cultural reformulation of the question is what makes Newbigin's invocation of the doctrine of election so persistently pointed and at the most elementary level makes his construction a unique invocation." *Bearing the Witness,* p. 95.

69. Wright, *The Mission of God,* chaps. 6–7.

under these terms: a choice by a personal God, in favor of a helpless people, with promises and gifts to be held as loaned and borrowed, never as possessed and owned, as signs of love rather than indicators of power, as goods to be shared instead of riches to be hoarded and defended."[70]

It is a serious limitation in this volume, open to serious criticism and perhaps inexcusable, that I do not follow the trail indicated by these words. Be that as it may, I confine myself to saying here that, notwithstanding the legitimacy of some protests against exclusivism, we dare not eclipse a privilege which is more than the privilege of a particular historical vocation. It is true that the eschatological postmortem fate of individuals within Israel is not directly in view when national election is in view, even when, in describing God's choice, we wander outside the preferred term, *bāchar,* which particularly focuses the idea of election in the OT.[71] We cannot correlate election as it applies to any particular *group* in the OT with the postmortem fate of *individuals* in that group.[72] The designation "group" is a loose way of picking out the diverse forms or levels of election which existed within Israel. When we attend to these different forms, we discover a vast territory, which can be marked "privilege," lying between the areas mapped as "temporal service to others" and "the eschatological destiny of individuals." This vast territory can more specifically be designated: "Communion with the living God."[73] At all levels of election, whatever its instrumental necessity in God's hands for carrying out his particular historical purposes, it carries with it the peculiar privileges of the elect — the privilege of communion. If the Lord is our life (Deut.

70. Quoted in Hunsberger, *Bearing the Witness,* p. 91.

71. As with formulations such as those we encounter in Neh. 9:7 and Isa. 51:2.

72. This is not so even in the case of the "remnant": see Ben Witherington III, *Paul's Letter to the Romans: A Socio-Rhetorical Commentary* (Grand Rapids: Eerdmans, 2004), p. 254.

73. I am highlighting "communion" in a different way than does Preuss when he sets out the principle of his OT theology: "The following presentation views the center of the Old Testament and thus the fundamental structure of Old Testament faith to be *'YHWH's historical activity of electing Israel for communion with his world' and the obedient activity required of this people (and the nations)." Old Testament Theology,* 1:25. See Preuss's reference to von Rad in this connection (1:278 n. 140). If we were to make "communion" a central theme of OT theology, it is to Th. C. Vriezen, *An Outline of Old Testament Theology* (Oxford: Blackwell, 1970), that we should turn. When he published the third Dutch edition of this work in 1966, he brought to particular clarity the theme of communion, central to his theology of the Old Testament, as he stated in the preface of this (2nd, revised and enlarged) English edition. See Vriezen's *Outline,* p. 151, for a description of the divisions of his exposition of "communion."

30:20), there is no higher privilege, and if he is God of the living, it is also an eschatological privilege which goes beyond the length of earthly days mentioned in Deuteronomy, according to the power of the Lord, who is the God of the living.[74]

The Form of Privilege

The privilege of communion with God impresses itself on us when we consider the two tribes which float onto our screen when we inquire into the election within election which took place in Israel. They are Judah and Levi, from which sprang monarchy and priesthood, respectively. The pre-Davidic history of Judah, as narrated in Scripture, is full of interest, and we could trace this back to the time when Judah, along with Reuben, is distinguished amongst the sons of Jacob for moderating his hostility toward Joseph and protecting Benjamin in Egypt, along with his less savory operations. We take it up, however, at the dedication of the tabernacle in the desert, when we learn that "the one who brought his offering on the first day was Nahshon son of Amminadab of the tribe of Judah" (Num. 7:12).[75] When, shortly afterward, the people of Israel resumes its march after being on pause since the book of Exodus, it is Judah and Nahshon that lead the way (10:14). The tribe first named in the book of Numbers to help Eleazar and Joshua in land distribution is Judah (34:19), and in the book of Joshua itself, after the case of the Transjordanians is sorted out, the allotment to Judah heads up the list and dominates the account

74. Having expressed painful awareness of the dangerously vast lacunae in my discussion of election in the OT, I flag up a further omission in connection with the particularity of Israel's election. Hendrikus Berkhof spoke of Israel's vicarious calling and role in respect of other nations as something which made her an "experimental garden." "In an experimental garden the soil and what can be done with it are tried out, so that other fields, to which these experiments are applicable, may benefit from it" (*Christian Faith: An Introduction to the Study of the Faith* [Grand Rapids: Eerdmans, 1979], p. 245). Berkhof's remarks in this connection on guilt, in particular, lead us deep into atonement territory, which can never be long out of sight in any detailed treatment of election. For discussion of this theme, see Thomas F. Torrance, *The Mediation of Christ* (Grand Rapids: Eerdmans, 1984). Berkhof takes up the question of "vicariousness" in relation to the NT in chapter 30 of *Christian Faith.*

75. Although Nahshon alone is referred to here under the weight of his own name, while all the other tribal representatives in this chapter are described from the beginning as "leaders," this probably has no significance in light of the lists of names in 1:5-15 and 2:3-31, where Nahshon's leadership is mentioned. Cf. 1 Chron. 2:10.

that follows (Josh. 15:1-63). The geographical positioning of the tribes as they are meant to settle in the land accounts for the order in which they are mentioned, but in the context of the wider OT narrative, this priority simply accentuates, and does not cause, the prominence of Judah in the tribal history of Israel. Geography is a sign of privilege, given the future significance of Jerusalem. As the dark book of Judges begins, God bids Judah go up first to fight the Canaanites (Judg. 1:2-10), and God bids it go up first to fight the Benjaminites as the same book draws to its harrowing end (20:18).[76] We have read all this before the book of Ruth discloses to us the proleptic kinship with David which springs from her marriage to Nahshon's grandson, Boaz, and after the striking profile of Bezalel the craftsman, of the tribe of Judah, found in the book of Exodus.[77] The personal piety — that is, faithfulness to God — of individual tribal members may account for the privilege of certain forms of service. Caleb was its stalwart exemplar in his day.[78] However, this is not the guiding cause of tribal privilege. What assumes that office is the divinely independent sovereignty of choice, culminating in David himself.[79] David could only be amazed at his personal place in God's electing economy. "The LORD, the God of Israel, chose me from my whole family to be king over Israel forever. He chose Judah as leader, and from the house of Judah he chose my family, and from my father's sons he was pleased to make me king over all Israel" (1 Chron. 28:4). Personal and extensive privilege fill him with awe: "But who am I, and who are my people, that we should be able to give as generously as this" — a gift for the building of the temple (29:14)?[80] We must grant that,

76. Of course, the concubine at the heart of the late story is from Judah (19:1) and the book of Judges is particularly interested in the southern tribes. Given Judah's original protective attitude to brother Benjamin, this conflict is particularly poignant.

77. He is first introduced to us in Exod. 31:2. (While it is scarcely surprising that the first tribe listed in Rev. 7, from which 12,000 are sealed, is Judah, Bezalel's worthy assistant, Oholiab the Danite, might have wondered what became of his tribe in that list.) Ruth, the Moabitess, connects Rachel, Leah, Judah, and David (Ruth 4:11-22).

78. Presumably, we are to assume that, when it came to dividing the land, Caleb represented Judah by virtue of his track record as a faithful spy, although we do not know whether the other tribal representatives were selected on account of their personal fidelity: see Philip J. Budd, *Numbers* (Waco, Tex.: Word, 1984), p. 367 on Num. 34:19.

79. "Culminating in David" is loose and includes the significance of Solomon and, more still, of Jerusalem.

80. To get the full force of this, we should read on from this point in the text. See the commentary offered by Roddy Braun, *1 Chronicles* (Waco, Tex.: Word, 1986), pp. 283-86. For the climactic nature of this prayer in this portion of Chronicles, see Richard L. Pratt,

even if the meaning of the phrase "a man after his own heart" (1 Sam. 13:14), descriptive of David before God, is "according to God's choice," it does not follow that God's election of David was unrelated to his personal qualities (15:28; 16:7). Yet, this fact does not make David a type of the elect people of God in either the Old or the New Testament. In any case, it is not the relation of election to personal worth which interests me here.[81] My aim is to emphasize the reality of communion with God and its significance for thinking of election as privilege.

The Davidic psalms disclose to us something of the caliber of this personal communion with God, even when they are designed for public use.[82] Bearing in mind the category of necessity introduced earlier, we might want to argue that monarchy constituted some sort of necessity within the electing purposes of God and that the stability of the throne was dependent on the perpetuation of tribal privilege.[83] This would have to be argued principally from a sociological or political point of view; in the biblical narrative, God's purposes for the Davidic throne express a most gracious accommodation to the unbelief which generated the clamor for monarchy in the first place (1 Sam. 8:14-22). But pursuing an inquiry into the concept of necessity in this connection will gratuitously plunge us into the conceptual thickets of the connection between dark historical contingency arising out of unbelief and the theological necessity of having on the throne of Israel a type of one who was to come. The question is certainly not without relevance to the broad topic of election, introducing us on a large scale to issues of accommodation, contingency, and conditionality in

---

1 and 2 Chronicles (Tain, Ross-shire: Mentor, 1998), pp. 271-76. See too J. G. McConville, *Chronicles* (Edinburgh: St. Andrew Press, 1984), pp. 204-6.

81. In following this investigative trail, we should have to explore the significance of, e.g., Neh. 9:7-8 and the connection between election, Abraham's faithfulness, and covenant. The text is an interesting reflection of the fact that what we customarily describe in English as "having faith" is not something quite different from what we customarily call "faithfulness." See I. H. Brockington, *Ezra, Nehemiah, and Esther* (London: Nelson, 1969), p. 172.

82. The point is not that people, then as now, may be more truly pious in private and more calculatedly formulaic in public, but, rather, that we cannot straightforwardly identify the theology of communion expressed in the Psalms with the reality of communion experienced in the individual, as though the correspondence must, in principle, be exact. However, I do not hesitate to believe that they can, in practice, often be so identified. "The prospect of communion with God is the loftiest expression of personal faith in the Psalms, both in the present . . . and in the future, after death." Vriezen, *Outline,* p. 178.

83. Of course, Saul was not of the tribe of Judah and, quite generally, the choice of king is the prerogative of God (Deut. 17:15).

the ways of God with Israel. However, the point of present interest is that David receives far more than the privilege of service. Election is about a depth of personal communion possible for its humble recipient. The high privilege of David's election is something in which Israel must rejoice; the high privilege of Israel's election is something in which the nations must rejoice; the high privilege of David's election is something in which the nations must rejoice. Election is not just a means to an end; it is peerless privilege for the elect. To be thus elected is not to be used only; it is to know the Lord. We do not know how the Lord was known in the privacy of many an Israelite heart (if we do not balk at the proposal that ancient corporate piety allows us to use such language without lapsing into inappropriate anachronistic individualism). We speak only of what we know, and we know that to be David of Judah is to be elect to a privileged opportunity to know the Lord.[84]

When we turn to the tribe of Levi, perhaps we can also speak of a kind of necessity attached to its election. Amphictyony may require that proper order can be kept only if responsibilities are tribally allocated, and someone has to perform the duties surrounding priesthood, so one clan — the Aaronic — possesses religiously distinctive responsibilities.[85] As in the case of Caleb of Judah, members of the tribe of Levi seem to have displayed exceptional personal loyalty to God and to Moses on a particular occasion. While Exodus 32:26 is spare and offers no commentary on the matter, it is a candidate for consideration under that description (of loyalty), and it has been proposed that "the loyalty of such men . . . provided in itself a kind of ordination to Yahweh's service that resulted in a blessing."[86] However, even if that is the case, Durham is right to add that "it is not likely that this 'ordination' . . . was regarded as ordination to the ministry of worship in Yahweh's Presence described, for example, in Exod. 29." Difficult critical

84. Vriezen speaks of the "two elements that are most characteristic of Israel's religious life: personal vocation and personal communion with God." *Outline,* p. 42.

85. On amphictyony in broad connection with his overall discussion of election, see Preuss, *Old Testament Theology,* 1:56-59. The OT contains a number of strong statements in connection with the election of Levi, e.g., Deut. 10:8; 18:5; 1 Chron. 15:2. See Preuss, *Old Testament Theology,* 2:59, for the special covenant with the priests presumed to lie behind the OT texts. If we were not sticking loosely to the narrative at this point, Jer. 33:17-26 would command special exegetical attention. For brief remarks on the connection between God's covenant with David and with the Levites in relation to this passage, see Gerald L. Keown, Pamela J. Scalise, and Thomas J. Smothers, *Jeremiah 26–52* (Waco, Tex.: Word, 1995), pp. 174-5. We recall that Moses was a Levite.

86. John I. Durham, *Exodus* (Waco, Tex.: Word, 1987), p. 432.

questions surround the matter of Levite ordination, but the narrative does not ground the election of the tribe of Levi in what was done on that awful day recorded in the book of Exodus — or, indeed, on any day.[87] So I should go further than Durham's "not likely." Douglas Stuart, noting the prior assignment of priesthood to the Levite tribe (Exod. 27:21; 28:1) and emphasizing the Levite devotion to YHWH on the occasion of the slaughter of the idolaters, goes too far when he says that "[w]hat this account does is to show further the correctness of God's choice."[88] We cannot confidently discern the motives of the Levites who rallied to Moses' side, as far as the Exodus account goes, although perhaps Deuteronomy 33:9 should be interpreted as a commendation of them on that occasion.[89] Anyway, even if the Levites acted faithfully in that instance, they were constitutionally as religiously unstable as any other tribe.

The question of privilege and service rears its head here again, but surely, if the story of the tribe is read against the background of God's original assignments, the Levite privilege is immense.[90] It is unlikely that a reader will pause, blink, or think twice when a commentator interprets Malachi 1:6–2:9 under the heading "A Privileged Priesthood."[91] The names of the clans of Gershon, Kohath, and Merari, sons of Levi, proudly fill the best part of two substantial chapters in the book of Leviticus (chaps. 3–4). Men functioned as priests in Israel prior to the inauguration and implementation of the Sinaitic covenant, but the covenantal priestly inheritance of the Aaronic priesthood portended a fine spectacle for all observers, the priestly robes being made out of the same materials as the tabernacle itself (Exod. 28:2-4). "When I struck down all the firstborn in Egypt, I set them apart for myself. And I have taken the Levites in place of all the firstborn sons of Israel," says the Lord in the book of Numbers, which has heavily underlined the position of the Levites from its beginning (Num. 8:17-18).

87. Though see Num. 25:13 on the covenant gain of Phinehas on behalf of the priesthood.

88. Stuart, *Exodus*, p. 682.

89. Can we dissociate this account from Levi's violence in the name (or on the pretext?) of honor in Gen. 34:25-31, which so displeased Jacob (cf. Gen. 49:5-7)? On the other hand, see Num. 25:6-13.

90. Timothy R. Ashley, commenting on Num. 16:9-10, remarks that God's call to the Levites was to service and not to privilege; *The Book of Numbers* (Grand Rapids: Eerdmans, 1993), p. 309. But Duane L. Christensen quite rightly speaks in terms of privilege, *Deuteronomy 1–11* (Waco, Tex.: Word, 1991), p. 200, on Deut. 10:8-9.

91. Joyce Baldwin, *Haggai, Zechariah, and Malachi: An Introduction and Commentary* (reprint, Nottingham: IVP, 2009), p. 243.

With privilege come responsibility and accountability. Nadab and Abihu are punished with great severity, and the tribe of Levi can be the source of the worst; not only did Aaron lead the people in the transgression of the golden calf, but Korah's rebellion was essentially a Levite rising, although Reubenites were also implicated in it (Num. 16:1-50). The Levites are a pretty violent bunch (Gen. 49:5-7). However, even if we posit a punitive component in God's dispensation, they are ultimately spared the privilege of land in Canaan because they have the greater privilege of the Lord as their inheritance in what is a sign of the privilege of dependence.[92]

The account of this being put into practice is found in the book of Joshua, which contains a remarkable reference to Joshua's own humble retirement in the land after he has been granted by his fellow Israelites an allocation of territory in Timnath Serah (Josh. 19:50). Even before Joshua is named as the one who divided up the land, Eleazar, the priest, is named (19:51). Samuel was a Levite (at least according to 1 Chron. 6:26), and two of the three major prophets — Jeremiah and Ezekiel — were priests. The latter concludes his prophecy with the description of the allocation of land, divided amongst all the tribes, but with a special portion to be offered to the Lord, and this is the "sacred portion for the priests" (Ezek. 48:10). The *central* portion of this special portion is the sanctuary of the Lord himself, reserved for the faithful Zadokites (48:11). The other Levites still have the best of the remaining land, which is especially "holy to the LORD" (48:14). Although a specific faithfulness is rewarded here in the case of the Zadokites, who replace the house of Eli, this faithfulness occurs within an already established order of election. This form of faithfulness was not open to everyone. Whatever the covenant of salt may be (Num. 18:19), perpetuity pertains to it, and the Davidic line enjoys that covenant too (2 Chron. 13:5). Where you are in the land and what you do in the temple signify the opportunity for spiritual communion, its very possibility being the measure and outcome of privilege.

> Blessed are those you choose
> and bring near to live in your courts! (Ps. 65:4)

92. Of course, Preuss, *Old Testament Theology,* 1:126, notes the celebrated unclarity surrounding this point. However, the actuality of privilege should surely not be overlooked by reducing YHWH inheritance to a matter of being supported by sacred dues and offerings from the other tribes; see, e.g., S. R. Driver, *Deuteronomy* (Edinburgh: T. & T. Clark, 1902), p. 123.

This need not be restricted to priesthood, but it includes priestly privilege.[93] Whatever forms of necessity attach to the socioreligious organization of Israel, the reality of communion is a privilege of grace. Ezekiel brings this to light.[94] The geography of its closing chapters is extremely interesting. Comparison with the geographical descriptions of tribal allocations of land in Numbers 34 and Joshua reveals that borders have drastically shifted around as though to provide an idealized description.[95] The territorial redefinitions appear to indicate a hierarchical principle in the prophetic mind, at least where the Levites are concerned. Tribal privilege is meant to generate corresponding devotion of the heart. When Jehoshaphat tells the Levites to "serve faithfully and wholeheartedly in the fear of the Lord" (2 Chron. 19:9), this is not just formulaic language; as Pratt says, "the Chronicler's ideal of sincerity and devotion from the heart" is in play here.[96] Under God, Levite musical leadership is not a mere formal affair, from a religious point of view. Here, David and the Levites are joined at the hip.[97] "He who sings well prays twice."[98] Braun rightly connects the Levitical singers' appointment for service with the fact that this task places them "in a special relationship with God."[99]

93. Marvin E. Tate, *Psalms 51–100* (Waco, Tex.: Word, 1990), p. 142.

94. See, e.g., Daniel I. Block's discussion in *The Book of Ezekiel, Chapters 25–48* (Grand Rapids: Eerdmans, 1998), pp. 644-45.

95. Of course, the judgment that Ezekiel should not be read as literally predicting such a scenario as a southward move of Issachar and Zebulun, e.g., depends on our wider hermeneutic of prophecy and interpretation of its genre. Actually, the category of the "literal" is not an undifferentiated one. In given cases, we might say that a fulfillment is literal in the sense that we do not read a given text as symbolically indicating an otherworldly fulfillment, yet insist that its fulfillment does not take place in the precise literal form given in the prophecy. On one plausible Christian reading of Ezek. 40–48, I believe we have what is perhaps the most marvelous sustained example of descriptive accommodation in biblical eschatology prior to the book of Revelation, an accommodation to the loveliness of temple and temple-centered geography.

96. Pratt, *1 and 2 Chronicles*, pp. 461-62.

97. For David's institution of Levite musical responsibilities, see 1 Chron. 6:31-32. (Was musical accompaniment itself a prophetic activity or just its accompaniment [1 Chron. 25:1]? On this, see Ralph W. Klein, *1 Chronicles* [Minneapolis: Fortress, 2006], pp. 480-81.) The connection between David and the Levites is generally advertised by the Chronicler, who presumably regards David as a kind of second Moses (e.g., 1 Chron. 23:1-32).

98. These words are usually attributed (apparently without sufficient reason) to Augustine.

99. Braun, *1 Chronicles*, p. 247. See too Martin J. Selman, *1 Chronicles* (Leicester: IVP, 1994), p. 233.

We began our reference to Levi with Malachi and we end it with Malachi. When one commentator simply says that the priests "had a constant communion with him [God]" and another talks of a "*group* blessed by God," it is as unsurprising as talk of the "privilege" of priesthood.[100] Levi experiences a somewhat symmetric election within election: "As the tribe of Levi had a special relationship with God within Israel, so the entire nation had a special relationship with God over against other nations."[101] Personal communion subsists in a relationship enabled by privileged election.

In a more comprehensive investigation into our subject, we would have to ask how the patterns of promise and conditionality, election and cutting off, which apply when we consider the emergence of the Davidic monarchy from Judah (with reference to Solomon's line) and the emergence of the Aaronic priesthood from Levi (with reference to Eli's line), instruct us more widely on the question of election. My limited purpose here presses, instead, toward the question: What higher privilege is possible than for a person to know his or her God, the Lord God of Israel?[102] It is tempting to interpret the words of Moses: "Let me see your glory," as evidence of a man stirred by a spiritual impulse which goes far beyond a passion to serve, recorded in a book centered on the presence of Yahweh (Exod. 33:18). Perhaps we should not resist the temptation, while remaining wary of anachronistic assimilation of Moses' piety to forms more familiar to us and not forgetting that glory as the promise of presence, the guarantee of approbation, is involved in the case of Moses.

100. Pieter A. Verhoef, *The Books of Haggai and Malachi* (Grand Rapids: Eerdmans, 1987), p. 248; Richard A. Taylor and E. Ray Clendenen, *Haggai, Malachi* (Nashville: Broadman and Holman, 2004), p. 293.

101. Taylor and Clendenen, *Haggai, Malachi,* p. 305.

102. I am not persuaded that the phrase translated as "knowing the Lord" in English Bibles always denotes personal existential intimacy between the knower and God in the form of what we might call "a personal relationship with God." E.g., David Firth interprets in terms of existential knowledge the case where it is said that the sons of Eli, in contrast to Samuel, did not know the Lord (1 Sam. 2:12, as rendered in ESV, e.g., and 1 Sam. 3:7). Firth, *1 and 2 Samuel* (Nottingham: Apollos, 2009), p. 27. The extremity of the contrast between Samuel and the actual condition of the sons of Eli or "the sons of Belial," a description which brings out the antithesis to "knowing Yahweh," seems to me to indicate that respect and obedience suffice here to constitute knowledge of God, whether we are speaking of the negative (Eli's sons) or the positive (Samuel). 1 Sam. 3:10 surely indicates the kind of knowledge of God of which 1 Sam. 3:7 speaks. Whether or not it is a linguistically felicitous translation, the NIV arguably captures the *meaning* of the terminology when it translates 1 Sam. 2:12 in terms of Eli's sons lacking *"regard"* for the Lord.

Tertullian interpreted this scene with charming fancifulness. Moses saw the hind region of God, but the Latin translation, rendering this as *"posterior,"* lured Tertullian into exploiting the double entendre: Moses would see not just the back, the posterior, of God, but would see God *in temporibus posterioribus,* that is, in later — posterior — times.[103] According to Tertullian, Moses' wish was fulfilled at the mount of transfiguration when he saw Jesus. However we interpret Moses' desire, and keeping in mind that he enjoyed communion with Yahweh into which we may not pry, it is certainly the case that communion with God will turn out to have no terminus in the grave. If election means the possibility of communion, it is neither limited to service in time nor limited to time itself. "The reward of the good man," said Kierkegaard, "is to be allowed to worship in truth."[104] "To the pure you show yourself pure" (2 Sam. 22:27); although the text does not say as much, it portends the truth that it is the pure in heart who will see God. I am not assuming the automatic transposition of earthly Levite communion with God into the communion of an unending eschaton. The point is simply that election placed people in a position of opportunity, the opportunity of communion, and communion with God does not end in the grave.[105]

We recall that Rowley, who believed that "the privilege and responsibility could not be divorced from one another" when priesthood was under consideration, remarked: "In thc service of God is man's supreme privilege and honour."[106] Is it a needless cavil to express the worry, at this junction, that this statement, with all the rich and important truth that it

103. Tertullian, *Adversus Marcionem* 4.22, translated in *The Ante-Nicene Fathers,* vol. 3 (reprint, Grand Rapids: Eerdmans, 1993), pp. 382-85.

104. S. Kierkegaard, *Purity of Heart Is to Will One Thing* (New York: Harper, 1956), p. 67.

105. Vriezen held that "*[t]he basis of Israel's conception of God is the reality of an immediate spiritual communion between God, the Holy One, and man and the world. . . .* This certainty of the immediate communion between the Holy God and weak, sinful man may be called the underlying idea of the whole of the Biblical testimony, for in its essence this basic idea is also found in the New Testament. . . . This communion between God and man . . . may be called the A-B-C of the Biblical religion and message." *Outline,* pp. 157-58. Vriezen remarks briefly on Exod. 33:12-23 (p. 161). Again: "If we are to do justice to revelation in the Old Testament we must take all forms of revelation in the Old Testament seriously, and we can only do this by relating them all to the essential purpose of revelation: *the communion between God and man*" (pp. 177-78). "In the living communion with Him the whole existence of man and the world was encompassed" (p. 430).

106. Rowley, *Biblical Doctrine of Election,* pp. 102-3, 45.

contains, privileges the able-bodied and able-minded adult?[107] Worry is more evidently in order when Rowley runs the risk of playing down the distinction between the election of Israel for a role as the bearer of revelation and the election of other nations by speaking of God's choosing "Greece to achieve cultural heights far beyond Israel's."[108] At a theological distance from Rowley and some years earlier, Abraham Kuyper, lecturing on "Calvinism and art," stated that "if Israel was chosen for the sake of Religion, this in no way prevented a parallel election of the Greeks for the domain of philosophy and for the revelations of art, nor of the Romans for the classical development within the domain of Law and of State."[109] Kuyper may not have been well advised to put it like this, although it is a parallel whose terms are decisively modified by his steady distinction between common and saving grace. Be that as it may, if we presume to use the language of "election" to cover Greece as well as Israel, the first thing we must do is to distinguish, rather than associate, the senses — not distinguishing merely the *spheres* (of religion and philosophy, for example) but distinguishing the very *meanings* of "election."[110] We should scarcely need to resort to justifying this point by appealing to the semantic field surrounding Israel's historical experience, a field that includes the language of purchase or redemption *(gā'al, pādă, qānă)* and our knowing, *yâdaʿ*.[111]

107. As far as I am concerned, it is not a needless cavil. Many people in or on the periphery of the churches, perceiving themselves unable to serve God actively in body or mind, are crushed in spirit because activity is proclaimed from the pulpit as the heart of Christian discipleship. In its deep and wide dimensions, the election of grace puts paid to the notion that the value of the elect is dependent on their physical or mental capacities.

108. Rowley, *Biblical Doctrine of Election,* p. 138. Rowley's comments conclude his chapter entitled "Election without Covenant." On non-Israelite peoples "chosen by God for a service that often carried no measure of privilege," see p. 122. In the course of citing these words, Hunsberger claims that "for Rowley . . . there is not a fundamental difference between the election of Israel for its role as the bearer of the revelation of God and the 'election' of other nations." Hunsberger, *Bearing the Witness,* p. 105. However, a balanced judgment on Rowley's view requires that we look at what he says specifically in relation to separate nations, including the comment that the Chaldeans, in Habakkuk's prophecy, "were chosen of God for no lasting service, and their election is in the completest contrast to that of Israel. Israel was chosen that God might lavish His love upon her . . . they [the Chaldeans] were chosen to serve a temporary purpose." Rowley, p. 128.

109. Abraham Kuyper, *Lectures on Calvinism* (Grand Rapids: Eerdmans, 1931), pp. 161-62.

110. For Rowley's comment on this point, see his response to Norman Porteous, in *Biblical Doctrine of Election,* pp. 39-40 n. 2.

111. The classic *bāchar* for God's election does not appear until Deuteronomy.

What shall we conclude? It is right that election as responsibility and election for service should be understood as the main thrust of OT teaching when the alternative is either to narrow or to distort the biblical vision opened out by its account of election. However, we do not aid the flow of responsibility by draining out of it the incomparable privilege of communion with the living God, and it is surprising how often this seems to happen at the level of theological declaration. It is true that election is a privilege capable of fostering not only irresponsibility but also pride in the elect. Vriezen wrote that "the truth of Israel's election is unacceptable if it is rationally understood to mean that *for that reason* God has rejected the nations of the world, and *for that reason* Israel is of more importance to God than those other nations, for Israel was only elected in order to serve God in the task of leading those other nations to God."[112] This is true to a large extent, but I question the final clause: "*only* elected [it should read 'elected *only*']." Is Vriezen's adverb accounted for by a persistent worry about the abuse of privilege? Back to Hunsberger: "This hunger for missionary humility and the rejection of everything which perpetuates human egoism leads to Newbigin's persistent assertion that election is not for 'special privilege' but for 'special responsibility.'"[113] Lesslie Newbigin personally exemplified the deepest personal and missionary humility from which the rest of us must learn, and it goes without saying that any balanced assessment of his missiological contribution would have to integrate those things to which I have drawn attention into a host of other worthy emphases in his work. Nonetheless, all things considered, are we not in danger of engaging in dubious commercial practice? We do not help religious trade if we risk exchanging a sense of the privilege of special communion for a sense of the breadth of God's universal concerns. Each is too precious to be so commodified in theological barter.

Readers of the biblical narrative who follow the order of books in the Hebrew Bible will want to hear from no one more than from Isaiah when they turn to the prophets, for only two of the writing prophets are mentioned before we come to the Writings, unless Zephaniah the priest (2 Kings 25:18) is to be identified with Zephaniah the prophet. One is Jonah, mentioned briefly in 2 Kings (14:25); the other is Isaiah. Isaiah has by far the higher profile in the narrative (19:2–20:18). Sennacherib, the As-

112. Vriezen, *Outline,* p. 88.

113. Hunsberger, *Bearing the Witness,* p. 92.

syrian, threatens Israel, and King Hezekiah is in despair. Then Isaiah enters and speaks to him of the sovereign God. Not only is God's might available in defense of Jerusalem, but also Sennacherib is where he is because God himself has ordained it. It is not just the threat to Israel that brings Isaiah onto the scene; it is the pride of the one who threatens it, namely, Sennacherib. What Isaiah announces in the narrative marks his prophecy: God's ordination of human affairs is the antidote to human pride. In the light of this prophecy, none can boast.

Of all that could be said on the subject of Isaiah, election, and divine ordination, we confine ourselves here to the truism that divine sovereignty and human humility are integrally connected in his prophecy. Along with the psalmist, Isaiah is the great teacher of humility in Israel. He it was who saw the vision of the Lord in the year that King Uzziah died (Isa. 6:1), that king who, after starting well, was felled by his pride and ended his days in leprous exclusion from the house of the Lord (2 Chron. 26:16-21). The issue of pride lights up like fire Isaiah's authorship.[114] The references to pride are striking in the late-seventh-century/early-sixth-century period of prophecy — Obadiah, Habakkuk, Zephaniah, and even Nahum, implicitly — although the prophecy of (canonical) Isaiah covers a vast span of time. In Isaiah's prophecy, the question of Israel's election is elevated into a transcendent context. It is set in a sphere of incredible breadth as well as of height: God has his eye on the nations. The more the prophetic eye is trained on breadth, the more certainly is it drawn upward to height, where we glimpse God's direction of human history emerging from his peerless counsel. Just as Sennacherib must learn humility, so Isaiah accents it as the need of the day for the people of Israel. Righteousness, justice, the holiness of obedience — yes, of course; who more than Isaiah exalts these? But when the nation has stumbled into mortal danger, what exactly will the righteous perseverance of the few avail the people as a whole? What, indeed, actually constitutes the divinely mandated form of righteousness? It may all be too little too late by too few. Even the virtue of a Hezekiah, even the faithfulness of a Josiah, will not stop the slide. Now is a time of crisis. As never before, we must look to God to dispose of things as he wills, and so faith is expressed not just in righteous ethical conduct but in spiritual peace, quietness, and trust. The tranquillity of

114. I have in mind here the canonical book of Isaiah associated with the figure of Isaiah in the historical narrative, so see the whole stretch from 2:9 to 66:2. 2 Chron. 32:25 records Hezekiah's pride.

humble faith is the need of the hour. The twenty-sixth chapter of Isaiah, not long before he arrives at one of the "potter" passages that inform Paul's reflections on election in the letter to the Romans, epitomizes much in Isaiah's prophecy to that point:

> You will keep in perfect peace
> him whose mind is steadfast. (26:3)

God has effectively spoken this to Ahaz earlier through the prophet (7:1-11). Thus he will effectively speak to Hezekiah through the same prophet:

> "In repentance and rest is your salvation,
> in quietness and trust is your strength." (30:15)

And so, at a time of crisis, those who will listen, that attentive remnant whom God preserves, will learn not only that God has plans for the nations, but also what spiritual effect upon the individual an awareness of God's sovereign election is designed to achieve.

> "This is the one I esteem:
> he who is humble and contrite in spirit,
> and trembles at my word." (66:2)

Isaiah is the book of grand unities — creation and redemption; salvation and judgment; God's glory and Israel's deliverance; the election of Israel and the blessing of the nations; right worship and social justice. It is also the book which tells us that the proper form of our missionary humility before others is to be shaped by the proper form of our personal humility before God, and that the very opportunity for the latter is a unique privilege when God is known as only Israel knows God.

In the Last Days

By virtue of its election, Israel enjoyed communion with God; by virtue of election within election, some enjoyed special communion. To underline these facts is not, for one moment, to displace the truth that the election of Israel was for service. It is a service which ultimately exalts the nations. Along with Moses in Deuteronomy, Isaiah, teacher of humility, is the great teacher of election in Israel.[115] Significantly, these are also books in which a positive prospect for the nations comes into view or, at least for Deuteronomy, we should probably say: "positive view of the nations."[116] Next to its disclosure of God himself, perhaps the most striking feature of the prophetic literature, as we enter it with Isaiah, Jeremiah, and Ezekiel, is the scope of prophecy, embracing the nations. The connection between the election of Israel and God's interest in the nations was briefly stated at the beginning of this chapter. The blessing of Abraham, which is God's response to the plight of fallen humanity, is intrinsically and not contingently designed to be extended to the nations, supremely through the coming of Jesus Christ. Israel serves God's purpose by cradling the Christ and also by being a witness to Yahweh. Israel is called to be holy, for holiness is what the Lord wants and, in showing holiness forth to the nations, Israel does them the greatest service. Israel's mission is to make the name of the Lord great upon the earth, and the psalmists celebrate it, longing for the nations to rejoice.

> O you who hear prayer,
> to you all men will come. (Ps. 65:2)
>
> May the peoples praise you, O God;
> may all the peoples praise you. (Ps. 67:3)

"If a psalm was ever written round the promises to Abraham, that he would be both blessed and made a blessing, it could well have been such as this."[117] But we can rise even higher. Psalm 66 bids all the earth to shout with joy

115. For statistical remark, see Preuss, *Old Testament Theology,* 1:28, who also notes that, in Deuteronomy and Deutero-Isaiah, the emphasis on the theology of election comes at a time of crisis in religious faith. If we bracket the book of Psalms with Isaiah in relation to humility, should it join Deuteronomy and Isaiah as prominent in the literature of election? The question is somewhat moot. Note John Goldingay's observation that "[t]alk of Yhwh's choice of Israel is surprisingly rare in the Psalms." *Psalms 1–41* (Grand Rapids: Baker Academic, 2006), p. 469.

116. Isaiah is again outstanding, and Preuss is right: "While Deutero-Isaiah was able to feature the election of Israel by YHWH (Isa. 41:8f; 43:10; and 44:1f.) as no other prophet did, he also was the one who at the same time expresses a positive view of the nations." *Old Testament Theology,* 2:291-92. See also p. 304 and the appeal to Zimmerli's support, p. 404 n. 123.

117. Derek Kidner, *Psalms 1–72* (Leicester: IVP, 1973), p. 236. For a brief but helpful discussion of the Psalms in connection with election and its Abrahamic root, see Wright, *The Mission of God,* pp. 230-35.

(v. 1) and the peoples to praise the God of Israel (v. 8); some LXX manuscripts add to its heading: "Of the Resurrection." Easter proclamation is not far out of sight. At first blush, we should not expect the nations to rejoice every time David praises God in their midst, including when the banner of praise is unfurled as David expresses delight in subduing nations (2 Sam. 22:10, 38-46). Yet even this praise can be interpreted in connection with "Israel's existence . . . for all creation."[118] The nations can be called to rejoice in what God does for Israel even against her enemies. Universal eschatological rejoicing, such as Psalm 96 expresses, is the grand climax of the vision of the Psalms.[119] Eschatology gathers up the particular and the universal in relation to election. "Enigmatic" as it may be, the simultaneous particularism and universalism of Psalm 87 are hermeneutically significant: precisely where the one (the particular) is exalted, so is the other (the universal).[120] The Psalms themselves are *tĕhillîm,* "praises." By the witness of contagious praise, Israel serves the nations, for Yahweh is made known when his power and majesty are acknowledged and celebrated in such praise.

It is possible to call this witness a form of mission, as long as mission is defined in terms of what Israel does rather than a priori.[121] The relation between election and mission in the OT is a contentious question. It seems to me that, if we locate the call of Abraham in the context of creation and locate the formation of Israel in the context of the covenant with Abraham, this means we should speak of election as the corollary of God's mission rather than Israel's mission as the corollary of her election.[122] What will

118. Firth, *1 and 2 Samuel,* p. 522.

119. Note too 1 Chron. 16:7-36, reproducing Ps. 96 and part of Pss. 105 and 106.

120. See John Goldingay here, *Psalms 42–89* (Grand Rapids: Baker, 2007), p. 632, although this is my formulation and not his. The word "enigmatic" pops up everywhere in commentators' vocabulary in connection with this psalm, as the relevant discussions in commentators as different as Goldingay, Kidner, and Tate reveal. In according a significant hermeneutical role to this psalm, I am aware of taking an opposite position to that implicitly taken by some other commentators, e.g., J. J. Stewart Perowne, *The Book of Psalms: A New Translation with Introductions and Notes Explanatory and Critical,* vol. 2 (London: Bell and Sons, 1882), pp. 132-33.

121. For an impressive defense of this, see Wright, *The Mission of God.*

122. I side here with Wright and Newbigin against Rowley (see Hunsberger, *Bearing the Witness,* pp. 110-12). In arguing in favor of "the corollary of that [Israel's] election in her world mission," Rowley agrees that Isaiah is the key witness. Rowley, *Biblical Doctrine of Election,* pp. 62-63. "Election was for service and . . . one element of that service was a universal mission to the world." Rowley, p. 95. Rowley is surely inconsistent here, for if

become of that mission? Whatever the answer, we might expect all God's creative purpose and power to be let loose in it not least because, on one occasion, the nations are actually regarded as the work of God's hands (Ps. 86:9).[123] Viewed in terms of redemptive purpose and power, God's commerce with his people promises to take a truly extraordinary turn when Isaiah foretells a "highway from Egypt to Assyria"; in the day that it is traveled, "Israel will be the third, along with Egypt and Assyria, a blessing on the earth. The LORD Almighty will bless them, saying, 'Blessed be Egypt my people, Assyria my handiwork, and Israel my inheritance'" (Isa. 19:23-25).[124] We encounter anything but a suspect and unhealthy exclusiveness here. Yet, it is to Israel alone that God says:

> "I give Egypt for your ransom,
>   Cush and Seba in your stead.
> Since you are precious and honored in my sight
>   and because I love you,
> I will give men in exchange for you. . . ." (43:3-4)

God has no other loincloth (Jer. 13:11). There is no monochrome egalitarianism here either, and this we must accept if we simply in our hearts let the Lord, who has no counselors, have his way.[125]

---

election is for service, and mission is an element of service, then election is for mission and mission should not be thought of strictly as its corollary. In God's *ordo essendi,* election is the corollary of mission.

123. This is the only psalm attributed to David in the third book of Psalms, expressing "a covenantal tradition that unrolls its cadence with an intellectual delight rarely equaled elsewhere," as S. Terrien puts it in *The Psalms: Strophic Structure and Theological Commentary* (Grand Rapids: Eerdmans, 2003), p. 617. See Terrien's whole commentary on this psalm.

124. Richard Bauckham observes that this is "the most remarkable echo of Gn 12:3 outside Genesis." *Bible and Mission,* p. 31. He notes that the description of Assyria is applied to a nation elsewhere in the OT only in Isa. 60:21, and that nation is Israel. Chris Wright comments: "Personally, I find this one of the most breathtaking pronouncements of any prophet, and certainly one of the missiologically most important texts in the Old Testament." *The Mission of God,* p. 236. On questions of authorship and emendation that surround a text whose description of Egypt and Assyria is "in every way a unique assertion in the entire OT," see Hans Wildberger, *Isaiah 13–27* (Minneapolis: Fortress, 1997), pp. 280-81.

125. John D. W. Watts rightly says that Isa. 43:4 "confirms the classic statement of Israel's election in Exodus 19:5." *Isaiah 1–33* (Waco, Tex.: Word, 1985), p. 133. I am aware of, but not persuaded by, the objection that we should minimize the relative nature of Israelite privilege here: see, e.g., Watts, p. 261, and John N. Oswalt, *The Book of Isaiah, Chapters*

Additionally, there is a note in the OT which needs to be heard along with all the others, and we need to listen to it rather carefully as we draw to our conclusion. It is at least possible that we are catching the sound of something very significant, but we cannot be certain. Does it herald the provision of a key to the closet in which election is hidden, whose opening might unlock a good part of our riddle? What I am swithering about here is the question of Israel's rule over the nations. Levi ministers in and to Israel through her priesthood. Israel's role in relation to the nations is sometimes described as a mediatorial, priestly role, although this is controverted.[126] Judah ministers in and to Israel through her government. Whatever we make of Israel's priestly relationship to the nations, what should we make of her governmental relationship? "If you fully obey the LORD your God and carefully follow all his commands I give you today," says Moses, drawing to its conclusion his farewell speech, "the LORD your God will set you high above all the nations on earth" (Deut. 28:1). What will that involve? I earlier quoted the NIV translation of Deuteronomy 26:19, which reads: "He has declared that he will set you in praise, fame and honor high above all the nations he has made and that you will be a people holy to the LORD your God." The text can be alternatively and perhaps more accurately translated as follows: "He will set you high above all the nations he has made for praise and for a name and for honor, i.e., for himself."[127] Even on this translation, Israel is exalted and, of course, it is certainly "a people holy to the LORD" (26:19). It is difficult and perhaps impossible to know how far to press the implications of this relationship to the nations. Granted, the above statement of it is general.[128] Granted, too, that ultimately — and perhaps immediately — it is Yahweh's honor that is at stake. Granted, further, that the triad "praise," "fame," and "honor"

31–39 (Grand Rapids: Eerdmans, 1986), p. 381. The exegesis of this Isaianic passage requires some reference to Deut. 32:9, but it seems to me that our interpretative decision should not lean too heavily on the freight which the relevant Hebrew vocabulary carries as a matter of linguistic *necessity.* Interpretation needs to attend to the wider OT data on the theological place of Israel. Broader hermeneutical issues significantly impinge on narrower exegetical decisions here.

126. For a brief discussion, see Wright, *The Mission of God,* pp. 329-33. I find Douglas K. Stuart quite convincing on this point; see his careful description of Israel's priestly ministry in *Exodus,* p. 423, including reference to Jethro.

127. Cf. alternative ways of interpreting, if not of translating, Deut. 10:21, where "YHWH is your praise" might mean that YHWH has made Israel worthy of praise or that YHWH is the worthy object of Israel's praise.

128. J. H. Thompson, *Deuteronomy* (Leicester: Inter-Varsity Press, 1974), p. 259.

appears in Jeremiah (13:11; 33:9) when it is Yahweh who must be honored among the nations. However, when we turn to Isaiah 60–66 (especially 60–64), the emphasis on the honor of Israel is, arguably, slightly clearer. According to Isaiah 61:6, Israel's people

> will be called priests of the LORD,
> you will be named ministers of our God.
> You will feed on the wealth of nations,
> and in their riches you will boast.

In this connection, Chris Wright remarks that "though there is a rhetoric of submission to Israel, this is probably no more than a figuration of the recognition that it is Israel's God who reigns supreme."[129] Is this to play down a privilege in order to play up what, of course, cannot be played up too highly, the *soli deo Gloria,* and is it played down in order to avoid any embarrassing perceived threat to theologically healthy egalitarianism? It goes without saying, of course, that, in honoring Israel, the nations honor God (Isa. 60:11-12; 61:5-6, 9). In general, I sympathize with the main line of exposition adopted by a commentator like Oswalt's exposition of Isaiah 60–62, where he is regularly and rightly at pains to emphasize Isaianic theocentricity. Nonetheless, I worry about his worry: "Israel's exalted position is to be one not of privilege but of responsibility."[130] Are we not back in unruly antithetical mode? Let us return to Deuteronomy: "You will rule over many nations but none will rule over you" (Deut. 15:6). Is this, in context, no more than to say that Israel will not be a creditor nation? No doubt, Israel is to be "a servant nation instead of a ruling nation."[131] Still, will not the servant, the privileged servant, be exalted in due course? "The LORD will make you the head, not the tail. . . . You will always be at the top, never at the bottom" if you obey (Deut. 28:13).[132]

If we keep our eyes trained on the OT, it seems right to emphasize Zion's obtaining the glory of the Gentiles, their wealth and possessions.[133] The nations are privileged, indeed: they will see, learn, worship,

129. Wright, *The Mission of God,* p. 487. Cf. pp. 256-57 and pp. 239-40 on Isa. 60:12.

130. John N. Oswalt, *The Book of Isaiah, Chapters 40–66* (Grand Rapids: Eerdmans, 1998), p. 571.

131. Durham, *Exodus,* p. 263.

132. Cf. the language of Deut. 28:44. In this whole discussion, it is important not to presuppose thoughtlessly the legitimacy of talking about "the nations" as a single entity.

133. In relation specifically to Isaiah, I am inclined to side with E. J. Young, *The Book*

even become as Israel itself (Amos 9:12). Nevertheless, does this mean that the peculiarly elect nation will not reign? What is implied by the fact that, in Psalm 47, the "nations are being asked to clap for YHWH because he is the God who defeated them through Israel"?[134] Is this a temporal victory that casts no eschatological foreshadow? There are already discriminations *within* the elect, as we have seen. Therefore, without prejudice to the answer to the latter question, we are bound to ask whether a theological sensibility that turns out to be inconsistent with our acceptance of intra-Israelite discrimination is liable to hinder our acknowledgment of the possibility of an eschatological distinction between the protologically elect and the protologically nonelect peoples when election is eventually extended to the nations. Vriezen is not alone in observing that we are looking at a mixed scene; in some prophetic expectations, "Israel will rule over the nations, the nations will serve Israel," but "[s]ometimes these hopes are more universalistic: the nations will come to know Yahweh . . . and share with Israel in the salvation of the Lord."[135] Is this not to assume a contradiction or, at least, a tension between universalism and governance? When "the LORD will have compassion on Jacob," says Isaiah, before his dramatic announcement of God's designs for Egypt and Assyria,

> once again he will choose Israel
> and will settle them in their own land. . . .
> And the house of Israel will possess the nations
> as menservants and maidservants in the LORD's land. (Isa. 14:1-2)

---

of Isaiah, vol. 3 (Grand Rapids: Eerdmans, 1972), pp. 462-63. Even though Oswalt insists that Cyrus is not the addressee of Isa. 45:14, he plays down the homage to Israel. *Isaiah, Chapters 40–66,* pp. 214-15.

134. See Wright, *The Mission of God,* p. 474.

135. Vriezen, *Outline,* pp. 442-43. I quote Vriezen in particular because, in connection with the thought, expressed in Gen. 11, that all the nations have sprung from a common ancestor (Noah), he earlier made the observation that "the Old Testament is the only ancient Eastern work in which we find this universal outlook, as far as we know" (p. 372). Preuss rather tentatively suggests that "[t]he different positions taken on the destruction or salvation of the nations or at least on many of them [by the prophets] are in part occasioned or harmonized by speaking (as, e.g., in Isaiah 65 and 66) of a distinction that is made within the world of the nations." *Old Testament Theology,* 1:301. He thinks that the OT is actually "of two minds in its expressions, hopes, and expectations when it comes to the salvation of the nations and the destiny of the world of the nations."

What does this mean? It is of a piece with what we learn throughout the OT: if ever Israel is regarded as *inter pares,* it is most certainly *primum inter pares.* Israel is the firstborn son (Exod. 4:22), the firstfruits of the Lord's harvest (Jer. 2:3). There is simultaneous exaltation: the nations will become God's harvest and Israel is the firstfruit. Israel is a people of God's own inheritance (Deut. 4:20). Unfortunately, commentators routinely either collapse or distinguish all too casually the notions of Israel inheriting Yahweh and Yahweh inheriting Israel.[136] Where the former is under consideration, attention is regularly drawn to the connection between inheritance and sonship.[137] The "firstborn" presumably implies others, but temporal primacy in the ancient world is not simply temporal priority, as though there is no preeminence attached.[138] It is true that we might emphasize the *service* rendered by the firstborn.[139] However, we must also remember that service is not antithetically related to the appropriate form of governmental primacy which applies to the firstborn.[140]

In our enthusiasm to pursue people and tribes, we cannot forget that election in the OT is not only of people, tribes, or monarchs. It is also of place. Indeed, in Deuteronomy, the importance of this point can scarcely be exaggerated.[141] The fervency of God's affection for Zion grounds the permanence of his choice (e.g., Ps. 132:13-14). If our study had concentrated on the account of the Chronicler, we should want to tell a story of election that had its root in Adam and fruit in Jerusalem. We do not need to press on beyond Kings to Chronicles to observe that an OT theology of election that gave due and proportionate weight to all its elements could not possibly detach a discussion of David from a discussion of Jerusalem, these two being "Yahweh's two great loves."[142] Even before the Chronicler, we

136. See the strong affirmation of the latter in Deut. 32:9.

137. Apparently, there is uniformity in the OT on the fact that only family members can receive family property; see Christensen, *Deuteronomy 1–11,* p. 87.

138. The reversal in relationship between Esau and Jacob (Gen. 27:1-40) and between Manasseh and Ephraim (Gen. 48:14-20) is dramatic in this respect.

139. So, e.g., Durham on Exod. 20:28-29, *Exodus,* p. 330, and Childs, *Exodus,* pp. 202-4.

140. See the remarks in Stuart, *Exodus,* p. 146, on Exod. 4:22-23. In challenging the antithesis, I resist the temptation to conceptualize the relation of service to government as "dialectical" instead.

141. The repeated reminders of this do not cease at the close of the chapter which makes of this point a refrain, namely, Deut. 12. A reminder reappears soon in Deut. 14:23-25 and 15:20, for example. See also 1 Kings 8:16 and 29, which take up Deut. 12:5.

142. Brueggemann, *1 and 2 Kings,* p. 144.

encounter the astonishing finality of the language of 2 Kings 23:27, where the ultimately chosen place appears to be ultimately rejected: "I will remove Judah also from my presence as I removed Israel, and I will reject Jerusalem, the city I chose, and this temple, about which I said, 'There shall my Name be.'"[143]

Here we encounter another crucial feature of election. *Once again* God will choose Israel, Isaiah has told us (Isa. 14:1). Election is "once again," and Preuss emphasizes this precisely as he embarks on the question of the temple and city of God — the Zion tradition — in connection with election.[144] Indeed, the very claim that "election is a fundamental structure for interpreting Old Testament faith," which drives Preuss's whole OT theology, is made good by the historical recurrence and not merely originating oneness of God's electing activity.[145] God renews his electing work as a temporal activity. Both aspects of this must be underlined — that election is a historical activity and that it is not properly understood according to the category of a once-for-all historical activity. Certainly, this latter point has to be nuanced. Preuss, who emphasizes both points, can quote favorably the observation that "[b]iblical salvation history is an ever new *consummation* of divine election and accordingly an ever new requirement for individual decision by the nation."[146] This formulation is acceptable as long as we do not, in the name of "consummation," water down the freshness of God's act. Here I find myself again crossing swords with a commentator with whom I am in considerable agreement in many other areas. Commenting on the "once again" of Isaiah 14:1, Oswalt avers that "[t]his election does not speak so much of Israel's status before God as it does of the individual Israelite's experience of him."[147] Does he not take

143. "Astonishing" is no exaggeration; see T. R. Hobbs, *2 Kings* (Waco, Tex.: Word, 1985), p. 339. The statements establishing the temple are equally "remarkable"; see Pratt, *1 and 2 Chronicles,* p. 343, and Martin J. Selman, *2 Chronicles* (Leicester: IVP, 1994), pp. 340-41 on 2 Chron. 7:16. Cf. the language of Ezek. 43:7.

144. Preuss, *Old Testament Theology,* vol. 2, chap. 8. The book of Zechariah is outstanding within the prophetic literature for its emphasis on God's election of Jerusalem. The "again" used of Jerusalem in 1:17 is more emphatic in that verse than the NIV conveys. Cf. 2:12 and 3:2.

145. Preuss, *Old Testament Theology,* 2:39.

146. Preuss, *Old Testament Theology,* 1:181, quoting F. Horst, my italics. Horst continues: "Subsequently, blessing is the ever new bestowed gift of God that operates within the framework of election and individual decision."

147. Oswalt, *Isaiah, Chapters 1–39,* p. 312. The prophecy of Zechariah in its entirety rewards scrutiny in connection with renewed election. Space has forbidden serious refer-

seriously God's decree of divorce (Jer. 3:8)? Isaiah is emphatically referring to God's activity, not to our perception. Wildberger makes the more plausible comment that Isaiah's language is explained by the fact that "election is related intrinsically to possession of the land. To be elected once again means to be brought in and settled in the land once again."[148] However, this follows a claim that "it would seem theologically impossible to suggest that election could have been rendered invalid and then would come on the scene once again." Perhaps that is so, but we need assurance that this is not a reasoning governed by the categories of Christian dogmatics rather than those of the OT itself.[149] We can certainly say that *electio* is or includes *electio continua*.

All this reinforces the inchoate conviction that we dare not anticipate out of the OT what the NT will bring. All seems precarious for Israel as we draw to a close with Ezra-Nehemiah or with Malachi. Its election is portrayed in Deuteronomy as a means to the end of fulfilling the covenant with Abraham (e.g., Deut. 7:8), and it is connected with the Sinaitic covenant (Deut. 29:25). The hope of Israel becomes concentrated on the Davidic monarchy, and the hope of David becomes bound up with the temple in Jerusalem, in whose shadow we increasingly observe election as the OT draws to its close. If the fate of Israel is in the balance, we recall that judgment is also in prospect for the nations.[150] Yet we have hope. The story of Israel is a story of hope for the nations in a world under judgment. It is a hope embedded in thanksgiving.

> Whoever is wise, let him heed these things
>   and consider the great love of the LORD. (Ps. 107:43)

Sovereignty and grace coexist at the heart of this election.[151] If Isaiah has not taught us this, he has taught us nothing. If the thought of God's sov-

---

ence to the Minor Prophets in my discussion, and no prophetic book has suffered from this omission more than has the book of Zechariah.

148. Hans Wildberger, *Isaiah 13–27* (Minneapolis: Fortress, 1997), p. 35.

149. Biblically and dogmatically, discussion of this point would entail exploring the possibility and potential of distinguishing between a nonrenewable covenant with Abraham and a renewable election of Israel.

150. Preuss, *Old Testament Theology*, 2:303.

151. Karl Barth begins his exposition of the doctrine of God under the rubric "The Being of God as the One Who Loves in Freedom"; *Church Dogmatics* II/1 (Edinburgh: T. & T. Clark, 1957), pp. 257-321.

ereignty both is entwined with the thought of his grace and generates the response of faith, then hope will flourish. In unpretentiously majestic summary, we shall expect that "[e]lection and the kingdom of God belong together."[152] We may be completely confident that there will be at least a remnant.[153] The significance of the remnant is more than just latent in the Old Testament and is most certainly patent in the New Testament.

We said that we dared not anticipate out of the OT what the NT will bring. However, we do dare to feel at the conclusion of the OT that if election in the NT will deserve anything less than praise in Israel and amongst the nations, we shall have lost or missed something. Indeed, we have already missed something. For the outline of a figure has appeared at the height of Isaianic prophecy who will surpass in greatness all that the word "elect" has referred to in our account of the OT. And the name of Zerubbabel, son of Shealtiel, the elect signet-ring of Haggai (Hag. 2:23), will appear again in both the Matthean and Lukan genealogies in the light of a far greater name (Matt. 1:12; Luke 3:27). Barth was right to make him the center of his thought. Barth also spoke of the riddle of the OT. "Throughout the OT, this riddle of Israel and therefore of man is a hard but also a hopeful eschatological riddle — a riddle which points beyond itself."[154] Perhaps the form in which the hope of Israel and the nations is fulfilled in the NT is where the riddle of election really appears. It may turn out to be intellectually easier to live with the riddle of expectation than with the riddle of fulfillment.

152. Preuss, *Old Testament Theology,* 2:285.

153. Micah, for example, is strong on this (2:12; 4:7; 5:7), although we must not ignore prophetic particularities and hurry to assume that the word "remnant" always applies to one and the same group of people.

154. Karl Barth, *Church Dogmatics* III/1 (Edinburgh: T. & T. Clark, 1958), p. 239.

CHAPTER TWO

New Testament Election

The Old Testament Story Continued

C. H. Dodd spoke of a "two-beat rhythm" in the salvation history of Israel: "judgment and restoration; covenant curse and covenant blessing."[1] As the OT closes, we know neither what the future of election will look like nor how its design will be accomplished, but we are bidden to be hopeful, for God has not abandoned the world which he has created and the prospect of salvation illuminates the horizon, enfolding many nations. Salvation and judgment are intertwined. The Day of the Lord will certainly bring, reveal, and vindicate the righteousness of the Lord. There is a saving and there is a judging righteousness. Even if there is a sense in which judgment is not the opposite of salvation, but rather a form of it, we cannot collapse into one uniform content the notions of reckoning and rescue. If it is not quite right to speak of two sides of a coin if the object is to emphasize sharp distinction, we go still further astray if we conclude that the notions of judgment and salvation which we distill from the OT account effectively describe in narrower or in broader terms the same surface on the same side. We arrive at the close of the OT prepared to wait and see how God will connect judgment and salvation in all their forms. The Lord will purify, and the sons of Levi will not be alone in knowing it.

Isaiah gave instruction in the way of faith so that the godly Israelite cultivated the patience of tranquil hope. Once this disposition is culti-

1. Quoted by Kevin J. Vanhoozer in *The Drama of Doctrine: A Cultural-Linguistic Approach to Christian Theology* (Louisville: Westminster John Knox, 2005), p. 387.

vated in the hearts of those who attend to the prophetic witness, faith survives any particular historical occasion which has summoned it forth explicitly into this form of expression. It is sometimes observed that the OT makes relatively little of faith and that, amongst the prophets, it is in Isaiah that we shall especially come across it, where its incidence forms not only a harbinger of but a specific preparation for the prominent role of faith in the NT. So great is God and so utterly dependent are we on his acts and his mercy, that there belongs to the core of faith a component of passivity which looks, trusts, and lives. Passivity is obviously not the whole story as regards faith, and it is a notion which can be constitutionally misunderstood or abused.[2] However, in alighting on that aspect of it in the light of the NT witness, Luther glimpsed a truth which should not be surrendered, whether or not he rightly discerned its comparative proportions.[3] Faith involves hope, and for that reason the dire condition of the nations, unfortunately so often replicated in the life of Israel, is not downplayed if we dare to believe that election's design is a saving design and we rejoice in our hope. The exaltation of Israel has been the object of praise, thanksgiving, and joy among some who are not of Israel, but who nonetheless know something — without understanding much — about the activity of God in and through Israel; who glimpse the hem of his garment, the outskirts of his ways (Job 26:14), but who know not from within, from experience, what it is to be one of his people. Will (or how will) erstwhile spectators of election become its beneficiaries, even partaking of it, and what is the relation of their gain and privilege to that of Israel? As we quit the narrative and prophetic pages of the OT, our hope is in place, bolstered by, if not grounded in, the fact that the temple is in place. It is to the temple of the God of Israel that the nations will be drawn to worship.

Of the four Evangelists who pick up their pens to continue the narrative of Israel's history, Luke alone has the distinction of extending his

2. In light of my references to Brunner's work in the next chapter, I note here his warning about the derivation of psychological from theological passivity; *The Christian Doctrine of God: Dogmatics,* vol. 1 (London: Lutterworth, 1949), p. 315.

3. This is picked up in the *pura passiva* which attaches to the will according to the second article of the Formula of Concord; see R. Kolb and T. J. Wengert, eds., *The Book of Concord: The Confessions of the Evangelical Lutheran Church* (Minneapolis: Fortress, 2000), p. 494. Bonhoeffer takes up Luther on the passivity of love as well, insisting on its theological, as opposed to psychological, interpretation, i.e., on our passivity *coram deo,* in *Works,* vol. 6, *Ethics* (Minneapolis: Fortress, 2005), p. 337 n. 141.

account to embrace the story of the early church. This is rather remarkable, for, presumably, he is the only Gentile author in the NT; so now we find Gentiles no longer aiding the construction of temples, but advancing the composition of (what will turn out to be) Scriptures, and doing so with conspicuous attention to the language of the OT, albeit in the form of the Septuagint.[4] If we follow the canonical order of the New Testament, we are introduced from the very beginning of Matthew's Gospel to the interest that the nations have in the Savior who comes out of Israel, its history shaped with reference to the two great elect figures of Abraham and David (Matt. 1:1-17).[5] When the Magi explain to a troubled Herod what they are doing in his part of the world, they quote a Scripture pertaining to a king of the *Jews,* a Scripture specifying that out of *Judah* "will come a ruler who will be the shepherd of my people Israel" (Matt. 2:6). Not only are the Magi interested in the Jewish question, they also become nonelect worshipers allied with the elect infant against anti-elect Herod.[6] At any rate, the distant Gentile East rejoices in the internal salvation and divine governance of a foreign and unrelated people, namely, Israel.

Nevertheless, the arrival of the Magi in the land does not herald the imminent flocking of the nations to Jerusalem and Mount Zion. The advent of the Messiah inaugurates a centrifugal, not a centripetal, process. Although Calvary, Easter, and Pentecost establish the land of Israel as the site of God's unsurpassable saving action for the nations, and although the temple with which Luke's Gospel begins and ends — or, at least, its gate — is the site of the first recorded post-Pentecostal healing (Acts 3:1-10), the river which will heal the nations does not flow from the temple precincts to fructify proximate land for the benefit of nations gathered on a redeeming pilgrimage. Rather, it is by mission that the nations become beneficiaries of election.[7] Mission begins in Israel, for it is first a mission to Israel by Israel, but the turbulent religious politics of the nation ensures that it continues by spreading abroad outside Israel. As disciples are pro-

4. Priest and monarch are there from Luke's first chapter in the figures of Zechariah the priest and Joseph, of the house of David (1:5-27). Luke summarily states the hopes of the OT in the following chapter as well (2:32-38).

5. At the beginning of Luke's Gospel, David is the means whereby the elect inherit the promises to Abraham (1:69, 73). Cf. 1:32, 55.

6. Herod himself may not have been Jewish, but those he stirred up in presumably Jerusalem were.

7. This is emphasized in the longer ending of Mark (16:15-20) as well as in the textually uncontested NT.

moted to the apostolate early in Jesus' ministry, so are nations promoted to the possibility of discipleship after his resurrection.[8]

When mission starts within and continues outside Israel, the report of it in Acts displays a consternating pattern of repetition of the Gospels' account. The acts of the exalted Jesus, which Luke now records, follow the pattern of the acts of the earthly Jesus, recorded in his Gospel. As healing in Acts is followed by proclamation of forgiveness and both are followed by persecution, we find ourselves observing a configuration of events similar to that witnessed amongst the people up until just a few weeks earlier, when Jesus himself ministered on earth. There are unexpected and paradoxical shame and glory in the fact that Jewish hostility can provide the occasion, even the means, for the gospel to reach the Gentiles, as Luke records. It is this very repetition of the pattern of Jewish rejection, already portrayed in all the Gospels, that causes a deep shadow to be cast over election, even as the nations are incorporated into God's saving plan. At the beginning of Acts, perhaps we were expecting to take our leave of the history of Israel at the end of the book with a heart lightened by the fulfillment of the promises in whose sound we took our leave of the OT. We are disappointed. Words ominously uttered in Isaiah and ominously recalled by Jesus in the Gospels are now ominously repeated at the end of Acts:

> "Go to this people and say,
> 'You will ever be hearing but never understanding;
> you will be ever seeing but never perceiving.' "
>
> (Acts 28:26-27; Isa. 6:9-10; Matt. 13:14-15; Mark 4:12; Luke 8:10)

"Therefore," Paul adds, in a conjunction that will only half gladden the heart, "I want you to know that God's salvation has been sent to the Gentiles, and they will listen!" (Acts 28:28). It seems that the gospel begins as good news for the Jews and ends up as good news for the Gentiles instead. The reality of exchange threatens to replace the ideal of inclusion. The resurrection of Israel's Messiah, far from uniting Jews and Gentiles in

8. I am picking up the word "discipleship" from the Great Commission in Matt. 28:19 and the concept of discipleship from Paul's *inclusio* in Romans (1:5; 16:26), irrespective of how we should read the genitive in his phrase "the obedience of faith." The presence or absence of the word "disciple" has an interesting post-Easter history; see I. Howard Marshall, *Beyond the Bible: Moving from Scripture to Theology* (Grand Rapids: Baker Academic, 2004), pp. 65-66.

joyous fulfillment of hope, appears to be moving Gentiles into the place of divine favor formerly occupied by the Jews, grimly following through the logic of Jewish complicity with Gentile political authority at the trial and crucifixion of Jesus. Jesus has warned: "The kingdom of God will be taken away from you" (Matt. 21:43). Will history, after all, prove to be the fulfillment not of salvation for the Jews, but of the chilling words of Moses in his farewell speech: "The LORD will send you back in ships to Egypt on a journey I said you should never make again" (Deut. 28:68)?

To Paul is given the privilege of seeing further than Luke tells. The story of election is a story of switchbacks; reversal and paradox inform its temporal shape (Rom. 9:1–11:32). Agonizing over the course of history, Paul tells his Roman readers that he does not want them to be ignorant of a *mysterion.* "Israel has experienced a hardening in part until the full number of the Gentiles has come in" (11:25). Yet, as regards election, the people of Israel "are loved on account of the patriarchs" and "God's gifts and his call are irrevocable" (11:28-29). What Paul teaches about the future of Israel is variously interpreted, including the referent of the word "Israel." On any reading, we must surely remain prepared for more paradox and reversal in its history, not least because Paul warns elect Gentile Christians that they, too, can be cut off (11:22). The fearful prospect forms at the edges of the reader's mind that church history will repeat the history of Israel. How many years, decades, or centuries of church history will pass before it becomes plausible to suppose that the story of the election of the church of Jews and Gentiles is the story of earlier Jewish failure mutating into a "medley of error and violence," as church history has been described — a church that has become effectively Gentile rather than Jewish-cum-Gentile in its de facto sociotemporal composition?[9] We are glad that Isaiah has inculcated in us peace, faith, and trust on account of the sovereignty of God over history. The incidence of Paul's use of Isaiah in Romans, especially in Romans 9–11, is very striking.[10] It looks as though election throughout all its historical phases is shaping up, at least in part, as an *electio interfata* (interrupted election), at least as external appearances and forms are concerned, as much as an *electio continua.*

At this juncture, we might attempt to conclude the NT narrative of

9. This phrase is quoted by Barth without attribution in *Church Dogmatics* III/3 (Edinburgh: T. & T. Clark, 1960), p. 205.

10. See Tom Holland, *Contours of Pauline Theology: A Radical New Survey of the Influences on Paul's Biblical Writings* (Fearn: Mentor, 2004), pp. 31-33.

election by turning to the book of Revelation and then proceed to gauge the doctrinal dimensions of election, speaking of such things as the elect Son and the vocation of the elect church of Jews and Gentiles. Yet a narrative element in the NT account supervenes to turn my own account into a *narratio electionis interfata* if not a *narratio electionis interfatae* (an "interrupted narrative of election" if not a "narrative of interrupted election"). Luke injects into his story a sentence whose theological life will not end soon and presumably not until the eschaton; its descriptive content stokes the theological fires and keeps them burning as much as does anything else in the NT. We must reckon with predestination.[11]

The Appearance of Predestination

The scene is Pisidian Antioch, shortly into Paul's first missionary journey. Paul is addressing the Gentiles. When his audience heard what Paul had to say there, "they were glad and honored the word of the Lord; and all who were appointed for eternal life believed" (Acts 13:48). There would appear to be no starker statement of predestination in the narrative portions of the NT, and it is scarcely equaled, if we discount the distinctive witness of John's Gospel.[12] The verb Luke uses is *tetagmenoi.* It is patient of more than one translation. It has been parsed in the middle voice to yield the meaning that as many as had set or disposed themselves to or for eternal life became believers. This is an unlikely reading, not least because of the way Luke characteristically writes of God's action in cognate spheres.[13] Commen-

11. It is the conjunction of this element in the Lukan narrative with the history of dogmatic debate that has been at least partly responsible for swaying me away from an alternative way of approaching election in this volume, which is to offer a studiously and rigorously narrative account of election. Horst Dietrich Preuss indirectly signals the possibility of this alternative approach in *Old Testament Theology,* vol. 2 (Louisville: Westminster John Knox, 1996), p. 160.

12. Darrell Bock states that this is as "strong a passage on God's sovereignty as anywhere in Luke-Acts." *Acts* (Grand Rapids: Baker Academic, 2007), pp. 464-65. This is a telling interpretation of sovereignty; in any event, he is certainly right in relation to sovereign predestination.

13. With, e.g., F. F. Bruce, *Commentary on the Book of the Acts* (London and Edinburgh: Marshall, Morgan and Scott, 1954), p. 283 n. 62, and also his *The Acts of the Apostles* (London: Tyndale, 1952), p. 275; also William J. Larkin, *Acts* (Downers Grove, Ill.: IVP, 1995), p. 207. The text in question should certainly not be interpreted independently of the wider Lukan witness. See, e.g., Richard Pervo's remark on Acts 2:39-40 that "[i]n both

taries on the text show evidence either of theological pressure to read it in one way rather than another, or of the weight of dogmatic history on the shoulders of the interpreter.[14] We are unlikely to come to a definite exegetical decision on this text without examining Pauline teaching, joining Paul to Luke in a textual company that perpetuates the physical company they kept in life. We are likely to add the Petrine witness to this already formidable alliance, so that Romans 8:30, Ephesians 1:4-14, and 1 Peter 1:1-2 are prominent amongst passages that could be hauled in to confirm our prima facie interpretation of the text in Acts. It is plausible to suppose that "perhaps it means that the Gentiles believed in virtue of the fact that God's plan of salvation included them," but the fact is that not all Gentiles believed and Luke is going further than saying: "Election or predestination is for Gentiles also."[15] He is saying: "*These* Gentiles were ordained to life." We note that, at the Jerusalem Council, James sums up the situation in terms of God taking *from* the Gentiles a people for his name (Acts 15:14).[16]

It is the Augustinian interpretation of the NT teaching on predestination which has caused the doctrine of election both to have the prominence and to take the form it has frequently taken in the history of Western ecclesiastical controversy. If Acts 13:48 is to be read in line with this interpretation, then, some will suppose, we have modified most somberly any note of joy struck in the narrative history of election which joins New to Old Testament. Indeed, we have transposed a song of joyful hope, where the election note is sounded (the Old Testament), into a collapsed minor key (the New). What has happened to that "vast explosion of love, joy and hope released into the world by the resurrection of the crucified and

---

structural position and specific content, the Pentecost address displays many affinities to Paul's address in Antioch." *Acts* (Minneapolis: Fortress, 2009), p. 85.

14. Thus, e.g., Howard Marshall allows that the text "could be taken in the sense that God had predestined certain of them to believe," but he regards this as an open question, in light of other options; *Acts* (Leicester: IVP, 1980), p. 231. However, in following up with the insistence that, "[w]hatever be the precise nuance of the words, there is no suggestion that they received eternal life independently of their own act of conscious faith," he has an eye more on the history of dogmatic theological struggle than on the exegetical issue. He is entirely right on conscious faith, but that should not be at issue in interpretation; only the history of theology introduces the question of whether or not "conscious faith" features; it is a truism, as far as the text is concerned. Of course, theological pressure cuts in all directions; I am certainly not implying that one party in the discussion is more liable than another to feel it or to succumb to it.

15. Marshall, *Acts*, p. 231.

16. Cf. Rom. 9:24, where Paul uses the verb "call."

rejected Jesus," to deploy a phrase Lesslie Newbigin often used?[17] In telling his story, Luke, along with fellow authors in the NT, clearly means us to take heart on account of Gentile predestination, even if it is announced in conjunction with Jewish unbelief. Why exactly are we supposed to take heart? The OT has encouraged us to suppose that those who are not elect may one day rejoice in election — that observers will become partakers. What kind of rejoicing is possible and appropriate if, in fulfillment of God's promise, incorporation into the body of the elect is determined by a *discriminate* predestination? Is the barrier between Jew and Gentile torn down only to be replaced by a barrier between those who are and those who are not predestined? If so, should we have smelled more than a mild whiff of this possibility in reading the OT, and has our discussion of election in the OT glossed over any hint or declaration that God regularly acts in this discriminating way in matters that bear on human destiny? Perhaps we should have approached our treatment of election in the OT with a more effective peripheral vision, even if we could not be expected to see everything at once when training our eyes on eschatological hope for the nations. Should we have been thinking about Proverbs? Should we even have been led to think about the length and breadth of shadows cast over human destiny in Sheol, even though it is only in NT retrospect that it occurred to us that they might impinge on the scene of historical election? Whether we indulge in rhetoric or stick to a strictly sober expression of these points, we must ask the following in relation to the NT: If divine determination of particular postmortem destiny constitutes a partial fulfillment of the hope that attends the OT teaching on election, is that the good news we have been led to expect? An Augustinian reading of Acts or of any NT text forces this question.

Of course, there are two questions here. One is whether the Augustinian reading of Acts 13 and of other NT "predestination texts" is correct. The other is, if it is correct, whether it casts a cloud over the fulfillment of God's electing purposes along the lines suggested above. In speaking of election and of predestination, we are neither distinguishing categorically nor eliding lazily any distinction between these words. In familiar theological English, the terms "predestination" and "election," deployed with greater or with lesser semantic sophistication, can overlap to a greater or lesser extent, according to different habits of use. "Predestination" often has a wider range than "election" in two respects. Firstly, it can include

17. E.g., early in *The Open Secret* (London: SPCK, 1978), p. 3.

events as well as people, whereas "election" refers only to people. (We are asking about familiar theological English; it has already been noted that election can apply to place.) Secondly, where it does refer to people, it is sometimes applied to those destined for perdition as well as to those destined for life and thus includes reprobation, whereas we speak of election in a uniformly positive sense as election to life. (Where it is insisted that "predestination" is "predestination to life," a word like "foreordination" is used to cover the antecedent decree of reprobation, although "foreordination," in turn, can bear the "positive" sense.) Translation of the biblical Greek (or, for that matter, the Hebrew) is another matter. For my own part, I cannot underline too strongly that there is no substitute for attending meticulously to biblical linguistic details and distinctions and to the exact context of biblical utterance — no substitute for it, that is, as the indispensable groundwork of dogmatic theology. Nor, correspondingly, can I plead too strongly that notice be taken of the explicit limits of what is being attempted within the confines of this single chapter. The limits are most severe, and reference to Acts 13:48 alone will illustrate that, for not only should we really be inquiring in proper detail about its language and theological content if we use it to base our inquiry, but the text invites the question of the extent to which strong predestinarian language in the NT, outside the Gospels, is associated with the specific incorporation of Gentiles into the family of faith. In raising the question, I am not providing a subtle hint as to what I think is the answer, and in denying that I am providing a subtle hint, I am not providing a further subtle hint![18] Suffice it to say that the formal reason for pursuing predestination when discussing election — whether or not we judge that, in accordance with biblical usage, the words often have theologically overlapping meanings anyway

18. The kind of relatively detailed linguistic work done by an author like William W. Klein, *The New Chosen People: A Corporate View of Election* (Eugene, Ore.: Wipf and Stock, 2001), is certainly necessary. However, his word-study method has its weaknesses. In the discussion of the Johannine literature, there is no treatment of John 10 (though see a reference on p. 155). Terminological confinement entails a weakness in the treatment of Hebrews; when Klein says that "[e]lection concepts do not have much place in the Epistle to the Hebrews" (p. 217), he really means "election words." In chapter 10, James is afforded not much less space than Hebrews in his discussion, and much more in proportion to its length. Parenthetically, we note that the question of election and privilege comes up in connection with Eph. 1:4: "Election exists not for privilege, but to produce a holy people" (p. 180). At the same time, "[h]e [Paul] intends to remind the Thessalonian church [1 Thess. 1:4] that it enjoys the privilege and responsibility of being God's chosen ones" (p. 182).

— is that Luke's narrative in Acts compels us to ask whether the form taken by election in the NT is or includes that of predestination to eternal life.

At the risk of cutting concerns and becoming captive to the dogmatic scene, as opposed to the biblical scene, we should probably mention two outstanding alternatives to the Augustinian reading. The first is that God's predestination is based on his foreknowledge of what an individual will freely and voluntarily choose. This position boasts an ancient pedigree, especially in Greek- and Russian-speaking Christianity, extending back through the fifth century semi-Pelagians of Provençal.[19] Within Protestantism, it is associated with Arminianism, critics of which have sometimes accused it of semi-Pelagianism. On this alternative reading, God predestines to life those whom he foreknows will believe. Thus, foreseen and foreknown faith constitute the ground of, or at least determine the substance of, the predestination of these believers. Predestination is sovereign and gracious, but it is, relatively speaking, a ratifying and responsive decree — responsive, not in the order of time, but in the determination of content. While it may be a sovereign initiative, its substance is shaped in response to infallibly foreseen faith.

Clearly, this interpretation should be considered not only in its own right but also in the event of a failure of Augustinian or any other interpretation. All I do here is indicate the prima facie difficulty, and it is familiar enough. "Predestination" statements in the NT show no overt signs of possessing this studied or formal relationship to foreknowledge and faith, and there is no sign of the contingency attributed to them on this interpretation. This is a point which would have to be argued, of course, in respect of such a text as Romans 8:29, partly on linguistic grounds.[20] It is surely strained, at best, to argue that, while the historical execution

19. See S. Lancel, *Saint Augustine* (London: SCM, 2002), pp. 430-35. Some will want to extend the semi-Pelagian heritage of the church back beyond Origen to the Shepherd of Hermas, but, unless we read it into Hermas 16.3, we do not very clearly find it there. See M. W. Holmes, ed., *The Apostolic Fathers* (Leicester: Apollos, 1990), p. 206. This position also has antecedents in pre-Christian Jewish thought.

20. If any text seems explicitly to invite a distinction between foreknowledge and predestination so as to make foreknown faith logically antecedent to predestination, it is this text. Although I do not go along with this interpretation and agree with reasons familiarly adduced against it, centered both on the meaning of "know" in this context and on what is said elsewhere in the NT about predestination, it is right to note that a fair-minded and careful Reformed commentator such as Douglas Moo, who also rejects this interpretation, considers it "unlikely that this is the correct interpretation" rather than rules it out as impossible. *The Epistle to the Romans* (Grand Rapids: Eerdmans, 1996), p. 532.

of a predestinating decision derives from the sovereign and antecedent decision of God to act upon what he foreknew, the religious substance of the decision is conditioned by the disposition of the human being considered apart from any special grace. It is one thing to correlate human disposition and the free response of faith in some way with predestination, another to align them with foreknowledge in the way this proposal does. The historically concrete person known to us is the predestined person, but a person whose disposition is foreknown apart from the influence of predestining grace and who, in that form, becomes the subject of predestination is something of a chimera. He or she is an abstraction from his or her concrete historical reality. God is viewing this putative person, in the original instance, in terms of personal disposition, without the attendant features of specifically saving grace. Even if God sees (i.e., foresees) such a person as an agent operating within the sphere of a universally prevenient grace that he has himself established as the all-encompassing context for human life, this is not the grace of predestination which eventually becomes effective in historical time.

It is surely difficult to conceive of persons in such an "idealized" mode. Can we really conceive of such foreknown persons as identical to those who actually turn up in history, belonging to a whole antecedent history, shaped by God's effective grace? Are not such persons, whose foreknown disposition shapes divine predestination, really bloodless, abstracted personae, identified by a quality of disposition or by some spontaneous inclination liable to produce faith independently exercised within the sphere of prevenient grace? We do, of course, conceive of persons independently of what they do, whether in more trivial cases (e.g., irrespective of whether or not they have drunk a cup of coffee that morning) or in more significant ones (e.g., irrespective of whether or not they have got married). However, the case is different here, when God is understood to be attending, in virtue of prior foreknowledge, to a disposition completely untouched by any specific grace effective for salvation.[21] Admittedly, this may be too philosophically contentious a matter to introduce into the question of choices in biblical interpretation, and it may be possible to adumbrate a good conceptual response. I am simply trying to envisage what a

21. If Robert Musil, in one the greatest novels of the twentieth century, wrote *The Man without Qualities* (to use the familiar, though rather imprecise, English translation of the title), it is tempting to wonder if the standpoint which I here query logically posits the qualities without the "man" as the subject of divine predestination.

person looks like on this first alternative to Augustinian exegesis and what notion of the person must be at least implicit in Scripture for this exegesis to work — and finding it difficult. However, my principal difficulty is that "predestination texts" show no sign of the proposed correlation between foreknowledge, faith, and predestination which we are examining, and this proposed correlation looks more like an attempt to meet a theological difficulty arising in connection with predestination than a compelling interpretation of the texts. Of course, reasons garnered from other texts or from biblical theology more widely may be offered for the interpretation I am rejecting here, and the failure of an Augustinian reading to account for those texts and square with that wider theology may be fairly adduced as a reason for rejecting its interpretation of predestination texts. I make no pretense to offer anything other than a provisional conclusion here, although I am myself persuaded of it.

The second alternative to an Augustinian reading is to regard predestination to life as a corporate and not an individual matter. As Israel is elect as a people, so the church of Jews and Gentiles is elect and predestined as a people. If the concept of remnant is in view, it is still the corporate meaning that obtains.[22] In response to this, we say, first, that a corporate reading per se need not challenge an Augustinian reading. It is true that if we take Augustine's soteriology as a whole and examine the exegetical decisions by which he arrives at it, a corporate reading of texts that he read individualistically might lead us to diverge significantly from the soteriology, considered comprehensively. However, on the narrower point presently at issue, the significant question is not whether election and predestination is corporate rather than individual, but how the corporate is constituted. Surely God's dealings are too personal, too particular, too intimate to permit a construction of the corporate which reduces the significance of the individual in this connection. When Paul, for example, speaks of those called from among the Gentiles (Rom. 9:24), we may argue about the exact meaning and force of "call," but there would seem to be a discrimination here which cannot be explained as the product of individuals autonomously inserting themselves into a class and, if that is not what is happening, they are incorporated into the body of the church by divine predestination, as the particular individuals that they are. The shepherd calls his own sheep by name (John 10:3); "I have other sheep," says Jesus, extending the application of his words

22. C. K. Barrett speaks of the remnant as "a nation within a nation." *The Epistle to the Romans* (New York: Harper and Row, 1957), p. 209.

beyond the first circle, "I must bring them also . . ." (10:16), and not just to service. If it be objected that I am fusing together different Greek terms by the invocation of different texts (even if it is supposed that they signify the same or a similar reality), we may turn to Ephesians and consider it independently.[23] When Paul tells the Ephesians that God has chosen *us,* God has predestined neither the temporal space into which an individual can come nor a company nameless on the occasion of predestination (Eph. 1:4). He apparently predestines that particular people which occupies in time the ecclesial space afforded to the elect.[24]

Of course, even if the considerations I have advanced have some force, this does not show that Augustine basically got it right. To repeat: even if a prima facie case can be made for an Augustinian interpretation of some "predestination" texts, it may have to be reconsidered and revised in light of the difficulty of providing a coherent account within an Augustinian framework either of other NT texts that do not mention predestination or of other themes in NT theology. This is very readily granted. I am not attempting a demonstration. I am asking what we can or should make of election if we find ourselves concluding that the balance of probability lies on the side of an Augustinian reading of NT texts on predestination and that, consequently, we must factor this into our understanding and interpretation of election in the NT.

What is the scope of the "Augustinianism" detected in the biblical text? Luke's reference to predestination to life follows after and is connected directly with the report of Paul and Barnabas's unavailing evangelistic effort vis-à-vis the Jews. The Jews oppose them. So Paul responds: "We had to speak the word of God to you first. Since you reject it and do not consider yourselves worthy of eternal life, we now turn to the Gentiles," and he quotes — who else? — Isaiah before Luke tells us that the Gentiles

23. See also the point made in the language of 2 Tim. 1:9.

24. Eph. 1 is a classic example of why *electio continua* has so little mileage in the NT. Expounding the corporate nature of election, Clark Pinnock is among those who take the further step, in this connection, of contesting divine exhaustive foreknowledge. "God knows that some will respond, but not (I submit) exactly who"; "Divine Election as Corporate, Open and Vocational," in *Perspectives on Election: Five Views,* ed. Chad Brand (Nashville: Broadman and Holman, 2006), pp. 276-314, here p. 289. Pinnock describes Klein as his "favourite exegetical source" (p. 278 n. 4), and understands election as "not a call to privilege but to service" (p. 287). For the influence of Robert Shenk on him, see Pinnock's essay "From Augustine to Arminius: A Pilgrimage in Theology," in *The Grace of God and the Will of Man,* ed. Pinnock (Minneapolis: Bethany House, 1989), pp. 15-30, here p. 29 n. 8.

rejoiced at the fulfillment of prophecy and that "all who were appointed for eternal life believed." The contrast here is not between those who are predestined to life and those who are foreordained to perdition or passed over for predestination to life. It is not merely that the *force* or *point* of foreordination language is not the contrast between those predestined to life and those not predestined to life. It is that the *substance* of the contrast as described does not admit of description in those terms. The contrast is between a call or summons which is both genuine and responsibly rejected, on the one hand, and a predestination to life, on the other. We do not need to flatten out the way in which the vocabulary "called" and "chosen" is used in Paul and the Synoptic Gospels to say that "many are invited, but few are chosen" (Matt. 22:14) seems to find an echo in Luke's narrative at this point in Acts.[25]

By an "Augustinian" reading of the few texts mentioned, I mean no more than what has often been called "single" predestination. Election in the NT incorporates that. Augustinianism has, of course, been pushed further, including in some of Augustine's own work, so that, corresponding to predestination to life — albeit in asymmetric coordination — there is a passing over of others in some form of antecedent reprobative decree. There are three grounds on which the case for an antecedent reprobative decision on God's part is advanced, whether we couch it in terms of active determination or "passing over" of those not predestined to life. The grounds are that it is (a) explicit in Scripture; (b) analytic in, implicit in, or entailed by the biblical teaching that God eternally ordains everything that comes to pass in the world; and (c) entailed by single predestination.

I discuss the third ground in the next chapter. It lies outside the bounds of our discussion to consider the second ground; it draws in the subject of providence, perhaps subsuming the particular decree of reprobation under it, and this introduces the question of the relation between election and providence. This omission is obviously a serious limitation in my treatment. By way of assertion, not of argument, I simply note that biblical statements about God's activity which come under the heading "providence" have in view the temporal scene, the world stage which is largely occupied and crowded by evil and sinful action vomited out into

25. It is often held that Luke and Paul use *kalein* in the sense of an effectual call to salvation. While I am not convinced of this (e.g., I do not believe that the whole Corinthian church is effectually called; 1 Cor. 1:2), the plan of my volume forces me to dispense with the linguistic arguments which I admit are the stuff of good exegesis and, therefore, of good theology.

the world by humankind. We may be led occasionally to peer beyond it into what we picture as the time of God before time began, even if we train our eyes more frequently vertically into the heavenly present than horizontally into the imagined past-eternal. At all events, it seems to me that we can scarcely gaze with clear vision into a "pretemporal," "preprovidential" decretive order on the basis of the providential order itself, when it comes to a putative decree of reprobation. Does the scope of biblical statements affirming God's sovereign providential operations implicitly include a sphere of pretemporal (or eternal) antecedent immutable reprobative determination? When we observe the providential order itself, we see it adapted to a fallen world, even if it exhibits continuities with a good creation. I do not myself think that we can schematically connect actions, decisions, and ordinations effected and displayed in providential time with an antecedent immutable pretemporal decree in respect of eschatological perdition in adumbrating a theological doctrine of providence.[26]

Here, I turn to the first ground — the direct exegetical evidence for an antecedent decree.

An Antecedent Decree?

Sometimes, theological defenders of belief in an antecedent, immutable decree of reprobation admit that it is infrequently explicit in the NT.[27] In

26. Although, as the editions of the *Institutes* progressed, Calvin altered the order of his treatment of topics, so that predestination eventually appears in book 3 and providence in book 1, his treatment of providence wraps up the question of predestination, from a logical point of view. The connection between providence and predestination is more immediate in a figure like Thomas Aquinas, and, from his perspective, it is asking for trouble to omit discussion of providence in a treatment of election. From my perspective, it is asking for trouble to reason as he does in *Summa Theologiae* (1a.23.3), vol. 5 (Oxford: Blackfriars, 1967), p. 117: "God loves all men and all creatures as well, inasmuch as he wills some good to all: all the same he does not will every sort of good to each. In that he does not will to some the blessing of eternal life he is said to hold them in hate or to reprobate them." What would we say of an earthly father or monarch whose love was expressed by supplying some food and water to a child or subject but who withheld all clothes, shelter, protection, and comfort? The answer on behalf of Aquinas might take the form of a counterquestion: "Is this not precisely the case with God when we consider the problem of evil and suffering?" True enough, the problems of evil and suffering are perplexing in relation to the love of God, but they are not satisfactorily handled by defining love in terms of willing some, but not other, goods.

27. E.g., Herman Bavinck, *Reformed Dogmatics,* vol. 2, *God and Creation* (Grand Rapids: Baker, 2004), p. 393.

approaching the biblical material, we need to bring a hermeneutical rule to the forefront. It is obviously not an exclusive rule for the determination of the textual meaning. However, we underplay its role at our peril. To put it programmatically, if blandly: we must accord narrative its full and proper hermeneutical function. In some theological circles, hermeneutical and theological interest in narrative has been succeeded, supplanted, or supplemented by interest in drama.[28] My choice of "narrative" here indicates no explicit preference over "drama," nor does it imply any view of the relationship between the two.[29] The plea is that the story of Israel as narrated in Scripture (or the dramatic account of God and Israel) be permitted a heavy hand on the hermeneutical tiller.

What is involved here can be illustrated in relation to two passages to which appeal is customarily made in support of an antecedent decree of reprobation: 1 Peter 2:8 and Romans 9:1-33.[30] According to Peter, the stone the Lord laid in Zion "causes men to stumble" and is "a rock that makes them fall. They stumble because they disobey the message — which is also what they were destined for." Peter is addressing a readership of whose constitution (Jewish/Gentile) we cannot be entirely certain, but which is hailed in the corporate terms applied to Israel: elect, sanctified, a chosen people, a royal priesthood (1:2; 2:9). It is a description which celebrates the realization of the Gentile privilege to which the OT looked forward. In contrast to those who believe, who treat as a capstone or cornerstone the stone that the builders rejected, those who disbelieve stumble and fall. Peter's exposition is surrounded by reference to Isaiah; the precious cornerstone is found in Isaiah 28:16 and the stumbling stone in Isaiah 8:14. Isaiah 28:16 is explicitly cited in the NT only here and in Romans 9:33. Yet,

28. Hans Urs von Balthasar's five-volume *Theo-Drama,* the second part of his theological trilogy, set the pace. Further contributions include those of Kevin Vanhoozer, *The Drama of Doctrine,* and David Ford's essay *The Future of Christian Theology* (Chichester: Wiley-Blackwell, 2011).

29. Actually, David Ford's work illustrates how one can speak of narrative and drama in the same breath. His volume *The Future of Christian Theology* takes up the notion of drama, but he speaks of the "narrative/dramatic" (p. 40), and, after owning that "[n]arrative is the most common biblical genre and, for Christians, the central one," he proceeds to discuss "the biblical theodrama" (pp. 71-72). Anthony Thiselton also brackets narrative with drama and refers to "narrative, drama or dramatic narrative." *The Hermeneutics of Doctrine* (Grand Rapids: Eerdmans, 2007), pp. 65-67.

30. Fuller discussion would take in Jude 4, e.g., which tells us that the condemnation of certain men was *palai progegrammenoi,* a phrase which "bristles with difficulties," as R. J. Bauckham puts it. *Jude, 2 Peter* (Waco, Tex.: Word, 1983), p. 35.

the canonical Isaiah, with the wide sweep of his vision, underlines what is in any case clear in the OT: it is the hardened heart of disobedient Israelites which brings on the judgment of God. Certainly, that judgment may take the form of a further hardening, and the further hardening, in turn, furthers God's purposes. Furthermore, God may know beforehand what humans will do and plan what he will do. However, it is not only with reference to, but it is actually on account of, the willful disobedience, which is in its very nature a self-hardening, that God acts in judgment. The vagaries of human agency bring on God's judicial action. Obviously, Peter assumes this. To read into or to append to this an antecedent reprobative decree is either to read the text while forgetful of the OT narrative background or to make a theological inference rather than exegete the text. Of course, defenders of an antecedent reprobative decree do not deny the importance and relevance of historical processes and of willful disobedience. On the contrary, they insist that the economy discloses the entirely culpable human heart. The trouble is that they also posit the antecedent and eternal decision, and this is not indicated in the text.

It borders on an insult to the discipline of exegesis to treat summarily the ninth chapter of Romans, the locus classicus of the position I am questioning, but Paul endured worse insults in his day. Following on from the discussion of Peter, we note first what Paul says about the hardening of Pharaoh (Rom. 9:17-18). Paul does not tell us that Pharaoh hardened his own heart; although that is said in Exodus, it is more often said there that God hardened it.[31] Some take it as obvious that any self-hardening described in Exodus is the result of divine hardening.[32] However, this is to approach the theological interpretation of Exodus with a restricted vision. In the stretch of history that we read, Pharaoh's self-hardening is frequently the product of divine hardening, although whether this is uniformly the case is a moot point.[33] Still, let it be granted that both Paul and the Exodus narrative in

31. Although the contest begins in Exod. 7:10, see already 4:21.

32. Gordon Clark went as far as to claim that "Exodus is so clearly Calvinistic, or Calvinists are so Exodus-ians, that the continued existence of Arminianism is a miracle of blindness." *Predestination* (Philippsburg, N.J.: Presbyterian and Reformed, 1987), p. 159. On his own account, this blinding is apparently the work of God, although I am not sure whether he would have put this down to the iniquity of Arminians.

33. The question here is the extent to which we read the Exodus narrative as implying that there are occasions where Pharaoh could have relented. There may be less significance to the variety of ways in which the situation is described in the original Hebrew than the English reader is immediately disposed to suppose. See Douglas K. Stuart, *Exodus* (Nash-

the Hebrew OT would have us understand that God hardens Pharaoh so that he hardens his own heart. This does not at all entail, or even imply, that divine hardening was not the product of prior self-hardening. What sort of man was Pharaoh prior to God's hardening? The question is anything but an attempt to evade the obvious. On the contrary, the OT narrative encourages us to believe that divine hardening is generically the consequence of human hardness. Israel's hardening was, unfortunately, a known quality as far as apostle, along with prophet, was concerned. If ever God's hardening seems to be prior to self-hardening, to the point of causing it, it is always the hardening of a people with an already proven persistent and enslaving liability to self-hardening. God's hardening is responsive to humans, even while it leads to further self-hardening. It is described as a historical action, but not one with an antecedent ground in an immutable decretive counsel.

While we may not be able strictly to demonstrate that Paul visualized God's hardening of Pharaoh in line with the hardening of Israel, the phenomenon of hardening, which, tragically, came to apply to Israel as well as to Pharaoh, was depressingly familiar to Paul from the whole history of his nation, and it is surely likely that he thought of divine hardening generically in altogether familiar terms.[34] Israelite hardening tragically replicates

---

ville: Broadman and Holman, 2006), p. 149, and the whole excursus (pp. 146-51), including the observations on Egyptian cultural context. In his own excursus, Brevard Childs resists both a psychological and a theological-causal explanation; *Exodus* (London: SCM, 1974), pp. 170-75.

34. Douglas Moo is among those who argue that, "if Paul had in fact wanted his readers to assume that God's hardening was based on a person's self-hardening, we would have expected him to make this clear in response to the objection in v. 19 ['Why does he [God] still find fault?']." *Epistle to the Romans,* p. 598. However, there would have been no need to make it clear if it was a deep assumption shared by all concerned. Decision on exactly what Paul is arguing is suspended on our more general judgment about Paul's disputatious and rhetorical style. Meanwhile, we have to attend to the meaning and the force of the *eti* (still) in verse 19. Its meaning is certainly not undisputed every time it occurs in Romans. Moo takes *eti* as a logical inference in 3:7 (p. 194 n. 87), while B. Byrne puzzles a bit about its force there; *Romans* (Collegeville, Minn.: Liturgical Press, 1996), p. 114. However, see the comment of F. Godet, *Commentary on Romans* (Grand Rapids: Kregel, 1977), p. 137, on this text, which he interpreted in the same way as he interpreted 9:19 (p. 356), observing the temporal force of *eti.* As Leon Morris puts it, we should read 9:19 as: "*Still,* after God has hardened him?" *The Letter to the Romans* (Grand Rapids: Eerdmans, 1988), p. 363. Then the argument implicitly goes: "Of course, Paul, we know that divine hardening is the product of self-hardening and you do not need to defend the justice of *that,* but now that God *has* hardened and there is nothing anyone can do about it, how *now* is fault *still* found?" The uses of *eti* in Rom. 5:6, 8 and 6:2 should be considered in this connection.

what God sometimes did to the nations. When Joshua went to war with the northern kings, we learn, at one point, that God had hardened their hearts; but we have long been sensitized to the evil ways of the Canaanites, and it should not even occur to the reader that the hardening was anything other than God's historical intervention in the lives of a wicked people on account of their culpable, temporal, prior wickedness (Josh. 11:20). We should not expect anything very different if the Philistines harden their hearts in the case of a warning which explicitly refers us back to the story of Pharaoh (1 Sam. 6:6). The Exodus narrative furnishes us with no biography of Pharaoh, but its account of his tussle with God and Israel, especially when read in the context of the entire OT, succeeds in disclosing to us a character whose actions God is directing along, and not against, its very grain. Of course, advocates of an antecedent decree of hardening do not doubt that point, but they visualize the grain of character in the wider and more fundamental context of that decree, whereas no antecedent reprobative decree is proposed or even suggested either in Romans or in Hebrew Exodus as in any way accounting for the state of affairs under description. That Paul wants to make a point about divine sovereignty and divine action is as clear in Romans 9 as it is in the whole prophecy of Isaiah, which suffuses Romans 9–11. Yet, the steady presupposition is that we are dealing with God's responsive action toward people responsible for their own wickedness.[35] It is not that the sovereign ways of God must be reducible, as far as possible, to what we can comprehend. All we are doing here is seeking to accord to narrative its appropriate hermeneutical status. By the time we reach apostolic teaching, we ought to have internalized the awareness that what accounts for any divine hardening action is the initially culpable actions of humans and not a culpable action viewed from eternity in subordination to an antecedent decree.

35. We should not flatten out all references to hardening; see, e.g., C. E. B. Cranfield's comments in *The Gospel according to Saint Mark* (Cambridge: Cambridge University Press, 1972), pp. 227-28, and those of William L. Lane, *The Gospel according to Mark* (Grand Rapids: Eerdmans, 1974), pp. 237-39 on Mark 6:52, and note the different situations mentioned in Mark 3:5 and 8:17. While the specter of the problem of original sin threatens to hover over our discussion at this point, we need not become embroiled in an attempt to get its measure. Although it is in order to speak of human possession of a common, generically fallen nature, the ways persons live out that nature differ. It is only a theological culture formed by post-Augustinian or post-Reformation disputes over grace that will fear a creeping Pelagianism in the element of truth in the claim that all humans are wicked but that some humans are more wicked than others.

The extent to which Romans 9–11 is a commentary on Isaiah is impressive, even to those impressed by the extent to which the whole of the NT is a commentary on Isaiah. The prophet prays to God in these terms:

> Why, O LORD, do you make us wander from your ways
> and harden our hearts so we do not revere you? (Isa. 63:17)

As Oswalt remarks, "No one could read this book and believe that Isaiah thought the people were forced to sin by God."[36] In fact, no one could read Isaiah against the background of the OT narrative and think of God's hardening as anything other than a response to the sin of Israel. That is not to wrap up the issue with conceptual ease. It is not to deny the sovereignty of Isaiah's God by hemming in his ways with our earthbound hermeneutics. It is to attempt to interpret God's word. Isaiah himself says shortly afterward:

> No one calls your name
> or strives to lay hold of you;
> for you have hidden your face from us
> and made us waste away because of our sins. (64:7)

In any case, in relation to Pharaoh in Romans, the question arises whether Paul has eschatological destiny in mind at all. Even if he does, it does not follow that he does in the case of Esau, and there he surely does not. "Jacob I loved, but Esau I hated" (Rom. 9:13). We cut the nerve of Paul's argument in this context if we identify in God's action a responsive element — responsive to Jacob and to Esau — and that is one reason why we should reject a reading of this particular text along classical Arminian lines. However, the question of personal reprobation seems clearly not to be involved here at all.[37] There is a unity to God's electing call in the case

36. Oswalt, *The Book of Isaiah, Chapters 40–66* (Grand Rapids: Eerdmans, 1998), p. 613.

37. James Dunn remarks that "being outside the elect people of God is no guarantee of final condemnation, just as being inside the elect people of God is no guarantee of final justification." *Romans 9–16* (Dallas: Word, 1988), p. 564. Cf. Ps. 78:67. In interpreting the scene in terms of individual salvation or reprobation, commentators such as John Piper, Thomas Schreiner, and Douglas Moo are forced to say that Paul is applying language that meant one thing in an OT context to a different problem, namely, the problem of individual destiny. "The issue in the context of Romans is salvation even if the OT texts about Esau and his descendants merely concern temporal destiny." Thomas Schreiner, *Romans* (Grand

of Jacob; it is both to a role in God's historical purposes and to a personal destiny, for he will sit down at banquet with father Isaac and grandfather Abraham in the presence of the God who is the God not of the dead but of the living (Matt. 8:11). However, it neither logically follows, nor is it required by any code of semantic or conceptual biblical symmetry, nor is it said in the text, that Esau, rejected for God's purpose in election, is also eschatologically reprobated in one and the same act. Even if we were to conclude that Pharaoh is eschatologically reprobate, we should not assume that Esau's and Pharaoh's cases are identical. Esau is not hardened in the course of history, and Pharaoh is not rejected in God's purpose within the family line of Abraham and Isaac, the men of promise. Pharaoh is an individual whose personal family tree is of no evident soteriological

---

Rapids: Baker, 1998), p. 502. That is implausible in the extreme on Schreiner's understanding of salvation. The persuasiveness of Paul's argument here depends on the fact that he is expounding OT theology, exactly as he had done in the fourth chapter of his epistle. The principal reason for seeing it otherwise is the perception that Paul's sorrow in the opening verses of the ninth chapter is because not all individuals in Israel have accepted the gospel, and if his subsequent discussion of election does not deal with that, it fails to address the sad problem which preoccupies Paul. Consequently, we must understand that it deals with precisely that and that Rom. 9 is teaching that some individuals are elect and some are reprobate. John Piper's way of putting it is that Paul had to take OT materials out of context because he had limited resources for dealing with eternal salvation, "since the eternal salvation of the individual as Paul teaches it is almost never the subject of discussion in the OT." *The Justification of God: An Exegetical and Theological Study of Romans 9:1-23,* 2nd ed. (Grand Rapids: Baker, 1993), p. 64 n. 38. This is an unnecessary convolution. Paul's discussion of election in chapter 9 is placed in a context where the destiny of those over whom he agonizes at its beginning is a subject to which he returns at the end of chapter 11. His preoccupation is with the collective, Israel, and the early verses of chapter 9 do not tell us what the end of the story is. Discussion of Jacob and Esau is not designed as a relatively self-contained response to the problem of individual Israelites failing to achieve their destiny. Esau *is rejected* and not chosen before he is born, but Paul's worry is about the Israelites who belong to Jacob's election and who *themselves* reject God in the course of time. Esau does not fail to pursue the righteousness that is by faith; those over whom Paul agonizes, do. In integrating into his argument both the sovereign action of God in election and the failure of an elect people through disobedience, Paul is dealing with more than one strand, and we have to follow his reasoning all the way to the end of chapter 11 to understand the fabric of the argument in its unity and diversity. It is significant that, however troublesome his admission may be for the overall coherence of his exegesis, Douglas Moo admits that "Paul is not clearly asserting that Jacob and Isaac were saved while Esau and Ishmael were not" (although we have to observe the context and nuance of his affirmation). *Epistle to the Romans,* p. 586. In attempting to understand the logic of Paul's argument in Rom. 9–11 — and we would all do well to avoid excessive dogmatism in interpretation — attention has also to be given to what notion of salvation, not only what notion of election, we presume that Paul is working with.

significance in Scripture. Esau names an individual, but he also figures and functions as the head of the Edomites, who are all rejected in Esau's rejection and in which role the prophet Malachi envisions him when he announces on God's behalf: "Yet I have loved Jacob, but Esau I have hated" (Mal. 1:2-3). Of the eschatological fate of Esau or individuals descended from him, we do not learn from Paul in Romans 9. Any inferences we make about it will be on another basis than that provided by Paul's teaching on election at this point, even if we interpret the election of Jacob as entailing predestination to life. Both Esau and Pharaoh illustrate the sovereignty of God in election, but the course of election winds through varied terrain, taking into account different conditions and elements, diversified in its forms of discrimination. We must not flatten out all of God's discriminating activities. Because we cannot conclude eschatological reprobation in Esau's case, we cannot infer that this conclusion is invalid in Pharaoh's case. However, if we conclude that the text which concerns Pharaoh does not have to be read in terms of eschatological reprobation, the inapplicability of eschatological reprobation to Esau strengthens any independently gained conviction that it is not clearly applicable to Pharaoh.

Adopting, then, the same unwillingly cavalier prima facie approach to exegetical argument as the one adopted in the case of "single predestination" texts, I have indicated why I believe that antecedent reprobation is not part of the NT witness. We must now return to the positive reading of Acts 13 and texts implicitly read along Augustinian lines. In relation to Acts, it was simply said that those who rejected the word were genuinely capable of responding positively to it. Is this assumption too hasty, to say the least? There are texts in the NT which impel us to ask whether they could have responded positively. If that question is answered in the negative, the theological question arises of whether there was an obligation to respond positively, for how can you be obligated to do that which you cannot do? However that is answered, let us first ask about the NT text. Acts ends on the ominous Isaianic note sounded already in the Synoptics: "Go to this people and say, 'You will ever be hearing but never understanding; you will be ever seeing but never perceiving'"; this is the product of a calloused heart that God will not (at least at this time) heal. This text is hermeneutically important. It seems to push us in the direction of saying that Acts has all along been concerned to indicate the impossibility of belief rather than its positive possibility for those who reject the gospel.

However we interpret Acts left to itself, our suspicion that this is part of the NT witness is enhanced when we turn to the witness of John. At times, John seems to couple responsibility for believing with the impossibility of believing. If we read Acts as coupling responsibility with possibility, we might be tempted to conclude that our account of the NT, taken as a whole, needs to specify meticulously times, places, people, and contexts, resulting in a distinction between those times, places, people, and contexts where there was and those where there was not a genuine possibility for positive response. Thus Luke and John would not necessarily collide. Of course, meticulous specification is important whatever we believe about the theological unity of the NT. But is the temptation to distinguish in this way to be resisted? While it is impossible to be too attentive to the nuance, detail, and differentiae of biblical narrative, the Johannine testimony invites us to consider whether it merely expresses in sharpest form a paradox that is implicit, if not explicit, in the Synoptic Gospels and Acts. The surface paradox in Acts is the paradox whereby the opposite of predestination to life is the genuine and rejected possibility of embracing the gospel. In turning to John, we are asking about the paradox involved in the claim that people are simultaneously responsible for and incapable of believing. The latter pole of that paradox collides with the way in which I have described the former pole of the paradox in Acts. It is with this in mind that we turn to John's witness. In any case, we need to heed it in its own right.

John

In chapter 12, verse 40, John quotes Isaiah:

> "He had blinded their eyes
>   and deadened their hearts,
> so they can neither see with their eyes,
>   nor understand with their hearts,
>   nor turn — and I would heal them."[38]

It is "for this reason" that "they could not believe" (12:39). "The importance in the NT of the quotation from Isaiah 6 can hardly be exaggerat-

38. Although I retain the NIV translation here, in accordance with the policy followed in this volume, I am not committed to it as the optimal translation of this verse. However, the course of my argument must, as far as possible, try to avoid dependence on linguistic judgments expressed in translations and accordingly go light on detailed or even definite exegetical decisions.

ed."[39] These words occur at a structurally vital join in John's Gospel. It has been plausibly proposed that chapters 1–12 expound 1:11, "He came to that which was his own, but his own did not receive him."[40] The narrative up to chapter 12 explains how we are to understand and why we arrive at the Isaianic conclusion, as had the OT narrative in the Historical Books. No limitation in the scope of grace, from God's end, is indicated in the prologue. As we read on through the chapters, we find that distinctions between people are the function of human response to Jesus, the Word made flesh, and a text such as 3:36 underlines human responsibility for decision. Jesus dwells among and ministers to those whose disposition is corrupt and whose openness or otherwise to the light is revealed in their response to him (3:19-21). His opponents are those who have not the love of God in their hearts (5:42). If the eyes of the heart are blinded by God, it is because people do not want to see.

The interpretation of *hina* in 12:38 is an exegetical crux.[41] Linguistic considerations and exegetical confidence apart, it is important to reckon with the "strong" interpretation of *hina* in order to see whether my reading of Luke can, in principle, survive the pressure of Johannine contrast. This is not in order to render the NT witness maximally isomorphic. The question is whether the construction of an NT theology of predestination which takes something of a steer from Luke is rather arbitrary in the sense that another (e.g., Johannine) starting point would yield a different construction. At the center of John's theological understanding is the realization

39. C. K. Barrett, *The Gospel according to John: An Introduction with Commentary and Notes on the Greek Text* (London: SPCK, 1978), p. 431.

40. Correspondingly, it has been argued that chapter 13 onward is an exposition of the verse: "To all who received him, to those who believed in his name, he gave the right to become children of God" (1:12). These words come from the prologue; 12:37-50 seems to form an epilogue to the first part of the Gospel. "Jesus' rejection by his own (1:11) is detailed in 1:19–12:36 and explained in 12:37-43." Craig S. Keener, *The Gospel of John: A Commentary,* vol. 2 (Peabody, Mass.: Hendrickson, 2003), p. 883.

41. Although grammarians warn that purpose and result may be hard to distinguish in this type of Greek construction, the force and context of the passage surely signal the need to retain the strong purposive sense of *hina.* Of course, Semitic considerations must also be taken into account; see B. Lindars, *The Gospel of John* (London: Oliphants, 1972), p. 437. Chrysostom's observations on this passage are worth noting here; see his *Homilies on the Gospel of John,* in *A Select Library of the Nicene and Post-Nicene Fathers of the Christian Church,* vol. 14 (reprint, Grand Rapids: Eerdmans, 1996), pp. 252-53, as are those of that thoughtful commentator Frédéric Godet, *Commentary on the Gospel of St. John,* vol. 3 (Edinburgh: T. & T. Clark, 1889), pp. 82-89.

that persistent, culpable unbelief of the kind Isaiah and other prophets had witnessed in Israel brought on then and brings on now judgment in the following form: God determines that unbelief will be the destiny of the disobedient. The metaphor which will inform our discussion is this: if God locks the door, it is because it has already been shut firm from the inside by those not wanting or willing to abandon unbelief and enter into the obedience of faith. God decides to ratify human decision.[42]

Those passages which, on their surface, appear to say that Jesus teaches that his Father does not simply seal culpable unbelief by sovereign closure, but even determines the initial unbelief, must be read in this narrative context. Two passages are outstanding, centered on 6:36-46 and 10:25-29. Of the former, Barrett says that it is an "excellent microcosm of [the Gospel as a whole],"[43] and of 6:37 in particular: "The verse sums up the individualism, the universalism, and the predestinationism of the gospel."[44] Yet, the narrative up to that chapter scarcely exudes predestinarianism. With reference to these passages, Bultmann gets it right: "The Jews do not have it in their power to form a judgement about the Revealer; they have indeed already passed judgement. . . . [T]heir thought, which always remains within the sphere of unbelief, is equally powerless to overcome their unbelief. Only God himself could alter that."[45]

At first blush, John 10 appears stronger. We may be justified in denying the presence of an explicit double predestination in John 6.[46] However, beyond the fact that the calling of the sheep by name appears predestinarian, the strength of the words "You are not of my sheep" in this connection can hardly be missed.[47] Don Carson concludes that "[u]nbelief can be explained by the fact that the unbeliever has not been chosen, a fact which neither decreases the unbeliever's responsibility to believe, nor permits

42. As D. A. Carson puts it, the guilty are "condemned to do and be what they themselves have chosen." *The Gospel according to John* (Leicester: Apollos; Grand Rapids: Eerdmans, 1991), p. 448. Calvin formulates it thus: "It is accidental to the Word of God . . . to blind men." *The Gospel according to St. John 11–21 and the First Epistle of John* (Edinburgh: Saint Andrew Press, 1961), p. 47. "[T]he revelation brings to light the authentic being of man." R. Bultmann, *The Gospel of John* (Oxford: Blackwell, 1971), p. 453.

43. C. K. Barrett, "The Dialectical Theology of St. John," in *New Testament Essays* (London: SPCK, 1972), pp. 49-69, here p. 65.

44. Barrett, *Gospel according to John,* p. 294.

45. Bultmann, *The Gospel of John,* p. 231.

46. See Lindars, *The Gospel of John,* on 6:37, p. 260.

47. Edwyn Hoskyns, *The Fourth Gospel* (London: Faber and Faber, 1947), p. 387, is evasive on predestination here.

boasting by the believer."[48] Yet, while those chosen are not chosen on the ground that they merit choice, the fact that someone has not been chosen is not adduced by John to explain what we may call the primal unbelief which shapes his or her character.[49] We encounter Gospel characters *in medias res.* As in the case of Pharaoh, we are encountering unbelief as the fruit of character, with an unseen background to men we meet in their (relative) maturity. What no one can do is to decide how long to persist in unbelief, presuming to keep a door open to the claims of God's truth. God decides that he will not call some, but we are not told that he caused them from the beginning of their lives to be headed inevitably for the condition they are in when we meet them in the course of the Evangelist's report. As far as we are told, what God determines is *persistence* in unbelief, not what we are calling *primal* unbelief. The thoughts of many hearts are revealed in the Gospels (Luke 2:35). Calvin is right: "It is their own fault if God does not wish to convert them, for they were the authors of their own hopelessness."[50] In line with John 3:20-21, God's judgment and verdict is an exposure. The reason a person cannot leave the room is that the door has been locked, but the reason the door has been locked is that the person does not want to leave the room. Both emphases must be preserved. Raymond Brown, for example, reckons insufficiently with the explicit nature of the "sheep" texts in 10:26-29 when he flatly says that it is wrong to assume that those who do not believe do not believe because they are not given to God by Jesus.[51] As an explanation of God's determination of the outcome of unbelieving attitudes to the point of stubborn unbelief, this is insufficient.[52]

48. D. A. Carson, *Divine Sovereignty: Biblical Perspectives in Tension* (London: Marshall Pickering, 1994), p. 203.

49. I am not persuaded by Robert Yarborough's way of putting it in relation to John 10:26-27: "Jesus associates this tragic behaviour [attacking his message] with failure to believe — but he attributes it more fundamentally to not being recipients of the gift that engenders belief." "Divine Election in the Gospel of John," in *Still Sovereign: Contemporary Pesrpectives on Election, Foreknowledge, and Grace,* ed. Thomas Schreiner and Bruce A. Ware (Grand Rapids: Baker, 2000), pp. 47-62, here p. 52. The fundamental problem is the failure to believe.

50. Calvin is commenting on chapter 12 here; *Gospel according to St. John,* p. 47.

51. Raymond Brown, *The Gospel according to John, I–XII* (London: Chapman, 1971), p. 276. However, I appreciate the general importance he attaches to the specification of audience (p. 388).

52. Neither does Rudolf Schnackenburg reckon with unbelief in its whole dynamic and variegated length and breadth when he remarks, in relation to 12:39, that "[w]e seem to be faced with the theologically dubious assertion of a divine rejection (reprobation) even

John's way of presenting his material is often described in terms of "antinomy," "paradox," or some broadly cognate or aligned language. If we plump for "paradox," the paradoxes potentially embraced in John's Gospel include both (a) the paradox of simultaneous responsibility and inability in relation to belief and (b) the paradox of the apparent universality of God's love, on the one hand, and his discriminating activity in relation to humans, on the other.[53] Such is the deliberation and force of John's prose that it is surely mistaken to suppose that his presentation can be explained in terms of the NT habit of giving "its explanation on a simplified level wherein all happenings are attributed to divine causality without any sharp

---

before any decision by human beings." *The Gospel according to St. John,* vol. 2 (Tunbridge Wells: Burns and Oates, 1980), p. 414. On the other hand, I acknowledge the hermeneutical issue here, one which affects our reading of the entire OT, in relation to texts that describe divine action. It is flagged up by a remark such as that of Augustine: "For God thus blinds and hardens, simply by letting alone and withdrawing His aid." *Homilies on the Gospel of John,* in *Ante-Nicene and Post-Nicene Fathers,* vol. 7 (reprint, Grand Rapids: Eerdmans, 1991), p. 293.

53. The word "antinomy" is not so easily handled as it appears to be on the philosophical surface. John Sanders has protested that it is inappropriate to use it with respect to any biblical teachings, including divine sovereignty and human responsibility. *The God Who Risks: A Theology of Providence* (Downers Grove, Ill.: IVP, 1998), p. 35. In terms of his definition of antinomy, he is right, and I do not deny the appropriateness of his definition. However, in the context of biblical scholarship, it may be used to describe a literary trope. "Antinomies were . . . standard fare both in Greco-Roman rhetoricians and in Jewish writings," remarks Keener (*The Gospel of John,* p. 685), with reference to Rodney Whitacre. Barrett, referring to John's simultaneous Gnosticism and anti-Gnosticism, comments: "Here too we have an antinomy that is written into the stuff of the Gospel." "The Dialectical Theology," p. 55. He apparently equates the antinomic with the dialectical. "Antithesis" has also been proposed; Schnackenburg, e.g., refers to it in the context of Johannine "technique"; *The Gospel according to St. John,* vol. 1 (Tunbridge Wells: Burns and Oates, 1966), p. 115. Of course, "antithesis" may be regarded as subject to the same problem as "antinomy." I remain with "paradox" or "sharp paradox" as long as nothing hangs on the allegedly superior felicity of this description. Don Carson speaks of "tension," which Sanders too quickly apparently identifies with "antinomy" in his discussion of Carson. *The God Who Risks,* p. 35. Whether or not we subscribe to the detail of his formulations, Carson protects himself better than Sanders supposes by studiously advocating "retreat to the nebulous expression 'tension theology.'" *Divine Sovereignty,* p. 218. There are, indeed, wrong uses of "antinomy," as, e.g., when N. T. Wright describes Pauline predestination in Rom. 8:29-30 as an "apparent" antinomy as well as paradox. "The Letter to the Romans: Introduction, Commentary, and Reflection," in *The New Interpreter's Bible,* vol. 10 (Nashville: Abingdon, 2002), p. 603. "[T]alk of God's building the new Temple does not mean that there will not be human architects and stonemasons." However, there is not even an apparent antinomy (nor apparent paradox) here more than there is when I speak of my building a house, meaning that I employed laborers.

distinction between primary and secondary causality."[54] That may apply to some of the NT, but there is a studied point in John's presentation, a deliberate purpose in drawing our attention to both human and divine "causality," if we may provisionally retain that word, without glossing it. Such deliberation of purpose should also make us think twice before embracing the conclusion that the relation of grace and predestination to freedom is simply not experienced as a problem for John.[55] If we speak in terms of "issue" as well as "problem," how can we be confident that there is neither an issue nor a problem involved?[56]

Whether or not we opt for paradox, the question arises whether John's witness, expressed in his narrative and reflective theology, brings to its sharpest expression in Scripture the general problem which led us from Luke to John. A writer's literary style is explained by more than one factor, but while the existential phenomenon of unbelief is limned by the peculiar literary form in which it is presented to us, the language may itself be shaped by existential realities which are painful and, to some degree, perplexing, so that literary form reflects existential reality.[57] Barrett observes that "[p]erhaps it is safest to say that in language as in thought John treads, perhaps not unconsciously, the boundary between the Hellenic and the Semitic."[58] This is surely the function of bringing to conceptual expression in Greek the fruit of theological reflection on a theme traceable through the OT narrative, reaching its dramatic climax — even apocalypse — in the ministry of Jesus.[59] To put it this way does not entail a specific view about the relative possibilities of the Hebrew and Greek languages. Tropes

54. Brown, *Gospel according to John,* p. 485. Brown hears echoes of Deut. 29:24 in John 12:37, observing, in connection with the OT text, that its "primitive thought shows no theoretical awareness of secondary causality or divine permissiveness as regards what is related to salvation."

55. Hoskyns, *The Fourth Gospel,* p. 295.

56. "Like most of his Jewish contemporaries, John felt no tension between predestination and freewill," according to Craig Keener, *The Gospel of John: A Commentary,* vol. 1 (Peabody, Mass.: Hendrickson, 2003), p. 685. Cf. pp. 824-26. Whatever the case with Jewish contemporaries, can the absence of an explicit admission that there is a tension be taken as evidence that it was not felt? Are the literary signals anything like conclusive in this regard?

57. Of course, issues deeper than we can address in connection with language and its relation to the world surface here. Note Bultmann's reference to *"paradoxical states of affairs"* (he italicized only the word "paradoxical"), in *The Gospel of John,* p. 34.

58. Barrett, *Gospel according to John,* p. 11.

59. Yet, the Johannine prologue does not have to conceptualize its matter in the mode of paradox, which gives us food for thought.

surfacing in John and identified as characteristically Hebraic may not be exclusively so.[60] It is to John's use of the OT, rather than to Johannine Greek, that we must attend for present purposes. Though direct citations from the OT are fewer in John than in the Synoptic Gospels, allusions to the OT and the way the OT infuses John's pattern of thought and narration are outstanding.[61] Perhaps, then, the clue to the way John treats the coexistence of opportunity and obligation with impossibility and divine decision lies in the OT materials. Let us briefly explore this.[62]

The Isaianic revelation of Israelite contumacy is a prophetic declaration about its manifestation at a crucial juncture in history, but the darkness of humanity had been previously detected in the pages of the OT and what Isaiah eventually saw was effectively prophesied earlier. In Deuteronomy 31:16 we meet what will strike some readers as a surface paradox: the people have been exhorted to live to the Lord, but it is foreknown that they will not. Readers' judgment will vary about the depth underlying what is on the surface. If we have proceeded no further than this narrative juncture, we have every reason to suppose that what is foreknown is something the people will freely do, in the sense that they could have

60. Barrett finds parataxis to be the most striking feature of John's style, as characteristic of Aramaic as it is rare in good Greek; *Gospel according to John,* pp. 7-9, but see Keener on parataxis in Greek, *The Gospel of John,* 1:69 n. 142. Of course, what Barrett says about parataxis in Aramaic does not entail the marginalization of hypotaxis in the Hebrew Bible.

61. This has long and frequently been acknowledged in modern scholarship. Following a reference to Isa. 12:37-38, B. F. Westcott, for example, observes that "[t]he writer of the fourth Gospel is penetrated throughout — more penetrated perhaps than any other writer of the NT — with the spirit of the Old." *The Gospel according to St. John: The Greek Text with Introduction and Notes,* vol. 1 (London: John Murray, 1908), p. cxxxix. I am not claiming that the connection with the OT can be properly described without attending to linguistic and literary considerations. The link between literary and theological considerations may be fruitfully explored in relation, e.g., to Wisdom; see Brown, *Gospel according to John,* pp. cxxii-cxxv. This often bears on our key passages; see, e.g., Westcott, p. 230, on 6:37 and the house of wisdom.

62. Carson, *Divine Sovereignty,* well shows the link with the OT on the subject of sovereignty and responsibility. I agree with him (pp. 209-10) that we should not look in the direction of the time/eternity relationship for resolution of this question, *pace* Godet, *Gospel of St. John,* p. 87. Carson does, however, closely connect the sovereignty-responsibility question with the christological question, the question of Jesus as God and man (e.g., p. 160). Cf. Andrew Lincoln's point: "The paradoxical Christology, in which Jesus has both human and divine origins, can only be grasped when there is also a paradoxical response, in which believing is a matter both of human responsibility and divine initiative." *The Gospel according to John* (New York: Hendrickson, 2005), p. 230. I do not pursue the question of a connection with Christology.

done otherwise. There is no clear sign that divine foreknowledge thwarts human "libertarian" freedom; it is presented as divine awareness, not as divine determination, of future action. To apostrophize: if this reading of Deuteronomy encourages us to construct a philosophical account of it, it should be along the lines that the problem of divine foreknowledge and human freedom must not be described in terms of God foreknowing that a human will do *x,* but in terms of his foreknowing that a human will freely do *x.* Then it is not the case that the human being is not free to do other than what God foreknows, for the deed is foreknown precisely according to its free form. However, the human being *will* never in fact do other than what God foreknows, for it is foreknown what the human will do.

Philosophical rumination aside, at the end of Joshua the formulation is couched in terms of an unmistakably craggy paradox. "Joshua said to the people, 'You are not able to serve the LORD'" (Josh. 24:19), judged "perhaps the most shocking statement in the OT."[63] It is sometimes urged that this is not an absolute statement, but a piece of rhetoric, constituting a dramatic exhortation.[64] Is it? Perhaps humble, faithful, courageous Joshua exactly discerns the nature of the darkness. It may, I think, be more plausibly interpreted along prophetic than along rhetorical lines, but prophecy with a harder edge than we have just encountered in Deuteronomy.[65] If Deuteronomy apparently entertains libertarian freedom on its surface, Joshua apparently does not. There is a moral incapacity or inability on the part of the Israelites to obey. This is the paradox brought to light in an exhortation to responsibility. Joshua saw Isaiah's day.[66] If liberty remains

63. Trent C. Butler, *Joshua* (Waco, Tex.: Word, 1983), p. 274. This is because Joshua "denies that the people can do that which he has spent the entire chapter trying to get them to do."

64. Pekka M. A. Pitkänen, *Joshua* (Nottingham: Apollos, 2010), p. 396. Cf. M. H. Woudstra, *The Book of Joshua* (Grand Rapids: Eerdmans, 1981), p. 353. David M. Howard denies that this is an "absolute, timeless statement"; *Joshua* (Nashville: Broadman and Holman, 1998), p. 438.

65. Richard D. Nelson with justification speaks of a "deep paradox" here; *Joshua* (Louisville: Westminster John Knox, 1997), p. 276. J. Gordon McConville and Stephen N. Williams, *Joshua* (Grand Rapids: Eerdmans, 2010), p. 90, allow for this possibility. I am discounting the interpretation which regards verse 19 as an interpolation into an earlier text; my interest is in the canonically finished product.

66. Nothing in my argument hangs on an interpretation which can surely be tentative at best. There is much force in the different (though not inconsistent) explanation we find in Butler, *Joshua,* p. 275, and Nelson, *Joshua,* pp. 274-75, in connection with divine holiness and the jealousy of divine love.

in Joshua, it is more like the liberty of spontaneity (to do what you want), than of indifference (to do other than you did).

I have suggested that we picture the situation in terms of the divine locking from the outside of a door already closed from the inside. Whether or not this is Joshua, it surely is John. The paradox that comes to light here is the paradox of responsibility and inability to believe, a paradox grafted onto any other paradoxes that we discover in the twisted self-governance of human beings. What Scripture implies or makes explicit is that if you have got yourself to the point of inability to believe, it does not follow that there is no longer any responsibility to do so. And one good apostrophe deserves another: if, again, we want to construct a philosophical account, it should be in terms of the fact that there is a relevant sense in which obligation cannot be sloughed off by the fact that one cannot meet it. If I cannot feed my child because I simply have no way of getting the food, having gambled away my money, my obligation is not thereby dispensed with. However, this sort of illustration is not meant to inaugurate a comprehensive explanation of the point at issue. We must always ask about the illocutionary nature of biblical speech acts — why and with what purpose or end in mind what is said, is said — and resist too readily assimilating them into an independently constructed philosophical framework.

Philosophical rumination aside (again), it is quite in order to conclude that the paradox of belief and unbelief is that, on the one hand, humanity is responsible for believing but, on the other hand, ability is the product of God's mysterious working.[67] Unbelief has a profoundly moral root. God decides that this morality should run its course, find its terminus. Therefore, he locks the door. Of the "divine impossibility" that none can come to Jesus unless the Father draws him, Westcott observes: "It is not anything arbitrary, but inherent in the very nature of things; it does not limit but it defines the nature of human power."[68] There is much truth in this, but we need to tighten up the formulation so that "the nature of things" does not marginalize or exclude divine determination. The appearance of tension between a moral explanation of unbelief and the word of John 6:44-45, for example, is appearance only.[69]

It looks as though John so brings the story of Israel to its terse, pithy,

67. With Andrew Lincoln, *Gospel according to John,* p. 305, on 10:26-27.

68. Westcott, *Gospel according to St. John,* p. 235. Cf. p. 122: "Judgement is not an arbitrary sentence, but the working out of an absolute law."

69. This somewhat contrasts with Schnackenburg's analysis; *Gospel according to St. John,* 1:405.

climactic expression as to land us in a profound paradox. The riddle of divine election is perched on the riddle of unbelief.[70] Only predestination rescues. Given a universal guilty state and wayward disposition, God *must* act sovereignly for any human to respond, and predestination is the antecedent divine decision to act in time in sovereign grace. Then how are we to understand the universality of God's love? Generally and as long as faith is not understood autonomously, Barrett puts it well: "While God loves the world . . . his love only becomes effective among those who believe in Christ. For the rest love turns, as it were, to judgement."[71] The prologue, presumably a theological summary of the Gospel, starts with all and moves to the many. In universal love, God summons all to faith. Such is God; such is the gospel. That is the baseline, as far as God is concerned.[72] Yet the God who loves the world and summons all to faith knows of a rejection which will culminate in a cross. That cross he has purposed to turn into the means of salvation. In God's dispensation, only when unbelief runs this phase of its course will the cross bring it to light and resolution. Predestination is a device contrived by love to rescue men and women for the kingdom under conditions of time in a godless world.[73] Just as inability does not remove responsibility, so prophetic knowledge of unbelief does not prevent ringing invitation to the world. Prophets preached in agony to a people they were sometimes told would not listen. In a cry that would fain shatter the barrier that separates those divinely predestined to life from those divinely confirmed in their unbelief, Jesus hurls out his appeal to the listening world: "If anyone is thirsty, let him come to me and drink" (John 7:37).

In John, we have an extremity of darkness corresponding to the ex-

70. Schnackenburg, *Gospel according to St. John,* 2:412, appropriately included "The Riddle of Unbelief" as part of the subheading for the discussion of 12:37.

71. Barrett, *Gospel according to John,* p. 215, on 3:16. Perhaps "as it were" is too mild; it depends on its precise meaning and scope. Bultmann's way of putting it is: "Unbelief, by shutting the door on God's love, turns his love into judgement." *The Gospel of John,* p. 154. See his whole discussion on pp. 154-60. Barrett quotes Bultmann favorably in this connection (p. 218).

72. J. Ramsey Michaels's account of the "tension" at this point is hard to follow. *The Gospel of John* (Grand Rapids: Eerdmans, 2010), pp. 226-27.

73. Admittedly, this is an infralapsarian formulation, but I cannot here either defend infralapsarianism or ask whether this point is capable of skillful formulation in supralapsarian terms. Nor is it possible to investigate whether the concepts "infralapsarian" and "supralapsarian" are potentially apt and suitable for containing the biblical materials within their mold. Michaels seems to me to mistake John's emphasis here by emphasizing divine election at the expense of human unbelief; *The Gospel of John,* p. 377 (including n. 66).

tremity of love.[74] There is nothing moderate here.[75] What, then, shall we conclude in relation to Acts? If John portrays the paradox of responsibility and incapacity for believing, then either the paradox in Acts is a different one or my earlier description of the Acts paradox has to be revisited. To recapitulate: meticulous distinction of times and places, that is, precise attention to particular contexts, is all-important in attending to the implications of biblical narrative. Yet should we not resist the temptation to distinguish John and Acts in this respect?[76] On the one hand, the biblical (OT, Gospels, and Acts) narratives encourage the supposition that there is a time for possibility and a time where possibility has passed. There is a time for everything under the sun. On the other hand, if Acts 28 functions as the hermeneutic for Acts 13, we must ask whether the appearance of positive possibility in Acts 13 is revealed as appearance only in Acts 28.[77] Either Acts describes a process of hardening, so that what was once possible during the course of narrated history becomes impossible at the end of it, or it is crafted in terms of disclosure, so that we see at the end that what we thought in Acts 13 was possible turns out not to have been.

I neither need nor propose to be dogmatic about this. If my initial description of the paradox in Acts is challenged by the possibility of a redescription in the light of John, advertising the force of Acts 28, this does not mean abandoning the outline NT theology of predestination sketched earlier in this chapter, starting with Acts 13. Even if, at the precise *time* when Paul preached to the Jews in Acts, those who rejected were locked up in their rejection, it is nevertheless in *time* that they have become responsible for their condition. The crucial point is that, taken in the round, the biblical

74. Bultmann introduces his discussion of Johannine theology in *Theology of the New Testament,* vol. 2 (London: SCM, 1955), by treating "dualism" (chap. 2).

75. Cf. Bonhoeffer, *Ethics,* p. 76, on the days in which he lived: "Today we have villains and saints again, in full public view. The gray on gray of a sultry, rainy day has turned into the black cloud and bright lightning flash of a thunderstorm. The contours are sharply drawn. Reality is laid bare."

76. I believe that Bultmann exaggerates the difference between John and the rest of the NT in part because he exaggerates the significance of linguistic distinctions; *Theology of the New Testament,* pp. 8-10. He remarks on election in this connection; cf. *The Gospel of John,* p. 21. It is superficial in the extreme to read what he reads into the absence of the notion of God's covenant with Israel in John, as though it were not presupposed in what John writes. In fact, without this presupposition, I wonder how much sense we could make of John's Gospel.

77. A similar question arises in connection with the (hexateuchal?) possibility of reading Deut. 31 in the light of Josh. 24.

narrative encourages the supposition that genuine possibility in time, not antecedent impossibility before time, governs unbelief, even when moral possibility is judicially commuted to existential impossibility at a particular time in the course and under the conditions of a time which had been a time of genuine opportunity to respond positively to the gospel. Both John and Acts describe gospel rejection by much of Israel. The situation they describe is accounted for by responsible temporal Jewish unbelief to the point of incapacity, after the Prophet of prophets, incarnate in history, had cried out to the people.[78] I shall not try to decide here between libertarian and compatibilistic accounts of the biblical data or whether we have both, depending on time and place.[79] I shall not try to decide about the relationship of John to the Synoptic Gospels and to the book of Acts — whether, in Acts 13, there was a genuine possibility for repentance and, in John 12, there was not. The salient factor is that where God intervenes to stop giving chances and determines to lock us up in unbelief, in a condition he uses to further his purposes, the temporal decay of those on the scene, and not a pretemporal decree, accounts for divine action. If paradoxes multiply, it is because evil multiplies. Evil creates a dizzying disorder too dark for us to peer far into. If the Lukan contrast which has informed my discussion needs any modification, it is neither from the direction nor on account of an antecedent reprobative decree.[80]

78. We should not omit reference to the Synoptic Gospels; as R. H. Gundry put it, "People have refused to understand, and the parables will always obscure the truth judgmentally." *Matthew: A Commentary on His Handbook for a Mixed Church under Persecution* (Grand Rapids: Eerdmans, 1994), p. 256.

79. In any case, it looks as though a net woven of alternatively libertarian or compatibilist materials or even, in different places, of both kinds of cloth, is altogether too big in its holes and too crude in its texture to catch everything which is going on in the biblical narrative on this score. This is impressed on us by Robert Alter, *The Art of the Biblical Narrative,* revised and updated (New York: Basic Books, 2011). From its opening chapter, it is indispensable reading in connection with election. Within the framework of his literary approach, note that he speaks in terms of "dialectical tension between these antitheses of divine plan and the sundry disorders of human performance" (p. 39).

80. One indication of the superficiality of my study is the failure to attend to various citations of Isaiah. See Raymond Brown's useful tabulation in *Gospel according to John,* p. 486. I feel under no compulsion to press biblical materials into maximal uniformity on the question under consideration ("uniformity" being taken in contrast with "variety," not with "contradiction"). Sometimes it seems to me that such "flattening out" can attend the discussion of John. So, e.g., if we consult the texts cited by Grant R. Osborne as examples of Johannine teaching on predestination "exceeded," as he puts it, only in Rom. 9–11, it is not at all clear that all of them are about predestination, especially when read alongside

Revelation

Luke's description of what happened in Pisidian Antioch has led us to narrow our gaze, if that is an appropriate way of putting it, so that we have been preoccupied with the belief or unbelief of individuals rather than the course of history. John 12:37-43 is a good point of reentry into the wider scene. Its subject is Jewish unbelief. What are the implications, as far as the election of Israel is concerned?[81]

Paul offers a relatively sustained account of election in Romans 9–11, and the eschatological question of Israel profoundly exercises him. If the eschatological question was posed for us in the OT in terms of Israel and the nations, it is posed here in terms of church and Israel. The eschatology of Romans 11 is variously interpreted. However we resolve the exegetical questions, what we do not find is any specific or immediate light on the question we raised in relation to the OT, which is about the eschatological primacy of Israel over the nations. It is to the book of Revelation, if anywhere, that we turn in the hope of illumination here. When we do so with Romans 9–11 behind us, we find that the question is transposed into the new and complicating terms dictated by the emergence of the church as a body separate from Israel. More generally, Revelation, more than any other NT work, encourages the conclusion that the riddle of election remains until the eschaton. If the resolution of the riddle is hidden somewhere within the folds of the book that closes the Christian canon, it is only if we are able to interpret Revelation aright before the eschaton that the riddle will be resolved before the eschaton.

Quite apart from any considerations arising from the book itself, the history of the reception and interpretation of Revelation in the West (let alone its Eastern fate) has prevented the churches from according to Revelation the hermeneutical function which is surely its prima facie due in NT and biblical theology. Consequently, it is not the force it should be in Christian doctrine. If Revelation is the climax of prophecy, it stakes a strong claim to taking over, in relation to the canon of Christian Scripture, the hermeneutical role that OT prophecy plays in relation to the OT.[82] The

---

Romans: "Soteriology in the Gospel of John," in *The Grace of God and the Will of Man*, pp. 243-60, here p. 244.

81. See, e.g., the way that connections are drawn by Godet, *Gospel of St. John*, pp. 82-83, and Carson, *Gospel according to John*, pp. 448-49.

82. I borrow the phrase "the climax of prophecy" from Richard Bauckham's volume of that name (*The Climax of Prophecy* [Edinburgh: T. & T. Clark, 1993]).

symbolic and sometimes even coded character of the Apocalypse, as it appears to the postapostolic mind, and the divergent interpretations it has spawned appear to rule it out a priori as a promising candidate for ordering our theological reflection in all its comprehensive range. Yet are we not in danger of misapplying here the sane rule that we should interpret the obscure by the clear? Much of Scripture is transparently narrative history, and some of it supplies us with doctrinal formulation. In Genesis and Revelation, transparency and formulation fade away at the protological and eschatological margins of Scripture respectively. To say that transparency and formulation fade away is not to say that history and doctrine fade away.[83] "And why should a picture be only an imperfect rendering of the spoken doctrine? Why should it not do the *same* service as the words? And it is the service which is the point."[84] "We must interpret the obscure by the clear"; but is it of no significance for biblical theology and for dogmatics that we find the bulk of Scripture held fast within bookends that do not deliver history and doctrine in uniform literal and propositional form? In Western theology, we have often connected a historical with a literal account, best suited, as we have supposed, to its subject matter — history. Somewhat accordingly, we have often connected doctrine with a propositional account, best suited, as we have supposed, to its subject matter — doctrine. Genesis and Revelation ask us at least to think again.

Whatever the outcome of our deliberations on this comparatively unwieldy question, we must surely consider the possibility that the book of Revelation be accorded hermeneutical centrality in our understanding of biblical theology and, correspondingly, in the construction of Christian doctrine. If the plenitude of the meaning of history is disclosed to us only in the fullness of eschatological time, the book which most vividly and deliberately displays that fullness before our gaze has all the potential for being grandly pregnant with theological disclosure. Although Revelation has been and is interpreted in many ways, we cannot gainsay the generality that it constitutes a grand depiction of cosmic and historical drama, culminating in the eschaton. This provides us with fecund possibilities in relation to election. Perhaps only when we acknowledge this will we

83. The Kantzer Lectures adapted for this volume were delivered in the bicentenary year of Tennyson's birth in 1809, so, instead of fading *at* the margins, perhaps we should speak of Genesis and Revelation as "an arch wherethrough / Gleams that untravelled world, whose margin fades / For ever and for ever," to quote Tennyson's poem "Ulysses."

84. Ludwig Wittgenstein, *Philosophical Investigations* (London: Macmillan, 1953), part II, p. iv.

make progress on election (as on other doctrinal subjects), even if progress means discovering the limits of mortal understanding. Given what a main stream in Protestantism — Luther, Zwingli, and, perhaps, Calvin — made of Revelation, this would be a far-reaching conclusion; to accord to Revelation a pivotal hermeneutical role would herald the appearance of Joachim of Fiore in the wings of our theological drama.[85]

If Romans 11:11-32 portends in sober, though stirring, language a further reversal in the story of election, Revelation inculcates in our minds that same possibility in the dramatic language of an imagery which strains, but does not quite burst, narrative form. Perhaps "reversal" is not precise enough to catch what Revelation is getting at, precisely because it places inappropriate constraints of descriptive precision on the text. Perhaps "further development," though very bland, is better. What we have in mind here is the disclosure that, after battles are done, the nations will walk by the light of the city of God and the kings of the earth will bring their splendor into it (Rev. 21:24). Nations apparently come to enjoy the privileges of the covenant people; the glory and honor they bring reflect the glory and honor bestowed on and offered to the Lamb by the heavenly choir of the redeemed. It may be going too far to say that "the nations balance up and even compensate for the adoration previously offered to the monster."[86] Nonetheless, a positive destiny for the nations is in prospect.

What is involved in that prospect is a matter of exegetical dispute. Are the nations converted? Who or what is included in "the nations"? Do the rebellious kings return on stage like characters in a stage play, smiling, united, joining hands at the curtain call after the brutal hostilities of

85. Joachim's work turned up in Venice in 1527 under the theological sponsorship of the Anabaptists. See Irena Backus, *Reformation Readings of the Apocalypse: Geneva, Zurich, and Wittenberg* (Oxford: Oxford University Press, 2001), p. xvii. (Jürgen Moltmann gives this date as 1519 in *The Coming of God: Christian Eschatology* [London: SCM, 1996], p. 157.) Backus observes that "[t]he most famous reformers either condemned the book (Zwingli, Luther) or ignored it (Melanchthon, Bucer, Calvin). Only Bullinger attempted to make it suitable reading for the faithful" (p. 29). Had Bullinger explored the logic of his belief that the Apocalypse combined the genres of Gospel and Epistle, would he have moved in the direction of an insight into the hermeneutical possibilities of Revelation in regard to both Old and New Testaments?

86. So W. Gordon Campbell in his very fine and illuminating study, *Reading Revelation: A Thematic Approach* (Cambridge: James Clarke, 2012), p. 155. Anselm memorably stamps on our hearts and minds the impression that we can never compensate for sin; "Cur Deus Homo," in *Anselm of Canterbury: The Major Works*, ed. Brian Davies and G. R. Evans (Oxford: Oxford University Press, 1998), pp. 260-356, especially p. 283.

the drama? "This is the form of vengeance that the grace of God takes: It converts the most rabid enemies of the church into her ardent lovers and champions" — are we to say this here?[87] Universalism does not appear on the horizon (see, e.g., 22:15), but do at least some privileged dead from the nations enter the city of God, by grace to join the elect?[88] Or is it precisely those alive who do so?[89] We may not be able to dig out any clear answer from Revelation itself. It perpetuates the persistent OT, indeed, whole biblical, habit of focusing our attention elsewhere where the relations of the nations to election are concerned, that is, focusing it on history rather than on individual postmortem destinies, although the depiction of the judgment of the individual dead is stark (20:12-15). It is difficult to suppose that "history" is not the appropriate natural category to apply to the last two chapters of Revelation, although it is not history literally told and we are entering a unique future-eschatological zone. At least we have to reckon with the strong possibility of ongoing history. The extent to which Isaiah, Ezekiel, Daniel, and Zechariah, whose presences pervade the book, encourage us to attend in any detail to the question of the individual dead is moot; but the presence of these prophecies in the book of Revelation tends to keep alive in us an underlying sense of history in motion, even while the book does not parade its images in the service of providing a unilinear depiction of history. The story of election runs out in massive hope for the joining of the elect by the nations. What occupies the center is a scene suggesting ongoing development and dynamic, following the descent of Jerusalem from heaven and the parousia of Jesus. It is not hard to see the appeal of a type of broadly premillennialist reading here, in the sense that the parousia of Jesus is not the end of history but inaugurates what we cannot help conceptualizing as "history." The Qumran Habakkuk *pesher* words it quite felicitously: "The final age shall be prolonged, and shall exceed all that the prophets have said; for the mysteries of God are astounding."[90] Revelation depicts a story not yet ended, and as we close the

87. A. Pieper, quoted by Oswalt, *Isaiah, Chapters 40–66,* p. 551.

88. Commenting on the scene whose description ends at 21:27, George Caird voices his conviction that "[n]owhere in the NT do we find a more eloquent statement than this of the all-embracing scope of Christ's redemptive work." *The Revelation of St. John the Divine* (London: A. & C. Black, 1984), p. 280.

89. Robert L. Thomas briefly lists nine options for the identity of the kings before tentatively proposing a tenth. *Revelation 8–22: An Exegetical Commentary* (Chicago: Moody, 1995), pp. 476-78.

90. Quoted by Richard Bauckham in *The Climax of Prophecy,* p. 262. However, he

book, the eschatological suspense with which we close the OT is scarcely removed, though it is transposed into a different key.

We have refrained from venturing any judgment on Paul's teaching on the eschatological prospect for the Jews, even though we are here at the large heart of NT teaching on election, and it would be perverse to venture an interpretation of Revelation in respect of them. The reappearance of the ark (11:19); the inscription of the names of the twelve tribes of Israel on the gates, accompanying those of the twelve apostles on the foundations (21:12-14); the very texture of the author's "Hebraized" or "Hebraic Greek," if we may call it that, combine to some degree to sow seeds of positive thinking about the future prospects for ethnic Jews. It was only the course of history, as interpreted in the NT, which disclosed to us the true meaning of the hope to which the OT beckons, inasmuch as its hope is fulfilled in the New. In the same way, only the eschaton will disclose the form of the fulfillment of the hope to which the NT beckons us. Perhaps Revelation provides us with the last earthly word on the riddle of election, and perhaps its last word is parallel to the one we encounter in the OT, defining the limits of dogmatic, as well as of biblical, theology. The word is simply this: that we shall not know how the story ends until we get there.

If Revelation be our guide, we are surely entitled (if not mandated) to hope that the terminus of God's electing and predestining ways will include a width of embrace far wider than the visible *ecclesia* in normal historical time comprehends. In light of our earlier question about whether predestination moderates the hopes raised in the OT, we must say now that to hope for this width of embrace is to hope that the advent and revelation of Jesus Christ will prove to satisfy a hope even greater than the OT can express. We must wait. In the meantime, we should indicate a possibility whose potential for shedding light on election and predestination we are bound to state without definitive dogmatizing. The latter is impossible not only because of the impossibility of pronouncing on the matter solely out of Revelation, but also because we should have to take into account a much wider swathe of biblical data than is explicitly connected even with the theme of election and to make assumptions on matters outside the terms of our remit. Nevertheless, while the following is speculative, it is not ungrounded or futile speculation.

---

quotes the passage from which I have extracted this reference to the Habakkuk *pesher* in order to *contrast* the *pesher* with Revelation in the context of his discussion.

How exactly should we interpret the fact that followers of the Lamb are destined to reign with him (20:4-6; 22:2)? Earlier in the NT, we have read that the disciples of Jesus will judge the twelve tribes of Israel (Matt. 19:28) and that the saints will judge the world and judge angels (1 Cor. 6:2-3).[91] A reigning group permits — though, in nonliteral discourse or discourse pertaining to a different world-order, it does not require — a people over whom to reign. We meet many "groups" in Revelation, including a mediating priesthood (Rev. 5:9-10) and martyrs, who are first-fruits (14:4).[92] "Reign" is a subject broached right from the beginning of the book of Revelation (2:27). Our familiar, Western egalitarian instincts may impel us to shy away from the thought of any gradation in reward, but the presence of the martyrs in the book of Revelation, quite apart from other hints in the NT, warns us not to transpose into apocalyptic key the assumptions or pretensions of modern democratic politics. Actually, Scripture has proved its democratic credentials, as it were, from the very beginning, with its declaration that not oriental kings, but humans as such are made in the image of God (Gen. 1:26). "Reigning" in Revelation surpasses the reestablishment of Genesis dominion, whose immediate scope is the earth, not its inhabitants. If we have surrendered to God the right to make temporal distinctions in election, we must surrender to him the right to make eschatological distinctions in terms of privilege and office, as well. Or are we about to accuse God of injustice? Jonathan Edwards, who was fascinated by the book of Revelation and, in 1723, began to devote a separate notebook to it, speaks edifying words in this connection.

> Not the least remainder of any principle of envy [will] be exercised towards any angels or saints who are superior in glory, no contempt or slight towards any who are inferior. Those who have a lower station of glory than others suffer no diminution of their own happiness by seeing others above them in glory. . . . Those who are highest in glory are those who are highest in holiness, and therefore are those who are

91. Although I provisionally share the tentativeness expressed by commentators such as Leon Morris, *The Gospel according to Matthew* (Grand Rapids: Eerdmans, 1992), p. 496 on the Matthean text, the possibility that judging entails ruling must be taken seriously, especially when the text is read against the background of the Wisdom of Solomon 3:8, where the just "will be judges and rulers over the nations of the world" (NEB translation). See also John Nolland, *Luke 18:35–24:53* (Dallas: Word, 1993), p. 1067 on Luke 22:30.

92. To put it like that is not to make any decisions about the identity, partial identity, or distinction between these various "groups."

most beloved by all the saints. For they love those most who are most holy, and so they will rejoice in that they are the most happy.[93]

Edwards speaks generally of gradation; I am speaking specifically of reigning. I do not renege on the judgment that it is only the eschatological manifestation of God's ways that will draw together for us the threads of what, until that disclosure, is only indistinctly foreshadowed in biblical teaching. However, if reflection on the *ecclesia* in Revelation impels us to think about gradation, reflection on the nations in Revelation impels us to think about the nature and scope of the reign of the elect. The mystery of the relation of the elect to the nations is deeper in the NT than it is in the OT. In the OT, we can sufficiently identify who the elect are (even allowing for the relation of ethnic Israel to the remnant of Israel) and who belong to the nations (even allowing for distinctions between them and representative individuals within them). The denationalization and depoliticization of the elect in the NT, relative to the OT, make the identification of "nations" harder at the end of the Apocalypse. The language of "nations" conjures up the territorial associations attached to it in the OT, but the church of Jesus Christ is not a territorial entity in the sense that Israel basically was and it is found in or among the nations. Further, there is the question of the Jews and Judaism. In Revelation, the "nations" are related to the one elect body of Jews and Gentiles, one component of which (the Gentile) was formerly itself of the nations.

Despite intricacies, the relation obtaining between the covenant and elect people of God, now Jew and Gentile, and the nations which appear to enter the kingdom at the end parallels what we appeared to read in the OT but could not interpret there with confidence.[94] I refer to the rule of

93. From his last sermon, "Charity and Its Fruits," in Jonathan Edwards, *Ethical Writings,* vol. 8 in *The Works of Jonathan Edwards* (New Haven: Yale University Press, 1989), p. 375. By way of contrast, when Clement of Alexandria conceptualizes gradation in terms of "the elect of the elect," those who have not attained the highest place will sorrow, knowing that they could have lived better lives; see Eric Osborn, *Clement of Alexandria* (Cambridge: Cambridge University Press, 2005), pp. 52-53. But see too chapters 13–14 of Clement's *Stromateis* in *The Ante-Nicene Fathers,* vol. 2 (reprint, Grand Rapids: Eerdmans, 1994), pp. 504-6. Exploring the difference between Clement and Edwards here would take us too far afield.

94. As Richard Bauckham puts it, "[n]ow that the covenant people have fulfilled their role of being a light to the nations, all nations will share in the privileges and promises of the covenant people." *Theology of the Book of Revelation* (Cambridge: Cambridge University Press, 1993), p. 131. (Perhaps "all" is a bit too strong.) Christopher Wright rightly observes that "the covenant includes God's blessing, but God's blessing is not limited to the

Israel over the nations. In Revelation, we seem to learn that the nations will *participate* in kingdom life, but there is no hint that they will *reign.*[95] If we could see further than John of Patmos, we might conclude that the saving blessing to the nations does not end simply with their incorporation into what took temporal form as the historical and visible *ecclesia.* Then the question of Israel's rule over the nations, now translated into the question of those new Israelites who reign in the book of Revelation, would be raised afresh. We cannot see further than John the seer, and anyone who claims to do so should scarcely command our theological allegiance.[96]

---

covenant." *The Mission of God: Unlocking the Bible's Grand Narrative* (Nottingham: Inter-Varsity Press, 2006), p. 204. Will the spiritual descendants of Japheth join the spiritual descendants of Shem?

95. It could be argued (as I am not doing) that healed members of the nations might eventually be numbered amongst the servants of God and thus reign (22:5). What we are told is that authority over the nations is given to the one who overcomes (2:26; cf. Ps. 2:8-9). Stephen S. Smalley is puzzled by Rev. 22:2: "Why . . . is therapy needed in the new Jerusalem . . . ?" *The Revelation of John: A Commentary on the Greek Text of the Apocalypse* (London: SPCK, 2005), p. 563. However, he is not reckoning with a process analogous to temporal-historical processes, which is surely a very strong possibility. It is most implausible to say, with David E. Aune, that the allusion to leaves of the trees for the healing of the nations "is simply mechanical . . . since there is no real place in the eschatological scheme of Revelation for 'the healing of the nations' contrasted to their conversion." *Revelation 17–22* (Dallas: Nelson, 1998), p. 1178. In similar language, Austin Farrer reads the phrase "of the nations" as an "almost automatic symbolical development." *The Revelation of St. John the Divine: A Commentary on the English Text* (Oxford: Clarendon, 1964), p. 222. As has often been pointed out, why supplement the imagery of Ezek. 47 with reference to the nations if the allusion is simply mechanical? See, e.g., Mitchell G. Reddish, *Revelation* (Macon, Ga.: Smith and Helwys, 2001), p. 420. Robert H. Mounce simply decides that there is no literal healing — that the imagery is borrowed from the present age. *The Book of Revelation* (Grand Rapids: Eerdmans, 1977), p. 387. I am not persuaded that Rev. 22:2 can be read at the level of generality that takes it to be no more than "figurative for the redemption accomplished by Christ, which will be consummated at his final parousia." G. K. Beale, *The Book of Revelation* (Grand Rapids: Eerdmans, 1999), p. 1108.

96. George Eldon Ladd starts his sentence sensibly but ends it much too dogmatically when he says, in reference to 22:5: "The text does not say whom they shall reign over, nor is it important." *A Commentary on the Revelation of John* (Grand Rapids: Eerdmans, 1972), p. 289. In one respect, Smalley is a bit more cautious: "Although the saints are said to 'reign for ever and ever' in heaven, it is not immediately apparent who will be their subjects, and in the vision such a consideration may not be important." *The Revelation of John,* p. 566. However, 22:5 speaks of reign on earth, not in heaven. Grant R. Osborne is amongst those who are far too swift and dismissive on 22:5: "Of course, this cannot be meant literally, for every saint will rule a kingdom that only the saints inhabit." *Revelation* (Grand Rapids: Baker Academic, 2002), p. 776. The position most completely opposite to the one I moot

Is this a truth about predestination that we need to consider: that God's predestination is a predestination to reign, whose proper opposite is to be described eschatologically as "not predestined to reign"? To couch the opposite in these terms is not to prescribe a uniform destiny for those not predestined to reign. Amongst them, there are the saved and the lost. The distinction implicitly picked out in the vocabulary of predestination and election, on the occasion when the terms virtually overlap, is not simply between those predestined to eschatological life and those who will never have eschatological life. Not numbered amongst the elect are those from the nations who will enter the new Jerusalem, along with those who reject the gospel and will not. Those who enter will not, however, reign there. Of course, the form of the reign of the elect is hidden from the mind's eye. Whether members of the nations are capable of upward mobility eventually to join the ranks of the reigning; whether such a form of reigning ceases; what eschatological stability attends the arrangement indicated in Revelation — this we cannot know and should not try to guess.[97]

I have deliberately been sketchy because the biblical foundations for this suggestion would need to be nailed down more firmly than I can do in this volume before attempting to adumbrate it theologically. If we entertain the possibility cursorily advanced, does it alleviate the difficulty widely felt with regard to Augustinian predestination? Some will think that it does; others that it offers, at best, a minor relief. (Of course, others will protest that no relief is needed.) If those who are not classified in the NT as elect or predestined may yet be saved, some will find that this demurral from the Augustinian tradition will help to reconcile them to that component in Augustinian doctrine which I have sought to retain. If those who are not classified in the NT as elect or predestined may yet be saved, but may not reign, others will judge that the grounds for their demurral from

---

here is the one apparently entertained by Ibson T. Beckwith when he quotes from *1 Enoch:* "Its fruit shall be food for the elect." *The Apocalypse of John: Studies in Introduction with a Critical and Exegetical Commentary* (New York: Macmillan, 1919), p. 766. It is the *nations,* not the elect, who are mentioned in 22:2.

97. Although I demur from this or that in their accounts and their accounts are, in any case, not identical, my reading of Rev. 21:24–22:5 strikes out in the same very general direction as those of Mitchell Reddish, *Revelation;* Robert Thomas, *Revelation 8–22;* and R. H. Charles, *A Critical and Exegetical Commentary on the Revelation of St. John,* vol. 2 (Edinburgh: T. & T. Clark, 1920). On the wider canvas of the book of Revelation, I find generally congenial the argument and conclusion of Poul F. Guttesen's study, *Leaning into the Future: The Kingdom of God in the Theology of Jürgen Moltmann and the Book of Revelation* (Eugene, Ore.: Pickwick, 2009), especially pp. 110-58.

Augustinianism remain firm. It should go without saying that those who partake of eschatological salvation, but not of temporal election, have not entered the city of God by some other means than the efficacy of atonement and the pardon of grace.

Of this we may be sure. How election stands in relation to nation, universe, and nonelect, and how it expresses divine love, mercy, and justice, will be entirely consonant with what John has told us: God is light, in him there is no darkness at all (1 John 1:5). It is a light by which the nations will walk and one whose dawning we must await. Where there is an eschatological perspective, we are suitably chastened in our dogmatics. "Where there is an eschatological perspective, arbitrariness is ruled out."[98] Indeed so, for an eschatological perspective is shaped by the promise of the glory of God. Its guarantor is the Word of God, he who is faithful and true, Jesus Christ. In him and for him all was created; in him and for him election takes place. The nations are his. The center of this whole chapter has been the Lamb on the throne. Jesus Christ is the center of our theological thinking, because what else is the election of grace about if it is not about him? He is the Word of God, faithful and true, and the NT testimony to Jesus, as the Word of God, partakes of that fidelity and that truth.

98. G. C. Berkouwer, *Divine Election* (Grand Rapids: Eerdmans, 1960), p. 66.

CHAPTER THREE

Dogmatic Limits

If our discussion of election up to this point is meant to gesture in the direction of a narrative doctrine of election, the gesture may not be a positively feeble one, as far as it goes, but neither is it any too vigorous. Although our discussion of election in the NT took off from the inclusion of Luke's statement about predestination in his narrative, no attempt was made to defend the methodological superiority — or even propriety — of discussing NT election in that way. Nonetheless, I have judged it appropriate, as long as we read the narrative mindful that election is in Christ. In the next two chapters, we turn respectively to questions of theological method and theological substance which arise in connection with the biblical theology outlined. In the course of treating the question of an antecedent reprobative decree in the NT, I alluded to the claim that, as long as we affirm anything like an Augustinian single predestination, we are impelled to conclude theologically that there is such a decree, because it is a straightforward and necessary theological deduction — elementary, inescapable, and scarcely a trick of the dark art of systematization. In probing this claim on dogmatic inescapability, attention to theological method is needed. Admittedly, it takes the place of a theologically wider and, indeed, richer exploration of election, but both the history of theology and the presence of predestination in the NT make it virtually inescapable.[1]

1. I am not unaware of the shortcomings of this procedure. As Bernard Lonergan simply put it: "Theology as a whole functions within the larger context of Christian living and Christian living within the still larger process of human history." *Method in Theology* (New York: Herder and Herder, 1973), p. 144. In emphasizing the function of theology within life, as I shall be doing, I shall be all too negligent of life within history. In that respect, the scope and balance of Wolfhart Pannenberg's treatment of election (irrespective of its substance)

Appeal to the biblical narrative in the previous chapter may have appeared portentous, the warning sign of a gaze turned in an antisystematic direction, if not of a face set resolutely that way. The first characteristic of "narrative theology" picked out in the article which introduces it in the *Dictionary for the Theological Interpretation of the Bible* is "antipathy towards forms of theology concerned with the systematic organization of propositions and grounded in ahistorical principles."[2] This is an opposition quite widely advertised in theological literature. However, the championship of narrative in the last chapter did not go so far as to threaten system and did not entail anything about system as such. "Narrative theology" was neither promoted nor denigrated, its dogmatic promise neither declared nor denied. The question of narrative theology puts in an appearance now only because it was stipulated in the last chapter that narrative be accorded a decisive hermeneutical role. This chapter takes the question of narrative no further. A narrative interpretation of or narrative approach to Christian doctrine demands a fair hearing in its own right, and Hans Frei's dictum that the "meaning of the doctrine is the story, not, the meaning of the story is the doctrine," deserves a fair consideration in its own right.[3] It may turn out that the position outlined in the following discussion lends itself more to some than to other ways of conceiving the relationship of narrative to system, but the relations of narrative to propositions and of propositions to system demand a careful attention that we neither can nor need to give here.[4]

---

are in a salient respect more satisfactory than my own; *Systematic Theology,* vol. 3 (Grand Rapids: Eerdmans; Edinburgh: T. & T. Clark, 1998), pp. 435-526.

2. Kevin J. Vanhoozer, ed., *Dictionary for the Theological Interpretation of the Bible* (Grand Rapids: Baker, 2005), p. 531. The author of the article is Joel Green.

3. Hans W. Frei, *Types of Christian Theology* (New Haven: Yale University Press, 1992), p. 90. This is not to say that Frei himself espoused a narrative theology or narrative interpretation of doctrine, however positively his work is related to such enterprises. Frei judged that his thinking about doctrine had an affinity with Wittgenstein's belief that the meaning of concepts lies in the way that they shape a form of life. In light of Kierkegaard's appearance later in this chapter, note Hunsinger and Placher's editorial observation that "the dissenting tradition in modern thought that has Kierkegaard urging 'existence is not a system' and that found Barth echoing that, if so, then all the more is God's self-revelation not a system, is perhaps continued by Frei on the hermeneutical plane," in Hans Frei, *Theology and Narrative: Selected Essays* (New York and Oxford: Oxford University Press, 1993), p. 27. Nor am I nailing my colors to the mast of the "narrative logic" impressively limned by Richard Hays in *The Faith of Jesus Christ: The Narrative Substructure of Galatians 3:1–4:11* (Grand Rapids: Eerdmans, 2002), pp. 220-26.

4. False disjunctions must be avoided. The Apostles' Creed encapsulates the way in which Christian doctrine can be described alternatively as a propositional summary of

The "dramatic" approach to doctrine was earlier mentioned as something of a successor or supplement to the narrative approach, but no position will be adopted on this more than is adopted on narrative.[5] It may be that what I argue lends itself to helpful elaboration in dramatic terms, but it is no part of my purpose to figure out whether this is so. Balthasar devoted his five-volume theo-dramatics largely to exploring how the question of freedom is illuminated when we conceive of Christian doctrine along dramatic lines, and a discussion of Balthasar is prima facie inviting, not to mention pertinent, in connection with election. According to Balthasar, "however much it [theology] tries to create a systematic presentation, it must leave room for this dramatic aspect [i.e., 'of revelation . . . the history of a struggle between God and the creature over the latter's meaning and salvation'] and find an appropriate form of thought for it."[6] Yet, he can still talk of a kind of system: "If theology . . . is full of dramatic tension, both in form and content, it is appropriate to . . . establish a kind of *system* of *dramatic categories*."[7] Balthasar's "kind of" turns out to be elusive. His conception of theo-dramatic theory is quite general in at least this respect: the way that its methodological contours actually limn his substantive discussion is vague.[8] In Kevin Vanhoozer's exploration of doctrine as drama,

---

narrative or as a minimal narrative set forth in propositions. "Jesus rose from the dead" is a propositional encapsulation of Gospel narrative. Yet, I confess sympathy toward John Goldingay's remarks on the limits of systematic theology in relation to the capacities of narrative in "Biblical Narrative and Systematic Theology," in *Between Two Horizons: Spanning New Testament Studies and Systematic Theology*, ed. Joel Green and Max Turner (Grand Rapids: Eerdmans, 2000), pp. 123-42, especially p. 135.

5. Mikhail Bakhtin's observation that Dostoevsky's "deep affinity for the dramatic form" was associated with the fact that he "conceived his world primarily in terms of space, not of time" invites the question of whether conceiving it in terms of time would have produced an affinity for narrative form and, if so, whether narrative and drama differ more significantly than I have implied; see *Problems of Dostoevsky's Poetics*, trans. C. Emerson (Manchester: Manchester University Press, 1984), p. 28.

6. Hans Urs von Balthasar, *Theo-Drama I: Theological Dramatic Theory; Prolegomena* (San Francisco: Ignatius, 1988), p. 126.

7. Balthasar, *Theo-Drama I*, p. 128.

8. The general nature of the theory — at least, general as regards the kind of dramatic categories that are of interest in connection with system, narrative, and theological method — is illustrated in the excessive and indulgent first volume of the *Theo-Drama*. For a variety of programmatic formulations of what Balthasar is attempting in this volume, see especially pp. 9, 11, 18, 66, 112, and 130. Balthasar's "dramatic resources" for theology, drawing on theater both as an illumination of existence and because it exhibits the character of existence, are spread out in part II of this volume. One way to discover what kind of thing

in which he builds on his earlier theological work on speech acts, there is certainly a place for the good, old-fashioned theological proposition and, therefore, for the requirement that we respect good, old-fashioned inference.[9] It is a question of what the place of proposition is, not whether it has a place. He demurs from the type of "propositional" approach taken by Charles Hodge, for example, but nothing in his approach rules out the theological legitimacy of discussing the question of inference from predestination to life in the form in which it has been posed in this volume.[10]

Balthasar has in mind when he advertises the usefulness of his account for theo-dramatic theory is to read his discussion of Schelling, pp. 566-77. Ben Quash is amongst those who note the looseness of the application of theo-dramatic theory to the detail of Christian doctrine in the subsequent volumes; "The Theo-Drama," in *The Cambridge Companion to Hans Urs von Balthasar,* ed. Edward T. Oakes and David Moss (Cambridge: Cambridge University Press, 2004), p. 146. The theological conception of human freedom assumed in Balthasar's first theo-dramatic volume emerges most visibly in, e.g., statements about divine love as necessarily cherishing human autonomy (p. 280) and the author's affirmation of Schiller (p. 359). Unfortunately, our discussion of Karl Barth in the appendix will afford us no opportunity to discuss connections with Balthasar in relation to election or predestination. For Balthasar's own study of Barth, see *The Theology of Karl Barth* (New York: Holt, Rinehart and Winston, 1971). Balthasar found that de Lubac's belief that all humanity and the whole universe are predestined in the church was an anticipation of Barth's discussion of election and predestination in *Church Dogmatics* II/2: *The Theology of Henri de Lubac: An Overview* (San Francisco: Ignatius, 1991), p. 41. See A. Scola, *Hans Urs von Balthasar: A Theological Style* (Edinburgh: T. & T. Clark, 2005), p. 103, for the formulation of a cognate way of thinking in Balthasar himself.

9. See Vanhoozer, *The Drama of Doctrine: A Cultural-Linguistic Approach to Christian Theology* (Louisville: Westminster John Knox, 2005). Vanhoozer follows this up consistently with the approach taken in *Remythologizing Theology: Divine Action, Passion, and Authorship* (Cambridge: Cambridge University Press, 2010). I find this essay generally very congenial and regret that I cannot take it into account in a chapter which explores just one angle on theological method and that constraints of space disable me from positioning my account more precisely in relation to it, e.g., to the discussion in chapters 6 and 7. "Whereas many accounts of divine sovereignty look for a causal joint between God and world, I shall explore the potential of thinking about this joint in the communicative terms of corporeal and penetrative discourse (i.e., word and Spirit)" (p. 367). I am not joining discussion of "a fresh way of thinking about the so-called 'causal joint' between God and the world, divine and human action" (p. 300). For specific discussion of the hardening of Pharaoh's heart, see pp. 339-42; for discussion of Dostoevsky, see pp. 310-11; and for the association of Bakhtin, Barth, and Balthasar, see p. 316. Vanhoozer believes that "Barth's attempt to shift the discussion surrounding the *concursus* between divine and human freedom from generalities about causal power to the specifics of Word and Spirit is a stroke of theological genius" (p. 370).

10. This emerges in an area germane to our discussion, namely, in relation to effectual call; Vanhoozer, *Remythologizing Theology,* p. 373. Even though "[d]octrines are less prop-

The phenomenon we encountered in the biblical narrative, namely, the contrast between a genuine offer and a predestination to life, grounded my provisional denial of the claim that predestination to life logically requires an antecedent decree of reprobation. Whatever obtains in the case of the NT text, how does that claim fare in the austere zone of dogmatics? Does not logic dictate that God *must* stand eternally in relation to those not predestined as he does to those he either (a) passes over in predestination or (b) actively predestines to perdition? One response is to say that it is presumptuous to figure out the logical necessities and possibilities which obtain for the relationship in which God, in his eternity, must stand in relation to humankind, including those who are not predestined to life. This response may be justified, but it undoubtedly creates the suspicion that we are simply halting logic where it suits us. In turn, that suspicion might be countered on the grounds that our intention is the theological preservation of the biblical testimony, not the philosophical refusal of its implications, and that, if the apparent implications undermine the testimony, the implications cannot be rigorously logical.

Still, we might risk taking a further step without blushing at the thought that this is to renege on our implicit principle of theological modesty. We might say this: the eternal relationship of God to those who are not predestined to life is not to be conceived of as a relation either to a company passed over in such predestination or to a company actively foreordained to perdition. Rather, it is a relation to those who will have the genuine opportunity in time to accept him, but who are not predestined to accept him in that time. If, purely for the sake of argument, we have conceded the right of theologians to form a conception of how God relates in eternity to those not predestined to life, we have here described the situation as it obtains in eternity in accordance with how it appears in time. It is only for the sake of argument that this exercise is allowed, but it is not an idle one even for those who doubt whether it is intrinsically theologically required and who regard this whole exercise as purely ad hominem.[11] It serves to indicate how

ositional statements or static rules than they are life-shaping dramatic directions," we can "save the proposition" (Vanhoozer, *The Drama of Doctrine,* p. 18; pp. 88-91). I sympathize with Vanhoozer in not following Hodge's approach to theology when Hodge assumes that theology is a science and that Scripture is — certainly for this systematic purpose — to be characterized as a book of facts. Hodge, *Systematic Theology,* vol. 1 (reprint, Grand Rapids: Eerdmans, 1993), pp. 1-17.

11. To state the matter in Dooyeweerdian language, the point here would be that human thought is bound to the cosmic law-order and, as God's thought is not so bound,

we are not bound to posit either a passing over or an active reprobation in the case of those not predestined to life. If it is claimed that, in fact, my formulation *does* entail that those not predestined to life are passed over, my response is this: it no more entails this than it does in Luke's narrative, or it only entails it to the extent that it is so presented in Luke's narrative.

With respect to the Lukan and temporal scene, it is entirely understandable that John Wesley at one stage toyed with the supposition that some were predestined to life but that others accepted life on the basis of their free will, grounded on God's prevenient grace.[12] It is equally understandable that he subsequently dropped this proposal.[13] Nevertheless, his suggestion does illustrate the impulse arising from such passages as Acts 13, which leads us to search for resolution, an impulse which must command our initial sympathy. Questions spring up all over the park in connection with the position I am adopting, including its appearance of bringing unseemly and unsatisfactory closure to a question which should be pursued and, if possible, resolved. What, for example, does my position imply about the relation of prevenient grace to sufficient grace? On an Augustinian account, God has not given sufficient grace to unbelievers for them to respond to his call. Unless sufficient grace is given, a positive response is not possible. However, he has given the predestined sufficient grace. Therefore, there must be a deliberate "passing over" of the others. So the argument goes. However, attempts to work things out along such lines as this simply advertise the impossibility of penetrating God's counsel, human nature, and the relation of the one to the other. Theological concepts must play the role of illuminating, not obscuring, biblical data, and if we employ the notions of sufficient grace, prevenient grace, efficacious call, responsibility, etc., it must be in order, as Wittgenstein said of philosophy, to leave everything where it is, as far as the biblical witness is concerned. Leaving everything where it is means insisting that a genuine

---

speculation about God's thinking seems pretty futile. Although it is an extremely general and rough account, L. Kalsbeek, *Contours of Christian Philosophy: An Introduction to Herman Dooyeweerd's Thought* (Lampeter: Edwin Mellen, 1975), succeeds in bringing out the force of this.

12. Henry D. Rack, *Reasonable Enthusiast: John Wesley and the Rise of Methodism,* 3rd ed. (London: Epworth, 2002), p. 388.

13. The grounds on which Wesley dropped it was that it conceded too much to Calvinism. Whether or not that was a good reason, it is impossible to distinguish biblically or theologically amongst responsible receivers of the word between those who attain life in virtue of predestination and those who attain life another way.

opportunity to respond positively is given to those who do not in fact do so, and if we cannot offer a satisfactory account of that in the conceptuality of sufficient, or prevenient, grace, etc., then it is the account or conceptuality that we must abandon, not the data for which we are trying to account.

To Wittgenstein we shall return at the end of the next chapter, but I summon here for help an earlier Cantabrigian: Charles Simeon.

According to Simeon

"The author is no friend to systematizers in Theology," said Simeon of himself.[14] "Beware of *systematizers.* Lay aside system and fly to the Bible; receive its words with simple submission, and without an eye to any system. Be Bible Christians, and not system Christians."[15] That is the negative. It is accompanied by the positive, and we shall devote some space to Simeon's position. Simeon believed that he was plowing fresh ground.

Charles Simeon lived from 1759 to 1836 and was incumbent at Holy Trinity Church in Cambridge for no fewer than fifty-four years. His impact on English Christianity was considerable. The great Macaulay himself, glancing back over Simeon's life in the decade following his death, observed: "As to Simeon, if you knew what his authority and influence were, and how they extended from Cambridge to the remote corners of England, you would allow that his real sway over the Church was far greater than that of any Primate."[16] As a matter of fact, his influence extended well beyond England, not only through the preaching and pastoral contact which affected so many who would later leave its shores, but also on account of his direct interest in the work of foreign missions, including the testimony to the Jews. Comparison is more instructive than invidious: "Bishop Wordsworth once declared that Simeon at Cambridge had a much larger following than Newman at Oxford, and for a much longer

14. Charles Simeon, *Horae Homileticae; or, Discourses (in the Form of Skeletons) upon The Whole Scriptures* (London: Richard Watts, 1819), p. 4.

15. A. W. Brown, *Recollections of the Conversation Parties of the Reverend Charles Simeon, M.A.* (London: Hamilton, Adams and Co., 1863), p. 269. "It is wonderful that among commentators none thought of taking Scripture just as it is. Men must have systems and make things bend to systems" (p. 211). Even Scott, perhaps the best of commentators, is "not free from system" (p. 344).

16. Quoted by Handley Moule in *Charles Simeon: Biography of a Sane Saint* (London: IVF, 1965), p. 148.

time."[17] The bishop of Calcutta asked: "At his death when did either of our Universities pay such a marked honour to a private individual?"[18] Simeon was a remarkable man and exemplary character. He was also a pioneer in a certain approach to biblical preaching, and it is in this connection that he appears on our dogmatic stage.[19]

In pursuing his three great aims in preaching — "to humble the sinner, to exalt the Saviour, to promote holiness" — Simeon observed that he loved "the simplicity of the Scriptures" and expressed the "wish to receive and inculcate every truth precisely in the way, and to the extent, that it is set forth in the inspired Volume."[20] It is as difficult not to believe Simeon as it would be to believe most others when we hear: "I never wish to find any particular truth in any particular passage."[21] To this desire he put down what he took to be his unique perspective on the Calvinist-Arminian controversy.[22] The controversy was lively during the course of his ministry.[23] Simeon gathered together his sermon outlines in more than one edition. There were the *Helps to Composition; or, Five Hundred Skeletons of Sermons, Several Being the Substance of Sermons Preached Before the University,* produced in 1801.[24] For an even snappier title, product of those

17. So Archbishop Coggan wrote in his Prideaux Lectures, *These Were His Gifts: A Trio of Christian Leaders* (Torquay: Devonshire Press, 1974), p. 17.

18. Quoted in W. Carus, *Memoirs of the life of the Rev. Charles Simeon with a selection from his writings and correspondence* (London: Macmillan, 1847), p. 838. Although neither Carus's *Memoirs* nor Brown's *Recollections* is a work of critical history, there is no reason to doubt the substantial reliability of their accounts, as far as they go.

19. Although it is not a critical treatment, if we want personal edification, the book to read on Simeon is still the late-nineteenth-century biography by Handley Moule, *Charles Simeon.*

20. Carus, *Memoirs,* p. 16.

21. So Simeon wrote in a letter to Bishop Burgess on the latter's acknowledgment of his copy of *Horae Homileticae.* Carus, *Memoirs,* p. 540.

22. It is only after time spent with Simeon that we shall give prima facie credence to the words adjacent to those I have just quoted: "My mode of interpreting Scripture is this. I bring to it no predilection whatever. . . . I never wish to find any particular truth in any particular passage. I am willing that every part of God's blessed Word should speak exactly what it was intended to speak. . . . It is by coming to the Scriptures with this mind that I have been led into the views which I maintain, and which no other person, as far as I am informed, has ever ventured to maintain, in relation to the Calvinist and Arminian controversy."

23. "North of the Tweed, the Wesleyans, being Arminians, are thought by many to be out of the reach of salvation. By many Wesleyans Calvinists are thought to be beyond reach of salvation. All this is very unchristian and false." Brown, *Recollections,* p. 292.

24. These were published by John Burges in Cambridge in that year.

market-driven days, try the next: by 1833, Simeon had published his complete *Horae Homileticae; or, Discourses (in the Form of Skeletons) upon The Whole Scriptures,* "emphatically the work of his life."[25] On completing the *Horae* for publication, Simeon wrote in a memorandum that one of the "tendencies" of this work was "to weaken, if not eradicate, the disputes about Calvinism and Arminianism."[26] Simeon's biographer doubtless speaks for the majority of the theologically interested when he says that "to a modern reader the Preface" of this volume "is the most valuable thing that Simeon wrote."[27] The preface has the Calvinist-Arminian controversy in view above all else, and Simeon was delighted when, in conjunction with the sermon sketches themselves, it had the effect of "the cutting down of high party spirit in theological matters."[28]

"Party spirit": scarcely anything grieved Simeon more. Nothing more manifested party spirit than the Calvinist-Arminian controversy, and nothing "under heaven," said Simeon, would "be more grateful to him than to see names and parties buried in eternal oblivion and primitive simplicity restored to the church."[29] He lamented that disposition of the heart which engendered such a spirit. To the issue of personal disposition, Simeon attaches the issue of scriptural "simplicity." Our sense of its simplicity ought to affect our disposition, and the way in which Scripture presents its matter dictates the way it should be preached. The way in which Scripture presents its matter and the way in which it should be preached are further connected with the question of system. As we have noted, Simeon was opposed to it and this is where he meets us. He is our contemporary because party spirit lives on today.

Approaching his task and responsibility as a preacher, Simeon declared himself interested in preaching the plain sense of Scripture. That is what "simplicity" amounts to.[30] What did that require or entail? Not

25. So Carus, *Memoirs,* p. 143. However, I shall be citing the preface of the 1819 edition, published by Richard Watts in London, which alluded to the preface of the 1801 *Helps.*

26. Carus, *Memoirs,* p. 719. The sentence continues: ". . . and thus to recommend, to the utmost of my power, the unhampered liberality of the Church of England."

27. Hugh Evan Hopkins, *Charles Simeon of Cambridge* (London: Hodder and Stoughton, 1977), p. 62.

28. Brown, *Recollections,* p. 191, with reference to the *Helps.*

29. *Helps,* p. x note m. The question of party and the need to steer clear of it appear from the beginning of Brown's *Recollections;* see p. xi.

30. Simplicity seems to have had a psychological attraction for Simeon. "I love simplicity. . . . I am in the habit of accounting religious as the simplest of all concerns." Carus, *Memoirs,* p. 615.

only in the context of his day, but as a normative principle of homiletics, Simeon believed that it meant the avoidance of system.[31] "I keep simply to Scripture, and not to system, and nobody *quite* likes me."[32] One way to avoid the temptation to system was to preach on texts in the context of the passages in which they cropped up.[33] While Simeon did not consistently deny the need to attend to the wider canonical context, all the emphasis lies on the immediate context; in his view, homiletic attention to this spells the death of system.[34]

What is at stake is so serious that Simeon does not mince his words. He fearlessly observed that "there is not a decided Calvinist or Arminian in the world, who equally approves the whole of Scripture . . . there is not a determined votary of either system who, if [he] had been in the company of St. Paul, whilst he was writing his different Epistles, would not have recommended him to alter one or other of his expressions."[35] Away from the printed page, Simeon could add: "The Calvinist wishes for some texts to be expunged from Scripture; the Arminian wishes the same as to others. They may say otherwise, but they secretly do so."[36] Guilt seems pretty evenly divided: "Half of Scripture is Arminian, half Calvinistic, and each party strains or else slurs over the other half of Scripture."[37] In a letter of July 1825, Simeon imagines Paul saying: "Today I am a strong Calvinist, tomorrow a strong Arminian."[38] Acute powers of historical audition — for the wave reverberates

31. Brown, *Recollections,* p. 11.

32. Brown, *Recollections,* p. 132.

33. "Always take the plain straightforward meaning of a passage and strive to find out what was the mind of God as clearly revealed in the text." Brown, *Recollections,* p. 176.

34. Allegedly, in 1831, Simeon remarked that, in preaching on a text or passage, "You must never wander beyond its true limits, you must not patch up your text by borrowing any extraneous ideas from other passages in Scripture." Carus, *Memoirs,* p. 678.

35. *Horae Homileticae,* pp. 5-6. Simeon wrote in 1808: "I am sure that the disposition to alter his words would have induced us to correct the Apostle Paul, if we had been at his elbow when he wrote the 7th of the Romans: or if we had been left his executors to publish his papers," quoted in Carus, *Memoirs,* p. xxviii.

36. Brown, *Recollections,* p. 274.

37. Brown, *Recollections,* p. 277.

38. Carus, *Memoirs,* p. 600. John Piper, seeking to reclaim Simeon for today, admits that Simeon "did not want to be labelled a Calvinist or an Arminian," but adds that "he was known as an evangelical Calvinist and rightly so." *The Roots of Endurance: Invincible Perseverance in the Lives of John Newton, Charles Simeon, and William Wilberforce* (Leicester: Inter-Varsity Press, 2002), p. 103. In insisting on this identification, Piper does exactly what Simeon urged us not to do. It is safest not to label Simeon. It is true that, in the context of saying that he believed "the great mass of Calvinists . . . wrong," Simeon could describe

and sweeps on today — are not required to hear the howls of injured protest on the part of biblical scholars and theologians who find their integrity questioned. Nor does it require acute powers of historical vision — for the mirror reflects also the third millennium — to observe the grimaces on the system-stained faces of dogmatic theologians who suspect that the next move of the Simeonite will be to put them out of a job, like the Ephesian silversmiths in Acts 19 (vv. 23-26). Yet pride, which is a much bigger problem for us biblical scholars and theologians than is incomprehension (for, whatever our glories or shortcomings, we remain part of the human race), should not prevent us from asking whether we need to heed Simeon's rebuke at this point.

Very well; but is it fair to describe in terms of an urge to system what is surely a worthy response to an imperative born of a prima facie difficulty in reconciling biblical statements and of the will to reconcile them? Where biblical statements are hard to reconcile prima facie, what is the preacher to do? What Simeon's preacher is certainly *not* to do is to reconcile truths that stand in tension with each other even to the point of giving the appearance of contradiction. If it is the case both that God really ordains and that humans really decide and Scripture makes no attempt to reconcile these truths, neither should we.

---

himself in 1815 as a "moderate Calvinist." Carus, *Memoirs,* p. 418. However, he said many other things as well, and, if we need to label him at all, Abner Brown's "semi-Calvinist" (*Recollections,* p. 75) is as good a label as any, or we could call him a specifically "Church of England" Calvinist. But why make the attempt? "You well know," said Simeon in a letter of April 26, 1822, "that though strongly Calvinistic in some respects, I am strongly Arminian in others." Carus, *Memoirs,* p. 563. This is an important letter, where Simeon speaks of striking a "harder blow at Calvinism, *as an exclusive system,* than it has ever yet received" (see pp. 563-66). "I certainly think that religious people are too much addicted to human system. Scarcely any one is aware that Calvinism and Arminianism are equally true, if rightly applied, and equally false, if pressed to extremes." Carus, *Memoirs,* p. 725. Simeon categorically says that he "will never agree with the Calvinists, that both election and rejection are irrespective of man's character; nor with the Arminians, that they are both dependent on it." Brown, *Recollections,* p. 277. He objected to nothing more in Calvinism than its failure to reckon with biblical passages on the possibility of falling away. "Thus he was wont to say that his Notes on the Epistles to the Seven Apocalyptic Churches would give a death-blow to Calvinism as a system; for that the ordinary common sense of readers could not but perceive, as pointed out in the 'Homileticae,' that if those seven Churches . . . *could* be overthrown, the system of Calvinism was virtually at an end." Brown, *Recollections,* p. 63. All I indicate here is some passages that should be taken into account by those who judge Simeon a Calvinist and, for my purposes, it is permissible to take the work of Carus and of Brown as sufficient evidence, while disclaiming any judgment on their merits as historians. The main point is that Simeon would be sorely tried by our attempts to label him.

> It may be asked, perhaps, How do you *reconcile* these doctrines, which you believe to be of equal authority and equal importance? But what right has any man to impose this task on the preachers of God's word? God has not required it of them; nor is the truth or falsehood of any doctrine to be determined absolutely by this criterion. It is presumed, that every one will acknowledge the holiness of God, and the existence of sin; but will any one undertake to reconcile them? . . . It is possible, that the truth may lie, not exclusively in either, nor yet in a confused mixture of both, but in the proper and seasonable application of them both; or, to use the language of St. Paul, "in rightly dividing the word of truth."[39]

With these last words, Simeon has told us positively what the preacher's responsibility is, what the preacher is to do. It is to apply.

Simeon denied that the truths in question formally contradicted each other and regretted it when doctrines were so stated as "to be really contradictory."[40] He was aware of the problem of implying that; to allege actual contradiction would be to impugn the integrity of biblical truth, which is internally consistent. Further, it is inaccurate to say that Simeon was simply flatly opposed to system. "Christianity is a system, but not according to human idea of system. It is quite *sui generis,* and often has incomprehensible and to us irreconcileable points, and we are nowhere required to reconcile them."[41] As a matter of fact, we encounter in Simeon remarks that go toward a reconciliation of relevant statements. He believed that there was a wider system in Scripture than adherents of either party allowed, and he was "disposed to think that the Scripture system, be it what it may, is of a broader and more comprehensive character than some very exact and dogmatical Theologians are inclined to allow."[42] Simeon often repeated this sentiment.[43] However, we neither do know nor need to know how to reconcile the truths in question. The contrary motion of cogs in a machine would appear to drive it in different directions, but they

39. Simeon, *Helps,* p. vi.

40. Simeon, *Helps,* p. x.

41. Brown, *Recollections,* p. 212.

42. Simeon, *Horae Homileticae,* p. 5.

43. See, e.g., Carus, *Memoirs,* pp. 566 and 580. Simeon observes here that "the key to the whole" of Scripture was "brokenness of heart." Carus makes the rather unexpected remark that Simeon hoped "to form a system of doctrinal, practical and experimental divinity eventually." *Memoirs,* p. 144.

do not actually do so and, if we knew the internal mechanism, we should see why not.[44] In this world, we do not know the theological mechanism. Our job is to know how truth *x* applies to our lives and how truth *y* applies to our lives, not the relationship between *x* and *y*. Simeon seizes here on what we may call the "point" of doctrine, as Scripture exhibits it to us.[45] On Simeon's terms, we can validly speak of this "truth" and that "truth," fearless of whether anyone will weigh in with an accusation of "propositionalism." We can also speak of principles:

> In Scripture, there are Calvinistic principles to act on man's hopes, and Arminian principles to act on his fears; both are needful, and combine to produce the right effect. Man has hopes and man has fears, and God has given us a revelation exactly suited to all the wants of our nature, and exactly adapted to *all* our capacities. He has mercifully adapted His revelation to our dispositions, nay, even to our vices. For the desponding and broken-hearted sinner, here is a salvation not depending on his own merits, or his own feeble efforts. For the sluggish, or confident, or easily quieted conscience, here is a salvation which we must work out, a danger of becoming a castaway even after preaching the Gospel to others, a danger that one who thinketh he standeth may nevertheless fall. Give an Arminian cup to the former class, and it is poison; give a Calvinist cup to the latter, and it is poison.[46]

He makes a further point, whose importance cannot be exaggerated. What perhaps cannot and certainly need not be reconciled conceptually can be reconciled existentially. All truths in question are readily integrated in the believer's life. In observing this, Simeon appealed both to experience in general and to the experience of prayer in particular.

> Pious men, both of the Calvinistic and Arminian persuasion, approximate very nearly when they are upon their knees before God in prayer;

44. Cf. Theodore Beza, *A Little Book of Christian Questions and Responses in Which the Principal Headings of the Christian Religion Are Briefly Set Forth* (Allison Park, Pa.: Pickwick, 1986), p. 68: "Did you ever . . . contemplate a clock, in which a certain very large wheel turning to the right, takes some others with it, some to the same right, but others to the left, with a completely contrary motion?"

45. See the approach taken by Schubert M. Ogden, *The Point of Christology* (London: SCM, 1982).

46. Brown, *Recollections*, p. 269.

> — the devout Arminian then acknowledging his total dependence upon God, as strongly as the most confirmed Calvinist; and the Calvinist acknowledging his responsibility to God, and his obligation to exertion, in terms as decisive as the most determined Arminian. And that which both these individuals are upon their knees, it is the wish of the author to become in his writings.[47]

I will not attempt a dispassionate investigation of the strengths and weaknesses of Simeon's position, and I will skate over a number of questions in relation to him which would need to be addressed in any thorough inquiry into his outlook. Amongst other things, investigation would require a study of over 2,500 sermon outlines, which apparently took thirty-two men to be fully employed for sixteen months to produce in print.[48] My objective is not a dispassionate critique of Simeon's thought but, rather, an inquiry into its potential to advance our dogmatic enterprise.[49] There are two related claims at the heart of his thinking. The first is that it is the preacher's task to relate doctrine to life, not to seek systematic doctrinal resolution. The second is that different truths (or aspects of the one overall truth), whose conceptual coherence is difficult or impossible for us to state, actually cohere in life; that is, truths cohere existentially. Both claims are modified by a third claim: that there is a wider system. Shall we agree with Simeon on these points?

Our immediate interest with regard to the first of these claims arises in connection with the task of dogmatics, not of preaching, even if what is decided with respect to the former should, upon examination, be dupli-

47. Simeon, *Horae Homileticae,* p. 7.

48. Hopkins, *Charles Simeon,* p. 60.

49. If I could develop one aspect in the exposition of Simeon's thought, it would be in connection with the extent to which he is to be explained as an Anglican, his theology conditioned by the liturgy of the prayer book, shaped according to the doxological unities of the Christian life rather than the conceptual tensions of system. In 1811 Simeon preached a course of sermons on "the excellency of the liturgy" and described his religion as "the religion that pervades the whole Liturgy, and particularly the Communion Service." Carus, *Memoirs,* p. 520. "No Dissenter dares to preach as I do," claimed Simeon, "one day Calvinist, another day Arminian, just as the text happens to be." Brown, *Recollections,* p. 221 (and see pp. 135 and 198 on Scottish Presbyterians). To specify doxological formation is not to overlook the influence on Simeon of the Thirty-nine Articles, which are neither prayer nor system. Despite this emphasis on his Anglicanism, Abner Brown is certainly correct in his judgment that when Simeon was seeking to discourage system in religion, he was "working for the whole Church at large." *Recollections,* p. 61.

cated with respect to the latter.[50] As far as dogmatics is concerned, Simeon surely underestimates the difference between the situation in which the theologian stands and that in which Paul and other NT authors found themselves. If it was not Paul's responsibility to reconcile or demonstrate the consistency of his words and thought with what Mark, James, or Peter wrote, it does not follow that the theologian who wishes to construct theology on a biblical edifice does not have that task. We receive Paul as part of canonical Scripture, and it is in that context that we are called on to seek to understand and apply him. The wider context than the one to which Paul addressed himself is not the object of purely peripheral vision as the theologian seeks to understand a particular letter or passage; it constitutes the very context in which theology (and, we may wish to say, homiletic exposition) takes place in the church. As far as I can judge, what Simeon discourages in the preacher, he discourages in the theologian.

Notwithstanding these criticisms, a modified and reformulated version of Simeon's strictures on system remains instructive for dogmatics. There is no law that requires the theologian to provide a conceptual scheme that reconciles diverse biblical statements at a conceptual level. However, he or she may be required to provide a reason why a failure to reconcile them at that level is not a failure to set forth Christian teaching coherently. It is better to speak of a failure to see how diverse aspects of the truth are to be *related* than how they are to be *reconciled.* Positing even prima facie irreconcilability risks posing the issue in terms of an assumption that systematic adumbration is in principle within our grasp, whereas it is the limits of the human mind and what is revealed to us, not the substance of the realities in question, that de facto generate our perplexities.[51]

50. We have noted Simeon's insistence that, in preaching, one should confine oneself to the text on which one is preaching. This is quite a dogmatic rule, and if we take exception to it, we may surmise that a hermeneutical error operative in his homiletical theory underlay restrictions which he erroneously placed on dogmatics. However, Simeon seems to have qualified these remarks; see Carus, *Memoirs,* p. 134. On his part, Simeon was quite self-reliant in biblical interpretation: "If you study the Scriptures yourself, all commentators will leave you in the dark." Brown, *Recollections,* p. 213; cf. p. 344. More weighty, when we consider the implications of Simeon's principles for dogmatics, is his conviction, apparently regularly expressed in sermon parties, that we should not make Scripture say more than it originally meant; Brown, *Recollections,* p. 51. Simeon's remarks on the discourse of covenant theology probably indicate that the strength of his aversion to nonbiblical expressions in theology arose from visualizing dogmatics in terms of strict systematics; see *Recollections,* p. 115.

51. An analogy is that we might speak of the difficulty of knowing how to relate, rather than of how to reconcile, the oneness and threeness of God.

That leads to the second claim, for Simeon does insist on a form of coherence. Here, Simeon seems to me to be right. Tautologically speaking, existence is the sphere in which we live, move, have our being, and, therefore, think. Embodied life is the proper sphere, and its spiritual enhancement and enlightenment are the proper goal, of theological thought. To ask how concepts are related in abstraction from the sphere of life and application is to ask a questionable question. Theological concepts treated in abstraction from the existential point at which they are biblically introduced or existentially surface will often stubbornly refuse to interlock because they are incapable of being directly joined. They are meant to interlock in and with life. Wittgenstein is with us again, philosopher, along with preacher, putting the squeeze on the theologian.[52]

What about the third point, Simeon's wider system? The upshot of his thought seems to be to identify paradox as the heart of theological form, at least where the doctrines of grace are concerned. Complementary realities whose relationship is hard or impossible to state, but whose conjoined reality is unaffected by our difficulty in stating it, meet us as paradoxes. Those who receive Jesus Christ are drawn in time by the Father who purposed from eternity to do so, and cannot join the Pharisee in thanking God that they are unlike other people. Those who do not receive Jesus cannot blame the Father for not having drawn them in time nor claim that they have been antecedently excluded from eternity. This way of putting it is drawn from John's Gospel, and here we advert to our discussion of John in the last chapter. John's Gospel is the most instructive of all NT writings in the context of our immediate discussion, directing us to consider the proposition that theological thought should not aspire to synthesis and resolution but that, on the contrary, paradox becomes *sharper,* and not eased, on theological reflection. Does John point us toward the way in which we should appropriate "the Hebrew mind" or a Christian frame of mind properly informed by the Jewishness of the Testaments under culturally different reflective conditions, where we have learned to trade in the merchandise of paradox, system, and such commodities? Simeon quoted John 5:40 — *"Ye will not come to me, that ye might have life"* — and John 6:44 — *"No man can come unto me, except the Father who has sent me draw him"* — in order to caution against system and to urge that the preacher's

52. We could still maintain that the task is remitted to philosophical theology of showing that Christian teaching is not demonstrably incoherent at that conceptual level on which Simeon warns us against operating in the interests of a system.

task is "the proper and seasonable application of them both."[53] The truth we need to know lies neither in the center, nor in a hybrid of elements, and not in systematic resolution, but at the poles of the paradox.[54] Had Simeon seen fit to develop a system, he would presumably have done so by delineating a scheme whose surface presentation was in the mode of paradox. We shall not pursue and so not commit ourselves to what he said about poles, but we need to say a little more about paradox.

From Simeon to Kant

"Paradox"! The word is a bugle call for theologians and philosophers to scurry back from the east and the west to join in an intellectual feast from which the Simeonite preacher has threatened to debar them on the grounds that the true feast is not that of the systematized theological concept. It is good to be back in business, is it not? However, our bugle gives a rather uncertain sound (something once said of Simeon).[55] It may appear that it is the task of the systematic theologian who aspires to sit under the ministerial instruction of Simeon to adumbrate a system that enshrines paradox. However, if such is the case, and if he or she does so convincingly, what then? Is the system to be preached? Presumably not. Then why is it needed, if that preaching which goes on while the system is being sought goes on just the same when the system is found? That is the gauntlet which Simeon casts down before us, although we are touching now on general questions about the relation of theology, dogmatics, and preaching that are much wider than those concerning paradox. What we must make sure of is that dogmatics is not a luxury item, as Kierkegaard observed of Hans Lassen Martensen's dogmatics.[56]

53. Simeon, *Helps,* p. v.

54. "Mr. Simeon used to say, justly, that 'when two opposite principles are each clearly contained in the Bible, truth does not lie in taking what is called *The golden mean,* but in steadily adopting both extremes and, as a pendulum, oscillating, but not vacillating, between the two.'" Brown, *Recollections,* pp. 74-75.

55. "It was said in religious periodicals of his day, — 'Mr. Simeon is more of a *Churchman* than a *Gospel-man.*' 'His trumpet gives an uncertain sound: who shall prepare himself to the battle.' True it was that his trumpet did give an uncertain sound in reference to party strife and party watchwords, but not in reference to any Bible truth, or any principles, doctrines, or rules of the Church of England. Such groundless charges have now died away." Brown, *Recollections,* p. 11.

56. See David J. Gouwens, *Kierkegaard as Religious Thinker* (Cambridge: Cambridge University Press, 1996), p. 41.

If we exclaimed: "Paradox"! earlier, it was only going to be a question of time before the exclamatory echo: "Kierkegaard"! boomed back at us. "The characteristic mark of Christianity is the paradox, the absolute paradox. As soon as a so-called Christian speculation annuls the paradox and reduces this characterization to a transient factor, all the spheres are confused."[57] Again: "Paradox is the source of the thinker's passion, and the thinker without paradox is like a lover without feeling: a paltry mediocrity."[58] Evidently, a proper exploration of the conceptual problem to which we are attending would require sustained attention for Kierkegaard.[59] If we undertook it, it would be with a view to keeping open the question of whether there is a wider, "Simeon-type," system out there at all.[60] What Kierkegaard said about paradox was integral to his claim that an existential system is impossible.[61] Systems stem from and cater to speculative objectivity, rather than stemming from and catering to the passion of faith. "An existential system cannot be formulated. Does this mean that no such system exists? By no means; nor is this implied in our assertion. Reality

57. S. Kierkegaard, *Concluding Unscientific Postscript,* trans. D. F. Swenson and W. Lowrie (Princeton: Princeton University Press, 1968), p. 480. This authorship was pseudonymous, but "Kierkegaard" stands in my description for the pseudonymous author (Johannes Climacus). "All Christianity," says Kierkegaard elsewhere, "is rooted in paradox"; quoted in Sylvia Walsh, *Kierkegaard: Thinking Christianly in an Existential Mode* (Oxford: Oxford University Press, 2009), p. 111.

58. Kierkegaard, *Philosophical Fragments,* trans. D. Swenson and H. Hong (Princeton: Princeton University Press, 1962), p. 46, also authored by Johannes Climacus.

59. For different interpretations of Kierkegaard, see C. Stephen Evans, *Kierkegaard on Faith and the Self: Collected Essays* (Waco, Tex.: Baylor University Press, 2008), p. 118. Needless to say, complexity surrounds Kierkegaard's notion of paradox. A striking example of it is found in a journal entry where Kierkegaard writes that what "I usually express by saying that Christianity consists in paradox . . . Leibniz expresses by distinguishing between what is above reason and what is against reason. Faith is above reason"; cited in Gregor Malantschuk's fine study *Kierkegaard's Thought* (Princeton: Princeton University Press, 1971), p. 75. However, Leibniz is moving in Locke's orbit at this point, where talk of faith as being above reason concerns the limitation of rational sources of knowledge, not the question of paradox. See John Locke, *An Essay concerning Human Understanding,* ed. P. Nidditch (Oxford: Clarendon, 1979), IV.17-19. For Leibniz, see *New Essays on Human Understanding,* ed. P. Remnant and J. Bennett (Cambridge: Cambridge University Press, 1996).

60. Perhaps this is to interpret "system" in Simeon too narrowly; he is probably not to be tied to a positive acknowledgment of system in a sense of which Kierkegaard would have disapproved in principle.

61. Kierkegaard proposes that "an existential system is impossible" in contrast to "a logical system" which "is possible." *Concluding Unscientific Postscript,* p. 99. His thesis extends beyond its particular application to Hegel.

itself is a system — for God; but it cannot be a system for any existing spirit. System and finality correspond to one another, but existence is precisely the opposite of finality."[62]

If Kierkegaard was right on the impossibility of an existential system, this ought to determine the course of our whole attempt to address that dimension of the problem of election which has set us off on this particular chase.[63] Resisting the task of attending to Kierkegaard in detail is made particularly difficult because the earliest theological entry in his journal was on the subject of predestination.[64] More generally: "In all his dialectical and existential presentations Kierkegaard always considers the doctrine of grace to be the ultimate and most central doctrine. . . . With grace as a fulcrum, Kierkegaard's dialectical reflections must also find a resting point. All his dialectical and existential thinking works towards this final and decisive boundary for all dialectic."[65]

Kierkegaard's philosophical adumbration, outlawing system, brings him into an ad hoc alliance with Simeon's homiletic adumbration, relegating system, in a confederacy which is the more impressive because both men were driven by theological concerns grounded in the passion for understanding Christian existence. Simeon thought that life reconciles what thought cannot, or cannot readily. This is surely both true and significant. If, on good grounds, we are convinced of the truths or realities in question, then we know that they are existentially true; if they are existentially true,

62. Kierkegaard, *Concluding Unscientific Postscript,* p. 107. In joining Kierkegaard to Simeon in discussion of system, the notion of "system" is being treated ad hoc. For a discussion of the different meanings of system, including the distinction between system as coherence and system as finality, see Anthony Thiselton, *The Hermeneutics of Doctrine* (Grand Rapids: Eerdmans, 2007), pp. 137-39. The question of coherence leads to the notion of paradox, which unites Simeon and Kierkegaard in my account, but Kierkegaard connects this with the question of finality. David Tracy wryly observed that Kierkegaard was willing to try any genre for explicating Christian truth — "diaries, music, exercises, dialogues, discourses, narratives. He will try anything except system"; quoted in William C. Placher, *The Triune God: An Exercise in Postliberal Theology* (Louisville: Westminster John Knox, 2007), p. 29.

63. This is not to say that I find persuasive everything germane in Kierkegaard's thought. My reading of Kierkegaard is much the same as that of C. Stephen Evans in *Kierkegaard: An Introduction* (Cambridge: Cambridge University Press, 2009) and Sylvia Walsh, *Living Christianly: Kierkegaard's Dialectic of Christian Existence* (University Park: Pennsylvania State University Press, 2005).

64. This was in May 1834 and, in relation to it, he began to present his own attitude to theological problems; see Malantschuk, *Kierkegaard's Thought,* p. 16.

65. Malantschuk, *Kierkegaard's Thought,* pp. 355-56. Amongst other germane references in this volume, see especially pp. 144 and 364-65.

the question has to be asked whether our inability to conceptualize their relationship to each other inhibits only our intellectual curiosity. To answer that question without being context-specific would be foolhardy. We have to ask what is theologically required in missionary, apologetic, and pastoral contexts and, above all, what enhances worship. Does this imply that theology does not possess its own peculiar and pressing task, a responsibility to think through Christian doctrine? No, it does not imply that. Simeon and Kierkegaard were as concerned about Christian doctrine as anyone. It is reflection on the biblical basis, content of, and approach to doctrine that leads them to their conclusions — their respective conclusions, for they are not agreed on everything in relation to the principles of doctrine.

The way in which various truths — or, if it is preferred, various aspects of the one great truth — apply to our lives can be spelled out in terms of responsibilities, warnings, humility, peace, etc.; this is Simeon's point, and this indeed is the primary objective of doctrinal thinking. It is true that where election embraces single predestination, many have existential perplexities and worries, and to this sort of concern we advert in the next chapter. However, if we are exercised by the *intellectual* problem of elaborating the conceptual relationship of the notions that we find bobbing around in this discussion, we have to ask ourselves why we are so exercised. Systematic irresolution is neither the issue nor the sign of an embarrassing theological failure which lets down Christianity, letting down Jesus Christ himself. On the contrary. The biblical realities in which theologians should be trading are the sheer deep ontological and existential realities, those realities by which we should understand and measure all things, not themselves subject to extrinsic canons of measurement. They are the true expression and proper manifestation of what is the case. Ours, as Duns Scotus put it, is *theologia nostra* and not *theologia in se.*[66] Simeon

66. Although T. F. Torrance makes some wider use of Scotus in his classic *Theological Science* (Oxford: Oxford University Press, 1969), the citation of these words in that volume (p. 281 n. 1) does not indicate the importance that Scotus's words come to possess in Torrance's work. See, e.g., Torrance, *Reality and Evangelical Theology* (Philadelphia: Westminster, 1982), pp. 21-22 and 116. The path of argument I follow in this volume is not meant to deny implicitly the immense potential gains of approaching theology, including the doctrine of election, in dialogue with the approach that Torrance sets out in these books and elsewhere, and it is important to make this point, which is why I pick up Scotus's words specifically from Torrance's citation of them. We should notice that Scotus's view of theology as a *scientia practica* does not stand in such contrast to the view of theology as a theoretical science as these terms might immediately lead us to think. See here Richard Cross, *Duns Scotus* (New York and Oxford: Oxford University Press, 1999), pp. 9-10.

aside, it is certainly appropriate and even important to ask questions about the conceptual form in which we grasp the interrelationship of truths (or understand the internal coherence of the various components of the one truth). However, just how important it is to provide a detailed adumbration of that form, one which goes beyond a simple and stark statement of it, is a subject for debate.

Citing Kierkegaard should not mean failing to see Immanuel Kant, whose distinction between things as they are and things as they appear, with his accompanying banishment of metaphysical knowledge, initially seems hostile to orthodox theology with its attachment to realist theological claims. It is certainly in order to quarrel with fundamental structural principles in the edifice of Kant's thought. In the *Critique of Pure Reason,* he early limits experience so that religious experience is effectively discounted. When he speaks of experience in both the first and the second preface of the *Critique,* we are not encouraged about the positive possibility of religious experience being included, and the subsequent "Introduction," followed by the launch into the "Transcendental Doctrine of Elements," sets a seal on the matter.[67] To read Kant after reading Scripture is to feel like a guest on the day after the wedding in Cana who encounters a man exhaustively examining the properties of water to see what capacities it has.[68] Kant reckoned on systematically investigating the compass of human knowledge without reference to the active power of God in revelation. If this is judged a philosophical necessity (in the form in which Kant approached matters), then philosophical necessity severely circumscribes philosophical competence in matters religious.

That said, a measure of significant disagreement at the level of presupposition or approach neither warrants wholesale dismissal of nor prohibits us from gaining much insight from and acknowledging agreement with major constituents of Kant's thought. Kant worried about the application of interpretive schemes to those things which lay outside the boundaries of our perception, and he thought the heart of his achievement was that he had "found a way of guarding against all those errors which have hitherto set reason, in its non-empirical employment, at variance with

67. Immanuel Kant, *Critique of Pure Reason,* trans. Norman Kemp Smith (London and Basingstoke: Macmillan, 1933). Kant exudes no sense of the presence of God, unless on the occasion of reference to the moral law. See Bernard M. G. Reardon, *Kant as Philosophical Theologian* (London and Basingstoke: Macmillan, 1988), p. 164.

68. However, to be fair, this feeling is stimulated more by Kant's *Religion within the Boundaries of Mere Reason* than by the first *Critique.*

itself."[69] He dealt thoroughly with our schematization of perceptibles too, but thought that, whatever you end up doing on that front, you cannot simply lift the scheme you use for perceptible things and apply it to the realm that transcends perception. We view things as earthly flatlanders, under the forms of space and time, and we factor into our perceptual and conceptual scheme a usable concept of "cause." Quit that scene and subsequently try your hand at conceptual understanding, and you are securely outside the realm of the knowable. Metaphysics becomes "a bottomless abyss," "a dark ocean without shore and without lighthouses."[70] If handling causality in empirical daylight is hard enough, what becomes of it in the metaphysical night?

> [T]he territory of pure understanding . . . an island, enclosed by nature itself within unalterable limits . . . the land of truth — enchanting name! — surrounded by a wide and stormy ocean, the native home of illusion, where many a fog bank and many a swiftly melting iceberg give the deceptive appearance of farther shores, deluding the adventurous seafarer ever anew with empty hopes, and engaging him in enterprises which he can never abandon and yet is unable to carry to completion.[71]

Kant's warning is not to be ignored on the easy ground that orthodox Christians trade in the commodity of revelation. It is true that belief in revelation establishes clear water between Kant's island and our theological homeland, but this does not mean that we are immune to the dangers of the ocean which he charts when we engage in metaphysics. And metaphysics there must be, whether we like it or not, as long as we demand of ourselves conceptual resolution in the service of a logical system.[72]

69. Kant, *Critique,* p. 9. On the notions of the schema of "the concept" (which can bear a technical meaning in Kant) and schematism of "Ideas" of "the understanding," see p. 182. As Korner puts it, for Kant, remoteness from sense-perception "is an ever-present source of danger . . . of *fata morgana* in intellectual deserts and logical fallacies." S. Korner, *Kant* (Harmondsworth: Penguin, 1955), p. 31. Where Locke wrestled with the limits of reason, Kant worried about its conflicts. (Locke features both at the beginning and the end of the *Critique* [p. 8; pp. 667-68]. Reckoning with empiricism is, of course, a leading concern in Kant's volume.)

70. Kant, *The Only Possible Ground for a Demonstration of God's Existence,* quoted in F. Copleston, *A History of Philosophy,* vol. 6 (New York: Image, 1994), p. 189.

71. Kant, *Critique,* p. 257.

72. For the metaphor deployed here, see Paul Engelmann's description of the early

What is of special interest to us here is not only Kant's weighty averment that pure reason lands us in antinomies, but also one of his examples, namely, the third one treated in the "Transcendental Dialectic" in the *Critique of Pure Reason.*[73] It concerns our freedom and it is the boiler house of Kant's treatment of reason.[74] According to pure reason, there both is and is not a causality attributable to freedom. A biographer tells us that two students in Kant's day fought a duel because one accused the other of not understanding the *Critique of Pure Reason,* saying that he needed to study it for thirty years before he could hope to understand it, and for another thirty before being allowed to comment on it.[75] So we youngsters had better prowl carefully. Certainly, if there is a single incontestable claim in the *Critique,* it is that this work can never be made suitable for popular consumption.[76] Therefore, it behooves us to call a halt to the exposition of Kant almost as soon as we have made a show of alighting on him. Behind Kant's delineation of the *parerga* — the nonrational elements in religious life — there is constant puzzling over radical evil in relation to freedom, and it is a puzzlement which should not only elicit our sympathy in its own right but also caution us against metaphysical confidence in the course of plotting the relation of divine to human action in the spheres of election and grace.[77]

Wittgenstein in Allan Janik and Stephen Toulmin, *Wittgenstein's Vienna* (New York: Simon and Schuster, 1973), p. 191.

73. Kant, *Critique,* pp. 409-15. We are back with our old friend, the "antinomy," here, in one of his or her many guises. Donald Baillie observed that "[w]e must neither be too impatient of antinomy nor too tolerant of it, if we are to advance to a clearer understanding of the deep Christian secret. Yet is it not altogether by thinking the matter out, but by living it out in daily Christian faith and love, that we shall arrive at a deeper insight in which the paradox will be less acute"; quoted in George Newlands, *John and Donald Baillie: Transatlantic Theology* (Bern: Peter Lang, 2002), p. 141. "These lines," says Newlands, "in many ways encapsulate his whole understanding of the Christian life." In light of what we have noted about John's Gospel and in Simeon, Baillie's remarks on the decrease of the acuteness of paradox are interesting.

74. This is highlighted from the outset of Henry E. Allison's careful study *Kant's Theory of Freedom* (Cambridge: Cambridge University Press, 1990).

75. Manfred Kuehn, *Kant: A Biography* (Cambridge: Cambridge University Press, 2001), p. 319.

76. Kant, *Critique,* p. 13.

77. Kant's remarks on the interests of reason in the conflicts which surface in his antinomies (*Critique,* pp. 422-30) and the conclusion of his discussion of the canon of pure reason (pp. 651-52) repay our consideration. Cf. the conclusion of part 1 of "Religion within the Boundaries of Mere Reason," in I. Kant, *Religion and Rational Theology,* ed. Allen Wood and George Di Giovanni (Cambridge: Cambridge University Press, 1996), pp. 96-97.

The reason why Kant's musings on freedom contributed to his skepticism about the scope of speculation was partly because he was perplexed about the relationship of moral freedom to moral evil.[78] It is too simplistic to remain content with the insistence that Kant had a shallow view of human nature and that this vitiates his treatment. Absolutely speaking, that is true, and when we judge him by the standards of that Protestant orthodoxy which constituted the deep background of Kant's heritage, we might be singularly unimpressed by him theologically in connection with the question of freedom, believing that he rose little higher than Pelagianism.[79] Yet, Kant puzzled instructively over human agency, and his puzzlement was generated by the coexistence of the conviction that humans are significantly free — which must be the case if they are moral agents — with the conviction that radical evil clings to human nature. Radical evil is apparently innate. This conviction, unimpressive to the orthodox, because it is taken for granted, dismayed fellow travelers on the Enlightenment and post-Enlightenment road. Kant thought that the will had willed itself into bondage. How? And how on earth can the will find a way out again? For, in Kant's philosophy, you are indeed meant to apply to earth and not to heaven in such a matter.

If Kant does not buy the witness to the Fall as it biblically stands, neither does he dismiss its illumination and treat it as a relic of the benighted and uninformative past which has no business instructing the eighteenth century. Goethe was disgusted: "Kant, who spent a whole lifetime cleaning his philosophical mantle from all kinds of prejudices which soiled it, has now ignominiously dirtied it again with the shameful spot of radical evil, so that Christians too can feel they ought to kiss the hem of it."[80] Yet anyone as aware of and puzzled by radical evil as was Kant is going to seek light from any quarter, and might the Christian Scriptures not have a little something to say about it? Gordon Michalson summarizes the outcome

78. Henry Allison does a good job of elucidating the proposition that "it is no exaggeration to claim that, at bottom, Kant's critical philosophy is a philosophy of freedom." *Kant's Theory of Freedom,* p. 1. In the preface to his *Critique of Practical Reason,* trans. Mary Gregor (Cambridge: Cambridge University Press, 1997), Kant states that "the concept of freedom, insofar as its reality is proved by an apodictic law of practical reason, constitutes the *keystone* of the whole structure of a system of pure reason" (p. 3).

79. See, in this connection, the first book of Kant's "Religion within the Boundaries of Mere Reason," in *Religion and Rational Theology.*

80. Quoted by Michel Despland in *Kant on History and Religion* (Montreal and London: McGill-Queen's University Press, 1973), p. 169.

of Kantian rumination thus: "In some profound and awful sense, I am opaque to myself, considered as a moral agent."[81] We are implicated in an altogether dire business here. Cutting to the chase, we find that the problem of evil "brings Kant closer and closer to the insight that reason is not fully self-governing, but is subject to forces too murky to specify" — forces hard, if not impossible, to understand.[82]

Although chucking around hunks of Kant in this chapter does not prove very much, we surely need to heed his voice. "Human reason," he said, opening the first edition of the *Critique of Pure Reason,* "has this peculiar fate that in one species of its knowledge it is burdened by questions which, as prescribed by the very nature of reason itself, it is not able to ignore, but which, as transcending all its powers, it is also not able to answer."[83] Our situation is characterized by the fact that "[h]uman reason is by nature architectonic. That is to say, it regards all our knowledge as belonging to a possible system."[84] That Kant's declaration turns out to be embedded in a scheme which does not reckon with revelation should not hinder us from asking whether it applies to regenerate theological reason; whether, in fact, a mass of Kantian material, which he works through in adumbration of this principle, is applicable with a none too loose *mutatis mutandis* to the theological task. Short of elaborating in detail on that possibility here, we must certainly ask this: If the preacher does not need resolution (Simeon) and the philosopher needs to live without it (Kant), will the theologian insist on creating his or her own alternative space?

I am not entirely binding myself either to Simeon or to Kant, unexpected bedfellows as they are; their concerns overlap rather than being identical, and I have selected only those elements in their thought that are patient of ad hoc alliance, as in the cases of Simeon and Kierkegaard.[85] Even so, it may be protested that they have been given too much opportu-

81. Gordon E. Michalson, *Fallen Freedom: Kant on Radical Evil and Moral Regeneration* (Cambridge: Cambridge University Press, 1990), p. 141. Michalson's fine study shows how this is anything but simply a small lacuna in Kant's philosophical comprehension.

82. Michalson, *Fallen Freedom,* p. 141.

83. Kant, *Critique,* p. 7, but see pp. 429, 556, 624-25, and 651-54.

84. Kant, *Critique,* p. 429. "By an architectonic I understand the art of constructing system" (p. 653), and "the unity of reason is the unity of system" (p. 556).

85. From a purely conceptual point of view, it is worth exploring possible parallels between Simeon's pastoral application and Kant on practical reason. We could take our bearings from the preface to the second edition of the *Critique* and the first section of the discussion "The Canon of Pure Reason," pp. 630-32; see too p. 642. Evans, *Faith and the Self,* has a useful account of "Kant and Kierkegaard," pp. 47-66.

nity to squeeze out the theologian, doing so, moreover, in objectionably assertoric or gnomic fashion. It seems scandalous to suggest that evangelical theology be brought to the bar of a philosopher who pronounces that "[t]he parties may be commanded to keep peace before the tribunal of reason; but the controversy none the less continues. There can therefore be no way of settling it once for all and to the satisfaction of both sides, save by their becoming convinced that the very fact of their being able so admirably to refute one another is evidence that they are really quarrelling about nothing, and that a certain transcendental illusion has mocked them with a reality where none is to be found."[86]

In particular, are Simeon and Kant being co-opted into too hasty an alliance in order to bolster the case for evading the responsibility of systematic theology to make an elementary deduction along the following lines: (1) those who are not predestined must be passed over; (2) to be passed over is to be actively passed over; (3) to be actively passed over is reprobation? Are we theologically and cravenly resting content with not flouting the requirements of homiletics or the claims of antinomy simply by keeping silence? The protest will go like this: "Never mind the difficulties of relating human freedom to divine call, with which we might be willing or bound to live. You have neither to be a rocket scientist nor a systematic theologian to make the deduction about reprobation which you resist in the cause of contrasting predestination with a genuine historical call — though perhaps only a systematic theologian who confines himself to a preacher (Simeon) and philosopher (Kant) is capable of missing it."

I hope that enough has already been said to turn aside this riposte, although a detailed Kierkegaardian elaboration is really needed to shore up our claims. What makes reference to Kant particularly apt is his conviction that it was only by musing over the relation of selfhood to temporality and pondering the relationship of empirical to transcendental ego that he could get anywhere with the problem of freedom.[87] For Kant, this was not purely an exercise in philosophically independent musing on the relation

86. Kant, *Critique,* p. 446.

87. "[T]o have the one or other disposition by nature as an innate characteristic does not mean here that the disposition has not been earned by the human being who harbors it . . . but means rather that it has not been earned in time. . . . This disposition, however, must be adopted through the free power of choice, for otherwise it could not be imputed." Kant, *Religion and Rational Theology,* p. 74. Theodore Green's older translation places the adoption of the disposition in the past; Immanuel Kant, *Religion within the Limits of Reason Alone,* trans. Theodore Green (San Francisco: Harper and Row, 1960), p. 20.

of selfhood, time, and eternity; it was a matter of being morally pressed to speak of an ego which must have the property of freedom. Lacking it, we could not be rightly indicted for our evil (or praised for our good) disposition. Yet, we are aware that, in its temporal appearance, we witness the ego in bondage. "The temporality of our agency is the necessary ransom that must be paid to the free will problem if our high vocation as moral agents is to be preserved."[88] Shortly before discussing the impossibility of an existential system, Kierkegaard voices a question in the same area: "In general, how does the empirical ego stand related to the pure ego, the I-am-I?"[89]

If any theologian promises to come up with a theological judgment along the lines I have followed here, it would appear to be Emil Brunner. Brunner regarded Kierkegaard as "the greatest thinker of modern times . . . the entire bent" of whose philosophy "seems to correspond with ours."[90] He immediately adds: "Our considerations are purely theological . . . hence they are not dependent upon the correctness or incorrectness of that philosophical undertaking which seems to run parallel — apparently or really — with our own." On the specific point at issue — the application of theological method to the conclusion that "the Holy and Merciful God, who in Jesus Christ has chosen all who believe in Him from all eternity, but who rejects those who refuse the obedience of faith" — Brunner appears to me to deliver, at least, generally.[91]

88. Allen Wood, quoted in Allison, *Kant's Theory of Freedom,* p. 47.

89. Kierkegaard, *Concluding Unscientific Postscript,* p. 107. Karl Rahner is a good example of a theologian who takes on board in his philosophical and theological anthropology the set of considerations entertained by Kant in connection with selfhood. "In spite of what Christianity says about the *history* of salvation, what it says about man always refers to him in the deepest origin and roots of his being." *Foundations of Christian Faith* (London: Darton, Longman and Todd, 1984), p. 40. Rahner works out the implications of this statement in chapters 2–4 of this volume. For a brief, but useful, entrée into how Kant features in Rahner's deep intellectual background, see Gerald McCool's introduction to *A Rahner Reader* (London: Darton, Longman and Todd, 1975).

90. Note the specific context in which Brunner makes these remarks in *The Divine-Human Encounter* (London: SCM, 1944), p. 57.

91. E. Brunner, *The Christian Doctrine of God: Dogmatics,* vol. 1 (London: Lutterworth, 1949), p. 337; see the whole discussion, pp. 303-53. The strength of Brunner's treatment in these pages is that of his work generally, which is that it keeps faith and history at the center, speculation at bay. Yet I should not commit myself to the detail of his adumbration and would even suspend judgment on the exact way in which he relates election to faith (pp. 319-20), pending a proper analysis of Brunner's notion of faith. Brunner is nothing if not stark: "Theoretical thought seeks the unity of system; the Theology of Faith insists on

Perhaps it is symptomatic of enslavement to modernity that conceptual inquiry has preceded confessional inquiry in this chapter. To turn in a confessional direction, is the position adopted here effectively the one given classic confessional formulation in the Lutheran Formula of Concord in its full and impressive article on predestination? The Formula denies that predestination to life is contingent on God's foreknowledge of humans' use of their freedom, but affirms that it does work that way with reprobation; that is, reprobation is contingent on God's foreknowledge of our sinfulness and sin.[92]

Religiously, the Formula moves in the right direction. Even so, to say the least, we should hesitate to be tied to a conceptual resolution advanced along these lines, especially where the resolution is proposed in the confessional statement of a church or churches and not limited to the speculative contributions of its theologians. The resolution may (or may not) turn out to survive the criticism I made of such positions as the Arminian one, namely, that they conceive individuals without those religiously determining characteristics which actually mark them as historical persons, and so "idealize" them. The reason why the Formula's teaching may not fall afoul of this criticism is that the foreknown person on the Arminian scenario is considered absent those characteristics that constitute the very identity of the concrete person, the latter being a recipient of saving grace. The foreknown person on the Formula's scenario, also marked by absence of saving grace, seems to correspond to the actual, concrete person as well, also marked by the absence of saving grace. However, this does not necessarily save the Formula. On deeper analysis, we might find ourselves back with our old problem, for it remains the case that, for us to conceive the person as foreknown, we have to strip him or her of the personal shape acquired in concrete history, a history of interrelationships including relationships with recipients of saving grace, a person who, as with the Jews in Acts 13, is marked by a temporally negative response to the offer of saving

---

the reality of existential decision." Brunner, *The Word and the World* (London: SCM, 1932), p. 7. Paul Tillich was right to note Brunner's consistency in the application of his dogmatic method; "Some Questions on Brunner's Epistemology," in *Theology of Emil Brunner*, ed. Charles W. Kegley (New York: Macmillan, 1962), pp. 97-107, here p. 102.

92. The terms of our discussion certainly do not need to be Protestant; see, e.g., the sixth-century pseudo-Augustinian *Memorandum against the Pelagians and Celestians* in the context of the controversy between Gottschalk and Hincmar. Jaroslav Pelikan summarizes this controversy in *The Growth of Medieval Theology (600-1300)* (Chicago: University of Chicago Press, 1978), pp. 81-95.

grace. A theological conceptuality along Concord lines may be defensible — indeed, I did not deny that classic Arminianism might come up with a conceptual response — but it is better to forswear speculation on the supposed form of an antecedent decision that is not a predestination to life rather than factor it decisively into Christian theology, especially when it takes confessional form.

The Formula does well to forfeit symmetry in its treatment of predestination to life and perdition and, if one formula be preferred to another in the Christian tradition, Concord scores high.[93] A theological statement can be like an arrow in upward flight, guiding our perceptions in one rather than another direction, and we can welcome its general trajectory while reserving judgment on its qualities as a precision missile in relation to the target. Concord scores high, but soars too high. The flight of Concord could never quite have found, and should not have been aimed precisely at, this target. In setting aside symmetry it does not in effect sufficiently shrug off the legacy of speculation. Its formulation presumes to trace phenomena which appear in time back to the eternal counsel of God and then proceed to order foreknowledge and determination in that eternal counsel in relation to those not predestined to life. It is doubtful if we can more break through to peer at the eternal counsel of God uninvited than could the Israelites at Mount Sinai. We might have that privileged invitation in the case of the positive salvation of the elect, but, even here, the door is only slightly ajar when we ask about the relation of time to eternity.[94] When we do not have the invitation, the theologian's motto, declared by the mouth of him who was most privileged at Sinai, must be recalled: "The secret things belong to the LORD our God, but the things revealed belong to us and to our children forever, that we may follow all the words of this law" (Deut. 29:29). The text does not allow a privileged body of theologians to do what the privileged body of Israelites were not allowed to do, which was to eat and drink and see God (Exod. 24:11). As Richard Baxter said, "One of the greatest sins" of divines is to "dispute unrevealed things about the nature of God."[95]

93. Brunner, however, criticizes it for its conception of faith. *Christian Doctrine of God,* p. 315.

94. It looks as though Brunner exaggerates with his remark that "we gaze beyond that [the historical act] at the eternal background, for a moment as it were, but we do not stay there." *Christian Doctrine of God,* p. 312. How great or serious an exaggeration this is can only be determined by working through his substantive theological work.

95. Quoted in Hans Boersma, *Richard Baxter's Doctrine of Justification in Its Seventeenth Century Context of Controversy* (Vancouver: Regent, 2004), p. 101.

We cannot safely make inferences about the relation of God's doings in historical time to the supposition of an eternal and immutable counsel in the case before us, unless it be, most tentatively, in the *negative* form. That is, where a fully responsible rejection of a genuine summons is described as it is in the NT, an antecedent, determining reprobative decree in relation to those who so reject can scarcely be what is reflected in historical time. Consider the complexities of inference which arise in other theological cases where the relation of time to eternity is concerned. Suppose that we ascribe to God both wrath and passibility. If we do so, we should affirm that they do not belong to God as do eternal love and peace, for there is no mutual wrath between the persons of the eternal Trinity nor is there perichoretic inner suffering.[96] Wrath and suffering are brought on by, are reactions to, human deeds. Yet, at least within a broadly classical view of God, we do not believe that wrath and suffering are eternally unknown to him who knows and foreknows all things, as though constituting for him an entire novelty occasioned by the world.

At the level of imagination, the possibilities involved here may not be difficult to conjure up. I can now anticipate the anger or grief which I will feel at some specific highly probable or even near-inevitable event in the future before it has happened. A perfect and infallible anticipation, impossible for humans, would mean that an event entirely novel in time is not novel in experience when it comes about in time. I can imagine that this is how it is in the case of God. What I cannot knowledgeably do is to translate this conceptually into terms fitting for God. The cases of wrath and passibility illustrate the problem in our attempts to conceive of the relation obtaining between the eternity of knowledge and the contingency of history in the eternal, immanent being of the triune God.

Yet, these involve less complexity than an inference to reprobation. The situation that obtains in the case of wrath and passibility introduces no threat of dichotomy or tension between will and nature; it just induces a confession of ignorance on the matter.[97] By way of contrast, dichotomy

96. Robert Jenson needlessly jeopardizes this principle by his attempt to push hard along a Barthian trajectory in his essay "Reconciliation in God," in *The Theology of Reconciliation,* ed. Colin Gunton (London and New York: T. & T. Clark, 2003), pp. 159-66.

97. See Brunner's appropriation of Luther in *Christian Doctrine of God,* chap. 14. "No modern theologian, perhaps no theologian at any period in the history of the Church, has grasped so profoundly the contradictory ideas of the wrath and the love of God" (p. 168). I assume that Brunner intends "contradictory" in the sense of "paradoxical"; cf. Brunner's *Word and the World,* pp. 6-7.

and tension are precisely what threaten in the case of antecedent reprobation: God is love according to nature but immutably decrees the reprobation of a creature good in the creatureliness of his or her nature although corrupted in her or his person, apparently given the opportunity in time to do other than he or she did. My objective is not to deny categorically the possibility of success in demonstrating the internal coherence of this position and even an appearance of coherence with the biblical witness — theologians can produce an impressive range of arts and crafts when a laudable concern for truth is at stake — but to indicate that the complexity of describing an eternal divine anticipation or experience of wrath or sorrow is compounded in the case of antecedent will and historical reprobation.[98] To argue for an antecedent decree of reprobation on the basis of the immutability of a divine will executed in time generates too many speculative metaphysical questions, both about what happens in time and about its relation to what happens in eternity. Where Scripture contrasts an effective call, rooted in predestination, with a rejected call which it roots in culpable stubbornness, we must not upset its proportions by an inference which is prima facie logical but turns out to be not only metaphysically complex, but also a threat to our hold on the reality of what is disclosed to us in time. Tentatively, inference is permissible in the case of wrath and passibility only for those who hold that the text teaches divine wrath and passibility and that we have theological reason to deny both (a) that these apply to God's immanent triune nature and (b) that they become novelties in God's experience. On the other hand, where an antecedent, determining reprobative decree is not clearly taught in Scripture, we have reason to believe that it cannot be inferred on the basis of what is taught.

As far as theological method and responsibility are concerned, why do we attempt some of the things that we do attempt theologically? The

98. As my concern is with the biblical witness and theological method, I have not attempted to outline in detail the logic of the position I am rejecting. This is simply because I do not think that either the biblical witness or the systematic task requires it of us. Those who believe that it is required by either or both have, of course, produced weighty historical defenses of this position. The most salient factors impinging on my discussion include (a) the insistence that the cause of our damnation lies within us and (b) the belief that the decree of reprobation is known in its execution, not *in se.* A figure like Polanus in Reformed orthodoxy represents these concerns; see Richard Muller, *Christ and the Decree: Christology and Predestination in Reformed Theology from Calvin to Perkins* (Durham, N.C.: Labyrinth, 1986), p. 160, in the context of the discussion in the whole volume. I have been careful to emphasize the antecedent, as opposed to the causal, quality of the putative decree of reprobation. The role of causality in this scheme seems quite complex.

cause of human sin and resistance lies within humans, and this is consistent with the belief that God can so harden, direct, and channel its expression in time (as well as reversing it in grace) that there can be *some* sort of concurrent divine-human agency when it comes to sin's particulars.[99] To my mind, the religious problem is not how to conceptualize all this, but why we feel impelled to do so. It is true that there is a danger of arbitrarily calling "halt" in theology. Failure to accept the logical implications of a belief or set of beliefs can amount to covering with the pious cloak of Scripture (a) a lack of *interest* in systematic exploration or (b) a lack of *competence* in systematic exploration or (c) a disingenuous lack of *willingness* to face systematic implication. Further, when we survey our theological operations in the round, we are probably all somewhat arbitrary in what we decide to explore or to leave alone. We all cry "halt" somewhere; theology, like philosophy, is knowing where to stop. Should we not accept not only the religious truth but also the virtual sufficiency of what Scripture discloses to us in the matter that is exercising us here? Are not the contours of the reality that we need to know laid out for us rather precisely in biblical revelation, when it comes to a question of this kind? It is not a revelation which inspires hand-wringing, quietly embarrassed confession of mystery. It is a revelation which exposes reality *precisely* according to its profoundest *existential* dimensions. It is surely a *fact* that those who are not predestined to life *were* given in time the real and not merely apparent opportunity to lay hold of it. It is a *fact* that God did not, by predestination, secure them for his kingdom. Theology is not now deprived of any explanatory job: it must inquire about the whole of the biblical revelation in a form which biblical authors were not called on to do and to consider both the intellectual and the religious implications of a broad theological integration. Doubtless, particular themes and particular contexts call out for more or for less "speculative" expenditure of theological time. What we must not do is to upset the biblical balance, threatening with obscurity or marginalization what is plain there or highlighting what is, at the very best, obscure or hidden there.

The question of human freedom does, of course, both lie at the intellectual heart of the matter and produce heart-anxiety, but why exactly do I need to know the nature and limits of human freedom in the

99. The language of particularity here does not imply that sin is to be thought of primarily in terms of particular, atomistic acts. Further, I am quite emphatically not saying that all forms of evildoing are to be thought of in the terms stated.

present context? "Morality does not, indeed, require that freedom be understood, but only that it should not contradict itself, and so should at least allow of being thought."[100] This applies to religion — Christian religion.[101] I am aware that I possess whatever kind of freedom that is attendant on and entailed by my responsibility before the living God, who summons me. I am aware that I can be held to account for resisting grace.[102] I am also aware that I cannot for the minutest second, to the minutest degree, congratulate myself on anything.[103] I am aware that the God who elects and predestines in love only bids me do anything because he is at work within me to will and to do (Phil. 2:13). This deep religious sense is no escape from rigor, the failure of some third-rate theologian or fourth-rate Christian to think honestly and thoroughly. On the contrary, what is existentially the case, at the deepest and most important ontological level of existence, is known precisely in existential mode, not necessarily in the mode of ontological speculation. Existential appropriation is not the product of failure to grasp the real; it is the form in which the real is grasped. Does it matter that I have no idea to what extent grace is theoretically resistible; no idea of how predestination

100. Kant, *Critique,* p. 29. This is essential to Kant's claim that the "final end" of reason is "in the sphere of the practical" (p. 34).

101. It is just after this remark on morality that Kant makes his celebrated observation: "I have therefore found it necessary to deny *knowledge,* in order to make room for *faith.*" *Critique,* p. 29. In quoting these words, I certainly do not fully endorse the whole way in which Kant relates faith and knowledge or the way in which he understands either. They should be read in conjunction with what Kant says about alleged antitheistic demonstrations concerning God, freedom, and immortality in his discussion "The Discipline of Pure Reason," p. 602. I certainly do not agree with what Kant says about what we do not need to know at the end of the first part of "Religion within the Boundaries of Mere Reason," in *Religion and Rational Theology,* pp. 96-97.

102. Brunner's *Man in Revolt: A Christian Anthropology* (London: Lutterworth, 1939) is a detailed adumbration of the claim that responsibility is constitutive of humanity.

103. A trawl through Augustine's anti-Pelagian writings reveals the ubiquity of 1 Cor. 4:7 — "What do you have that you did not receive?" — and the impression this text made on him. Nor can he stay away from it in correspondence relevant to the Pelagian dispute, such as when he cites it early in the letter to Paulinus written in 417; *Saint Augustine: Letters 165-203,* in *The Fathers of the Church,* vol. 30, trans. Wilfrid Parsons (Washington, D.C.: Catholic University of America Press, 1955), letter 186, pp. 191-221, here p. 194. At the same time, we must heed Kierkegaard: "There is a pious suspicion about subjectivity, that as soon as the least concession is made to it, it will promptly become something meritorious"; quoted in C. Stephen Evans, "Salvation, Sin and Human Freedom in Kierkegaard," in *The Grace of God and the Will of Man,* ed. C. Pinnock (Minneapolis: Bethany House, 1989), p. 181.

works in relation to freedom; no idea of how divine decision works in relation to the rejection of the gospel?[104]

Kuyper was surely mistaken to call, in the terms that he did, for a "clear reflection of the wisdom of God in the logical consciousness of humanity."[105] He is more helpful when he somewhere makes a remark to the effect that it is in prayer that we unite the diverse fragments of our lives, and it is this orientation to religious existence that Simeon expressed when he said it is in prayer that we unite those diverse truths applied to our lives which are presented through the medium of biblical speech acts. It is not that the act of prayer guarantees theological insight and integration. It is not implied that, in prayer, God is automatically transparent to us or that we are transparent to ourselves. Self can block out God in prayer. In my honest moments, I may admit that I try to project an image before others in the public arena. It might even occur to me that the habit is so deeply ingrained that I am unaware of it, though most everybody else is aware of it. In my wiser moments, I may admit that the perception others actually

104. For an important defense of the claim that "[t]he causal joint (could there be said to be one) between God's action and ours is of no concern in the activity of religion," see Austin Farrer, *Faith and Speculation: An Essay in Philosophical Theology* (Edinburgh: T. & T. Clark, 1967). These words are found on p. 66. Farrer is an altogether fruitful philosophical-theological source if we want to ponder the relationship of divine and human action. "God," said Farrer, is "uniquely unique" and "has the secret key of entry into all his creatures; he can conjoin the action of any of them with his will"; quoted in Douglas Hedley, "Austin Farrer's Shaping Spirit of Imagination," in *The Human Person in God's World: Studies to Commemorate the Austin Farrer Centenary,* ed. Brian Hebblethwaite and Douglas Hedley (London: SCM, 2006), p. 129. As Basil Mitchell put it, Austin Farrer "took it for granted that human personality transcends our attempts to grasp it conceptually — yet, if we know anything, this is what we know best." "Austin Farrer — the Philosopher," *New Fires,* Winter 1983, pp. 452-56, here p. 454.

105. A. Kuyper, *Encyclopaedia of Sacred Theology: Its Principles* (London: Hodder and Stoughton, 1899), p. 283. Although Kuyper does not use the word "logical" narrowly in this work and it seems sometimes interchangeable with "rational" in English translation, my demurral stands in the light of Kuyper's earlier remark: "The logical is not a temporal form of our human consciousness. . . . God Himself is logical, for in Him all knowledge is assumed, and between our knowledge here and that which shall be ours in eternity, there is no essential, but only a proportional difference: now in part, then perfect" (p. 245). To be sure, this should be examined carefully and certainly not dismissed *tout court* (I should dismiss in this fashion hardly anything written by Kuyper). Kuyper ruminates on election in this work, connecting the questions of election and logical consciousness (pp. 297-98). He also speaks of election to service (p. 516). Kuyper's brief work *The Biblical Doctrine of Election* (Grand Rapids: Zondervan, 1934) contains much that is very welcome and consistent with my account, even if the framework is quite different.

have of me is certainly not the one that I think they have of me and even less the one that I have tried to cultivate and project. However, all that seems far behind me in private prayer, when I go to the quiet place and, with ingenuous sincerity, admit all this, and much else, to God, who sees in private as well as in public. How self-deceived I am! Are we not often more self-deceived in that place than anywhere else, precisely because we feel protected from ourselves? We carry even into that quiet and private place an image of ourselves. As Bonhoeffer put it with characteristic candor: "Even in my little room I can produce quite a remarkable public demonstration," subconsciously making myself "the observer of my own prayer before God."[106]

Prayer is not the guaranteed secure place of theological insight. Yet, it is a place where the human spirit is most profoundly aware both of its responsibility and of God's sovereignty, even as we admit how little we know about how human responsibility and divine decision are intertwined. Both human action and divine action are a mystery to us, rendering their relationship a double mystery, and because evil is in the mix too, their relationship is a dark grey mystery.[107] Prayer means awareness of sin as well as awareness of God, and the former awareness can itself check the urge for speculation. "The dialectic of sin," as Kierkegaard put it in *The Sickness unto Death,* "is diametrically contrary to that of speculation."[108] Mine is to take responsibility for rejecting a summons genuine in my time; God's is to take responsibility for what is antecedently known and done in the eternal counsel of unalloyed holiness, goodness, uprightness, and love.

106. D. Bonhoeffer, *Discipleship* (Minneapolis: Fortress, 2001), pp. 153-54. It is completely mistaken to maintain that "dishonesty is spiritually impossible in prayer." Jeff Astley, "Evolution and Evil: The Difference Darwin Makes in Theology and Spirituality," in *Reading Genesis after Darwin,* ed. S. C. Barton and D. Wilkinson (Oxford: Oxford University Press, 2009), pp. 163-80, here p. 171.

107. We recall that Paul makes much of sin's agency in Rom. 7:13-23, complicating any theological account which reckons only with human and divine action.

108. Kierkegaard, *The Sickness unto Death: A Christian Psychological Exposition for Upbuilding and Awakening,* trans. H. Hong and E. Hong (Princeton: Princeton University Press, 1980), p. 120. The relation of logic in general to existence in general occupied Kierkegaard: Is the logical an abstraction from existence, or is it a pure abstraction without any relation to existence? See H. Diem, *Kierkegaard's Dialectic of Existence* (Edinburgh and London: Oliver and Boyd, 1959), chaps. 4–7. For the variety and richness of Kierkegaard's understanding of dialectic, see Walsh, *Living Christianly,* pp. 6-7.

CHAPTER FOUR

Dogmatic Difficulties

Justice and Mercy

Our discussion up to this point has not been designed to foster a cavalier attitude toward intellectual dilemmas in theology, as though their persistence had no significant existential fallout. A desire to make sense of the connection between God's particular choice and his wider call has often been fueled by worry about the notion of God's electing choice in the first place. It seems to cast a shadow over God's mercy or God's justice or both. A common response to this worry goes like this: mercy is undeserved. Both by definition and as a truth of the matter defined, mercy is not owed to us. Neither deserved by us, nor owed by God, it is to be distinguished from justice, which is what we deserve and what God delivers. None can complain when mercy is not meted out, for the alternative to it is justice and not injustice. There is no injustice involved in predestination, and the wonder is that God should have mercy upon anyone.

This response is both well motivated and justified up to a point. It should not be queried too hastily. On the contrary, if this response does not strike a deep, positive chord in us, self-searching is in order. That we have no claim upon God's mercy — that grace must never be understood except as grace — is religiously and theologically fundamental. We shall scarcely think luminously upon anything in theology without an accompanying sense of sin, which, as it deepens, deepens also our wonder at God's mercy. Yet, surely, this response is incomplete and, in its incompleteness, both unsatisfactory and liable to mislead. Paradoxically, it risks looking at matters too much from our point of view, and too little from God's. From our point of view, we can stake no claim to mercy. However, is God internally constrained to exercise it and to do so in a form which eludes our capacity to describe or conceive? What if God has an inner constraint *not* to leave sinners to perdition, a constraint which banishes any suggestion that his is a liberty of indifference when it comes to choosing to save or not to save? Anselm observed that, as God has purposely created humanity for communion with him, it would be self-defeating if he did not come to its rescue.[1] My point is consistent with but not identical to his and does not assume it. My question pertains to God's nature, not to his particular purposes, although this way of putting it gives an exaggerated impression of distinction from Anselm. The question is: Can we deny that God's nature, his very being, may be such that he cannot leave creatures without saving hope? Can we with confidence describe the relation of God's will to God's nature, as though his will could go either way as far as offering salvation were concerned, both ways being in equally consistent accord with his nature? Are we so conceiving of will and nature in God that, in matters of salvation, no necessity of nature requires that his will be anything but contingent in this matter? Can we deny that, as far as *God* is concerned, the power of love may be expressed in a world of sinners *only* by his having mercy?

While I shall not fight shy of declaring sympathy with what is implicitly proposed in the questions in their rhetorical form and with those who believe that the questions should be answered plainly and without dissimulation, it suffices for the purposes of the present argument simply to say that we cannot know God's mercy to be other than is implied in the line of thought advanced in the questions. That is, we must answer them in the negative. Beyond that point, quite apart from the advantage which accrues from adopting the principle of minimum theological commitment needed to secure an argument, we should need to tread carefully for both religious and conceptual reasons. The relation of freedom to necessity in God may be (and presumably is) quite different from anything we can conceive on the basis of earthly analogy; a fuller knowledge than mortals are privileged to receive might lead us to see that contrasting ascriptions of relative freedom and necessity to God soon lose traction or, at least, do not take us as far in the knowledge of God as we might have hoped. The

1. Anselm, "Why God Became Man," in *Anselm of Canterbury: The Major Works,* ed. B. Davies and G. R. Evans (Oxford: Oxford University Press, 1998). Here, Anselm takes a tighter logical line than is taken by, e.g., Athanasius, in *De Incarnatione,* on the fittingness of salvation by the Word: *"Contra Gentes" and "De Incarnatione,"* trans. R. W. Thomson (Oxford: Clarendon, 1971).

question of the relation of nature to will in God is a subject of discussion in itself. Grace may both be entirely free *quoad nos* and simultaneously subject to an inner determination in God that either is or accords with his nature. We must surely leave to God himself the relation of necessity, nature, freedom, and grace. From a religious, let alone a conceptual, point of view, we have to grope most tentatively in formulation. This is not because we are paralyzed by the fear of being caught cunningly flouting the boundaries of God's accommodated self-revelation, sneaking in speculation by the back door while placarding metaphysical agnosticism at the entrance of our theological house. It is just that it is not easy to state clearly what the biblical depiction of God allows and what it requires in any proposed account of the relation of his will to his nature or the relation of divine freedom and necessity.

All we can do is to make the absolutely minimal statement that such is the nature, power, and reality of a mercy unleashed in history that we cannot be sure that it could have been otherwise with God, while being entirely sure that we deserve it not a whit. It is the *name* of YHWH, YHWH, that is declared in Exodus 34:6 — "a God merciful and gracious, slow to anger, and abounding in steadfast love and faithfulness" (ESV) — and it seems entirely apt to describe this as God's nature.[2] If we insist that mercy was purely optional from a divine point of view, the exercise of power held in equilibrating liberty of indifference, we had better be careful that we do not end up like Chesterton's fictitious chief of the Paris police, "one of the great humanitarian French freethinkers"; with such types, the "only thing wrong . . . is that they make mercy even colder than justice."[3] Hooker's formulation is worth pondering: "The being of God is a kind of law to his working."[4] Barth's singularly impressive treatment of the being of God as he who loves in freedom, a treatment which underpins his subsequent exposition of election, addresses this.

I conclude that a standard response to the worry about the consistency of God's predestination with either justice or mercy — the response that we justly deserve punishment and that mercy could have been withheld — risks joining to an important truth (that we do not deserve mercy) a

2. So, e.g., Brevard S. Childs, *Exodus: A Commentary* (London: SCM, 1974), p. 652, and John I. Durham, *Exodus* (Waco, Tex.: Word, 1987), p. 454.

3. "The Secret Garden," in G. K. Chesterton, *The Penguin Complete Father Brown* (Middlesex: Harmondsworth, 1981), p. 24.

4. Quoted by H. R. Mackintosh, *The Christian Apprehension of God* (London: SCM, 1929), p. 210.

questionable dogmatism on the nature of God (that he could have withheld mercy). The claim that God could have withheld mercy might be impeccably motivated by the conviction that we do not deserve mercy, but we are leaving open the possibility that it goes beyond (and, some will judge, against) what Scripture testifies and unveils. What we do not leave open is any doubt about the truth that we deserve justice and not mercy. This is an axiom of theological thought which must be held fast in religious consciousness.

At the outset of this discussion we mentioned two distinct worries: that predestination is unjust and that it is unmerciful. How should we plot the relation of justice to mercy? As long as we contrast the antecedent predestination of some to the antecedent reprobation of others, we are offering a contrast potentially patient of treatment in terms of mercy (shown to the first group) and justice (shown to the second). I have used the phrase "potentially patient of treatment" because some contend that antecedent reprobation does not attain even to justice, let alone to mercy. However, it has been the burden of our earlier discussion to insist that this is not the biblical contrast. If, instead, we highlight the contrast between predestination and a genuine, rejected summons, we have to revise our way of formulating the issue in terms of mercy and justice. What we should really be describing is a case of one form of mercy in relation to another form of mercy. That predestination is mercy goes without saying; but what is a genuine summons to genuinely responsible repentance if not also an expression of mercy? "Mercy," as Melanchthon put it in his classical Apology to the Augsburg Confession, "has the clear mandate of God. For the gospel itself is the mandate which commands us to believe that God wants to forgive and save on account of Christ."[5] Luke tells us that "the Pharisees and experts in the law rejected God's purpose for themselves" (Luke 7:30). Even if we resist the temptation to let the text lure us into indiscriminately bundling together every example of God's summonses or purposes, we must ask: What was the rejected purpose, if not merciful?

In light of this, we must redescribe and reenvision the question of predestination as it is familiarly posed. In reflecting on the question of

5. R. Kolb and T. J. Wengert, eds., *The Book of Concord: The Confession of the Evangelical Lutheran Church* (Minneapolis: Fortress, 2000), p. 167. Clyde L. Manschrek, quoting these words in *Melanchthon: The Quiet Reformer* (New York and Nashville: Abingdon, 1958), p. 294, juxtaposes to it some important remarks by Melanchthon on the connection between mercy and election, remarks echoed in the Formula of Concord in *The Book of Concord,* p. 518, nos. 8-9.

predestination, it is certainly appropriate to consider the relation of God's justice to God's mercy.[6] However, while the intellectual problem remains, the existential mood of human questioning should change if we now conceive predestination as one mercy placed alongside another. It is one thing for an anxious soul to ponder the relation of mercy to justice; it is another to ponder the relation of one mercy to another. Yet, if predestination to life is properly contrasted with a genuine, albeit rejected, summons and opportunity to repent, the question about the relation of one type of action to another — that is, of predestination to summoning — is not immediately about the relation of mercy to justice. It is about the relation of one form of mercy (predestining) to another (summoning). It is understandable, whether or not quite justifiable, if our ignorance of the relation of God's mercy to God's justice generates existential anxiety; but why should ignorance of the relation of one mercy to another do so? Those not predestined cannot say that no mercy is extended to them. We should not cavil because we do not understand how one mercy is related to another. The word of God on the matter, that mercy is always in the equation, suffices.

If it is right to redefine the issue in these terms, will caviling automatically cease, even as intellectual puzzlement remains? Unfortunately not. Perseverance in caviling brings to light an unworthy reason for our commotion over predestination (which is not to say that all reasons are unworthy). "There is usually a snake in the grass," said Cotton Mather, "when [this] doctrine of godliness [predestination] . . . is hissed at."[7] Irrespective of Mather's specific reasons for saying this, what I seem all too often to be saying in my subconscious, while consciously caviling away, is this: "Well, if nobody can enter the kingdom unless predestined, God *ought* to have predestined everyone." With the word "ought," I accuse God of injustice. Predestination, if applied to any, is owed to all. Thus what

6. These concepts are frequently used in theology without precise alignment to the language of Scripture itself, and systematic theology requires constant vigilance and correction on this score. I am looking at the issue in the terms in which it is characteristically set up in theology, irrespective of whether it is more or less justified in terms of biblical vocabulary. Dogmatics should never proceed without attention to biblical vocabulary. However, conceptual distinctions can be validly made within the discipline of dogmatics which not only use vocabulary not found in Scripture (that is obvious and inevitable) but which use the vocabulary in a different way, as long as everyone is clear on what is going on.

7. "Free Grace Maintained," quoted by Richard F. Lovelace, "Cotton Mather: 1663-1728," in *The Pietist Theologians,* ed. Carter Lindberg (Oxford: Blackwell, 2005), pp. 115-27, here p. 116.

appears, at first glance, as an appeal against predestination to the universality of God's mercy turns out to be an appeal not to God's mercy, but to what his justice requires. What I am actually doing is reproaching the quality of divine justice. God has no right to show mercy to some and not to others. That is unjust. If I persist in my objections even after conceding that predestination stands in relation to rejected summons as one form of mercy stands in relation to another, I am displaying a distorted sense of justice, cloaked under appeal to the mercy of God. Does this not reveal my innate obduracy?

The suspicion that God is unjust surely lies pretty deep in human nature. It is not a suspicion that should be painted in monochrome black. Puzzles about the apparent nature, operations, or absence of divine justice may arise from agonizing questions surrounding human evil and suffering, and I am as far as can be from dismissing every question and questioner as infidelity or infidel. Where those perplexities have never tormented us in connection with belief in the power of God, we have probably had no serious exposure to evil. However, in our present context, where predestination is concerned, we need to search and question ourselves more than God. "God is not just": thus hisseth the snake. "God is not truthful; he has not set up his relationship with humankind transparently, and truthfulness is the first requirement of justice. You shall not surely die." What is God told by Adam? "The woman you put here with me — she gave me some fruit from the tree, and I ate it" (Gen. 3:12). Indisputably correct, Adam. Now reason on. "Granted that she was given to me for companionship — a gift of love. Granted you let me name her. Granted we could discuss the matter of where I was when she took the fruit. Yet, Lord, consider this: (a) she is the one who took it; (b) she is the one who gave it to me; ergo (c) in justice, you will surely take this into due and proper account." Is Adam, if we go fancifully no further than the biblical text, not taking inchoate issue with divine justice, conjuring up the elements of a demand as inchoately confident of its own justice as of the justice of him to whom demand is made?[8]

Eve's response to God's question — "The serpent deceived me, and I ate" (Gen. 3:13) — is probably too cryptic for us to know just how far she is

8. "Inexplicable Thy justice seems," says Adam to God in Milton's *Paradise Lost* (book 10, lines 754-55), although the mood is not the same as I have outlined above in this most moving and memorable book of that most moving and memorable poem. In parentheses, as Milton comes onto the election of Israel, an editor is at pains to point out that Milton "by no means rejected the doctrine of 'election to personal salvation.'" John Milton, *Paradise Lost,* ed. Alastair Fowler, 2nd ed. (London: Longman, 2007), p. 652.

palming off responsibility at this point, though she is as correct in the letter as was Adam. Still, perhaps it is rather arbitrary to be silent about Eve if we make insinuations about Adam. What we know is that she succumbed to *maya* — illusion, as Hinduism understands the deceptive realm of appearances which we take for reality — in her perception that the tree combined desirable looks, desirable food, and desirable wisdom. Sustained illusion is insanity. Therefore, we must reckon with the possibility that, when we take issue with divine justice, we lack a *mens sana* and are constitutionally unable either to see or to think straight. Adam and Eve had yet to acquire the experience of sin which Israel acquired, an experience which, said Jeremiah, prophet of the heart deceived, qualified it to be the instructor of the nations by force of faithless example.[9] He tells the people this in what is perhaps the single most poignant chapter on sin in the whole Bible. Yet the people are puzzled at the incipient injustice of exile. So God asks: Why do you bring charges against me (Jer. 2:9)? Perhaps sin is itself so puzzling that the puzzle is only a little compounded and not greatly increased when sinners launch a complaint at the injustice of deserved punishment.[10]

If Genesis begins the exposure of sin in the Bible and Jeremiah reaches its high point, Malachi, concluding the OT, exposes the same state of affairs. It is surely a twisted condition which gives rise to the questions recorded in his prophecy, questions that bear on God's justice. Malachi begins with the starkest announcement of election from God: "I have loved you. . . . I have loved Jacob, but Esau I have hated" (1:1-2). He closes with the direst of warnings that God could strike the land with a curse, a passage the order of whose verses is reversed in the LXX so that the prophecy ends with a softer recollection of Moses. Of all the prophetic books, Malachi most sustains the disputatious style that we occasionally encounter in the prophets.[11] The divine-human exchanges which open the OT dialogue be-

9. This becomes clear on a plausible translation of Jer. 2:23 which is sometimes just permitted, e.g., by J. A. Thompson, *The Book of Jeremiah* (Grand Rapids: Eerdmans, 1980), p. 185, and sometimes adopted, e.g., by Peter C. Craigie et al., *Jeremiah 1–25* (Waco, Tex.: Word, 1991), p. 42.

10. The paradoxical extreme of puzzlement over sin is reached in Henri Blocher's observations on its possibility in Eden in *Original Sin: Illuminating the Riddle* (Leicester: Apollos, 1997), p. 57, and "The Theology of the Fall and the Origin of Evil," in *Darwin, Creation, and the Fall: Theological Challenges,* ed. R. J. Berry and T. A. Noble (Leicester: Apollos, 2009), pp. 163-64.

11. Although we might defend the technical employment of "disputation" — see, e.g., Andrew Hill, *Malachi* (New York: Doubleday, 1998), section 1C, especially pp. 34-37 — I use the term here in a relatively neutral sense in respect of literary analysis.

tween God, Adam, and Eve may not yet constitute a wrangle, but those which close the divine dialogue with a people redeemed and elect look very much like one. The people hurl questions. "How have you loved us?" (1:2). "How have we shown contempt for your name?" (1:6). "How have we defiled you?" (1:7). "How have we wearied [the Lord]?" (2:17). "How do we rob you [God]?" (3:8). Even where the stark wording of the text does not make it explicit, historical and canonical context, embracing the long and weary history of Israel, makes clear that these inquiries are not born of innocence, though, perhaps, of ignorance, fruit of a prolonged and accustomed insensitivity not banished from the spirit by return from the banishment of the body in Judah's exile.

Nor is the prophet himself always faultless. Jonah, son of Amittai, is supposed to prophesy against Nineveh. He goes there under duress. "I know what you are like, Lord. You tend to relent from sending calamity. In the case of Israel, that is all to the good. But *Nineveh* — a place which is a military threat to Israel, idolatrous in the root principle of its urban life? People who know nothing about your law and probably cannot even tell the right hand from the left? *It* does not deserve the chance to repent. Where is the justice in sparing some Ninevites and threatening some Israelites?" I hope that the measure of rhetorical indulgence in this presentation of Jonah's point of view does not obscure the point. Desmond Alexander rightly urges us to find in Jonah a protest against God's justice.[12] In response, the reader should ask: "Deep down, Jonah, if you have no right to be angry, why are you angry?" (cf. 4:4).

Paul is different. "Who are you, O man, to talk back to God?" (Rom. 9:20). Paul's challenge is not a sign of perversity, irritably dodging the hard questions about God's justice in election, a "helpless mode of argument," as Troeltsch put it.[13] It is true that our interpretation of the point and force of his question depends on our interpretation of the logic of his overall argument and the position of his interlocutor. Whatever our conclusions, it is hard to contest the claim that what the apostle is doing is expressing a sentiment axiomatically presupposed in godly thought and not wheeling in a testy interrogative when his argument runs out of steam. We may be unsure of much in relation to election, but what we can be sure of is that God is

12. D. W. Baker, T. D. Alexander, and B. K. Waltke, *Obadiah, Jonah, Micah* (Leicester: IVP, 1988), pp. 51-131.

13. Ernst Troeltsch, *The Social Teaching of the Christian Churches*, vol. 1 (New York: Macmillan, 1931), p. 74. Although Troeltsch does not pick out this passage, it is a classic instance of what he does pick out.

righteous and just and that divine election does not give the lie to this. This is not a conclusion to be suspended until we have explicated God's ways. It is fundamental in biblically formed consciousness. We can be equally sure that the self is no paragon of righteousness and is not even righteous enough to assume that the question about God's justice is born of innocent integrity.[14] (Whatever the wider application of the foregoing points, I am *not* taking into account the question as it is raised in connection with God's power and love in the light of every form of human evil and suffering.)

It is more important to acquire a consciousness of God and self which knows God to be without injustice and ourselves to be mired in it than it is to resolve the riddle of election. "In his own eyes," the psalmist says of the wicked, "he flatters himself too much to detect or hate his sin" (36:2). In the West of the third millennium, if we have one highly developed moral capacity, it is our lightning ability to detect any trace of injustice toward ourselves. Morally, we have the sensitivity of hothouse plants. When shaped in disproportion to wider and deeper moral sensibilities, this capacity of ours blunts more than hones a proper appreciation of justice. The very speed of our detection of injustice toward ourselves, moving at a pace no faster than its bosom friend, self-defense, has scarcely slowed since the days of Adam. Traveling at the rate it does, all is in a blur around it as the moral world whizzes by. I am not denouncing cynically all human detection of injustice done toward ourselves. That would be to make the opposite error and deprive us of a positive moral capacity which we must retain. It is just that, in the context of our present inquiry, we humans need to fess up before we interrogate God.

That said, those of us who stand in the Protestant tradition cannot be satisfied with our magisterial forefathers here.[15] Calvin, as we know, particularly accented predestination. "Let God be true" is "the primary axiom

14. Erasmus surmised that Paul "would reply very differently to a prudent and faithful servant, modestly seeking to learn from his master why he wanted a thing to be done which at first sight seemed useless." "On Freedom of the Will," in *Luther and Erasmus: Free Will and Salvation,* ed. Gordon Rupp (London: SCM, 1969), pp. 35-97, here p. 67. One might not want to put it that way, but the supposition that Paul would not have always replied in those terms is plausible enough. Quite generally, conservative Protestants should not allow Luther's dialectical superiority to Erasmus and any substantive shortcomings in Erasmus's position to prevent them from taking far more seriously than they usually do some of Erasmus's essential concerns.

15. As Zwingli's direct influence has been less or less easily traceable than that of Luther or Calvin, I do not allude to his position or to that of any other magisterial Reformer.

of all Christian philosophy."[16] This is where we should start our thinking. Calvin consistently insisted that divine justice is not a lawless operation. To suppose the contrary is abhorrent. At the same time, the justice of God is often hidden and not transparent. "If a mortal man should pronounce his will and command and make his volition a sufficient reason, I admit it would be tyrannical. But to transfer the principle to God would be sacrilegious folly."[17] How dare we judge God's justice by our natural standards? The whole question of predestination hinges on the impossibility of making such a judgment, Calvin tells Pighius, that is, on the question "whether there is no justice of God except what we can conceive."[18] Calvin unremittingly insists that the cause of damnation lies in ourselves, but he insists with equal resolution that God's decree lies behind our sins, as it lay behind Adam's fall. Pressed on whether this entails that God decrees not just actions but also the state of the heart, Calvin, never one to avoid biting the bullet, agrees. "The hand of God rules the interior affections no less than it superintends external actions."[19] Calvin's discussion of providence in his *Institutes* seems to reveal a commitment to divine causal action which lies at the heart of this.[20] How all this is to be reconciled with a justice which holds humans to account for their sin and responsible for their own damnation, Calvin does not profess to know. As far as he is concerned, we do not need to know. Our business is to submit ourselves to the truth.

I am not directly engaging here with Calvin's substantive position on reprobation, only with his associated appeal to divine justice. It is surely inadequate.[21] Against Calvin, we must underline that problems with God's

16. Calvin, *The Epistles of Paul the Apostle to the Romans and to the Thessalonians* (Edinburgh: Saint Andrew, 1961), p. 60. He is commenting on Rom. 3:4.

17. Calvin, *Concerning the Eternal Predestination of God,* trans. J. K. S. Reid (London: Clarke, 1961), p. 117.

18. Calvin, *Concerning the Eternal Predestination,* p. 58.

19. Calvin, *Concerning the Eternal Predestination,* p. 175. "He has in his power also the depraved actions of the ungodly" (p. 174).

20. Calvin, *Institutes of the Christian Religion,* trans. F. L. Battles, vol. 1 (Philadelphia: Westminster, 1960), 1.16.

21. Did Calvin produce anything more remarkable and revealing than his *Sermons on Job* (1574; reprint, Edinburgh: Banner of Truth, 1993)? Susan Schreiner is right: "No biblical text . . . drives Calvin further into the realm of hiddenness [the hiddenness of God] than the Book of Job." *Where Shall Wisdom Be Found? Calvin's Exegesis of Job from Medieval and Modern Perspectives* (Chicago: University of Chicago Press, 1994), p. 121. Brian Gerrish is also right to say that "[s]triving after clarity in the concept we should entertain of God" is "a fundamental mark of the Calvinistic mind," quoted by David F. Wright in "Calvin's

justice in some relevant cases (antecedent reprobation is one of them), whether or not they can be resolved, are not bound to arise solely from what he regarded as a theologically illicit appeal to canons of natural justice external to Scripture. Questions arise on the basis of internal biblical considerations, especially from God's justice manifested there. For example, the Pentateuch records God's meticulous provisions for ordering social life, provisions which, as becomes increasingly clear when we study the prophets, manifest God's heartfelt love for social justice and do not constitute a dispassionate and negotiable agenda.[22] The rationale behind these provisions is not always obvious to us and pertains chiefly to the external ordering of human life. In connection with justice, the importance of the cluster of issues thrown up by, for example, feminist approaches to Israelite patriarchy must be granted. A detailed response to Calvin requires proper nuance and circumspection. However, even those who agree with (e.g., feminist) indictments of the ways of Yahweh's justice as set out in the OT should agree, ad hominem, against Calvin, that the biblical material is presented as expressing a justice which Calvin ought to have taken into explicit systematic account in adumbrating his argument. On Calvin's own premises, the various senses of God's justice, whether culled from a study of biblical vocabulary or theologically formulated on a biblical basis, must

---

Accommodating God," in *Calvinus Sincerioris Religionis Vindex,* ed. W. H. Neuser and B. G. Armstrong, vol. 36 of *Sixteenth Century Essays and Studies* (1997), pp. 3-19, here p. 3. In his *Sermons on Job,* Calvin develops the theme of God's double righteousness — hidden and revealed. What is remarkable here is not the affirmation of an utterly hidden righteousness in God. It is that there is a righteousness far transcending that which is revealed in the law, such that God can find fault not only with humans but also with the most perfect of angels. See, e.g., pp. 238 and 302. But the most revealing sermon of all is on Job 15:11-16, and see especially pp. 273-74. Job rightly sees that he could be perfect, yet still falls short of this higher righteousness (p. 188). If God wanted to, "he might justly condemn us" even though "we had performed all that is contained in the law" (p. 414). At the other extreme, Calvin intimates that God himself could go too far in commanding or permitting excessive barbarism in the Israelites; see David F. Wright's formulations of this point in "Accommodation and Barbarity in Calvin's Old Testament Commentaries," in *Understanding Poets and Prophets: Essays in Honour of George Wishart Anderson,* ed. A. G. Auld (Sheffield: Sheffield Academic Press, 1993), pp. 413-27, here pp. 414-19. For an important study, see J. Balserak, *Divinity Compromised: A Study of Divine Accommodation in the Thought of John Calvin* (Dordrecht: Springer, 2006). Calvin is quite extraordinary!

22. In its biblical sense, "justice" has been described by W. Dietrich as the scarlet thread which runs through the OT, making it the center of OT theology. Horst Dietrich Preuss, who reports this in *Old Testament Theology,* vol. 1 (Louisville: Westminster John Knox, 1995), p. 23, is not convinced.

yield a theologically consistent view of God, even though that does not entail understanding all God's ways. It is not good enough for Calvin to accuse his interlocutors of being basically secularized.

Above all, in Scripture, there is Jesus, the implicit or explicit center of all our thinking about justice and election because he is the proper center of our thinking about everything. Jesus, the Word, is the hermeneutical center of all Scripture. I shall not be found to demur from Barth on this point of general principle and, in discussing him, will defend myself against the charge of failing to practice in this volume what I have just announced in principle and systematically disregarding this rule. As election must stand the test of Christology (election takes place in Christ!), so must our theological understanding of God's justice. We are bound to consider God's justice, best we humbly can, in the light of the revelation of God in Jesus Christ, clothed with the perfections of the Father, which are also his own perfections in the unity declared in the *homoousion.* We do not here need so much to pursue the hermeneutical principle as to bolster the particular point that our questions about God's justice do not necessarily stem just from assuming the relevance of an extrabiblical or normative natural justice. Calvin was too ready to be suspicious at this point, and his discussion is consequently damaged.

Equally, the early Luther leaves something to be desired. *De servo arbitrio (The Bondage of the Will)* had an interesting sixteenth-century career. In lectures he gave on Genesis, sometime subsequent to the production of *De servo arbitrio,* Luther digressed at Genesis, chapter 26, to say that he was worried about how his words in that earlier volume might be interpreted when he spoke there of the absolute and necessary unfolding of all things.[23] He tells us now that what he really believes and wants to teach is that we should look to Jesus Christ to understand the will of God. Apparently, by the time of the Formula of Concord in 1577, "no mention of *De servo arbitrio* sufficed" in Lutheran discussion without supplementary reference to Luther's Genesis commentary, "specifically chapter 26."[24]

23. While there is some disagreement amongst interpreters of Luther here, it seems hard to get round the analysis in Robert Kolb's thorough study, *Bound Choice, Election, and Wittenberg Theological Method from Martin Luther to the Formula of Concord* (Grand Rapids: Eerdmans, 2005), especially pp. 27-28.

24. Kolb, *Bound Choice, Election, and Wittenberg Theological Method from Martin Luther to the Formula of Concord.* In another work, Kolb says that Luther's *Bound Choice (= The Bondage of the Will)* "comes as close as Luther came to speaking of God abstractly." *Martin Luther: Confessor of the Faith* (New York and Oxford: Oxford University Press, 2009), p. 97.

Nonetheless, let us take *De servo arbitrio* in its own right. There, Luther maintained that when Ezekiel says that God does not desire the death of the sinner, he is speaking "of the published offer of God's mercy, not of the dreadful hidden will of God," which is another thing.[25] It is to the published mercy of God that we must attend. "God in His own nature and majesty is to be left alone; in this regard, we have nothing to do with Him, nor does He wish us to deal with Him." As far as his righteousness is concerned, "I say that the righteous God does not deplore the death of His people which He Himself works in them, but He deplores the death which He finds in His people and desires to remove from them." On the other hand, as for "God hidden in Majesty," he "neither deplores nor takes away death, but works life, and death, and all in all; nor has He set bounds to Himself by His Word, but has kept Himself free over all things."

Like Calvin, Luther believed that we are not to inquire into but, rather, to adore God's will. Like Calvin, Luther quotes Romans 9:20 in this connection. To say that Luther's thought exhibits a tension here is to say the least. According to Luther, God, in the Word which is the Bible, reveals that he is not bound by his Word spoken to us. Simultaneously, he tells us to look to his Son. In terms of Luther's theology, what we see in the Son is not God himself, but God *quoad nos, quoad nos* believers, not unbelievers. This is most unstable ground if God is not bound by his Word and, if we shift into nautical metaphor, the soul's anchor is not firm. However, I pursue Luther on predestination per se no further than I have pursued Calvin.[26]

How it is that God loved the world in Christ, we shall know only at

25. Luther, *The Bondage of the Will,* trans. J. I. Packer and O. R. Johnston (Cambridge: James Clarke, 1957). The following quotations from Luther are all from pp. 169-70 in this translation.

26. If the records of what Luther said are accurate, he was capable of holding that certain things which were true of God are nevertheless dangerous for us to believe. See the example given in Harry Buis, *Historic Protestantism and Predestination* (Philadelphia: Presbyterian and Reformed, 1958), pp. 54-55. In connection with the Reformers' concept of God, issues of great importance in intellectual history arise. See the discussion of the connection between Ockham's thought and modern European nihilism in Michael Allen Gillespie, *Nihilism before Nietzsche* (Chicago: University of Chicago Press, 1995), especially pp. 14-28. (I assume an intellectual connection between the Reformation and the Ockhamist legacy.) Radical Orthodoxy encourages us to take a step further back to muse on Scotus, drawing Calvin and modernity into his inheritance; see James K. A. Smith and James H. Olthuis, eds., *Radical Orthodoxy and the Reformed Tradition: Creation, Covenant, and Participation* (Grand Rapids: Baker Academic, 2005), p. 19 and chap. 4.

the end of time. The riddle of election awaits eschatological resolution. Meanwhile, we believe that we truly see in Jesus Christ the merciful face of God, and nothing in that face is deformed and distorted, save by the pain of the cross where justice and mercy meet. That face has incomparable majesty and beauty, but we cannot read off it a doctrine of election, although we can learn of love. We must ever keep in mind the way Scripture brings to our attention the glad election of grace and the sad reality of resistance. To know much more, we must wait until we know as we are known. Prior to the eschaton, Christology will yield less in relation to election than some suppose. That is one reason why Christology has not been given independent treatment, although election in Christ is always assumed.

In *Till We Have Faces,* surely C. S. Lewis's greatest fictional work (not immediately seen that way by many of its contemporary readers), Orual, queen of Glome, is permitted to utter her complaint before the gods. Sad and bitter deprivation has marked long, weary years in her life. Justice is at issue. Orual launches into her speech. As she speaks, the force of her words disintegrate before her ears and before the eyes of her mind. When she is through, the presiding deity says only one thing. "Are you answered?" "Yes," says Orual.[27]

"There is much edification," said Kierkegaard, "implied in the thought that against God we are always in the wrong."[28] As he puts it in his sermon entitled "The Unchangeableness of God," God is "eternal clearness in eternal unchangeableness."[29] It was a leader in Israel, professionally acquainted with justice, who spoke what is the penultimate word for us on election on the occasion that his family was judged. "He is the LORD; let him do what is good in his eyes" (1 Sam. 3:18). It is a trustworthy word on which the light of the most trustworthy Israelite shines, that ultimate Word who enlightens all, Jesus Christ. He is the light of the world, whom to follow is not to walk in darkness, but to have the light of life. For God

27. Lewis, *Till We Have Faces* (London: Fount, 1956), p. 304.

28. Although these words are found in his *Either/Or,* Kierkegaard significantly returns to them in *Concluding Unscientific Postscript,* trans. David F. Swenson (Princeton: Princeton University Press, 1968), p. 239.

29. This translation is taken from Kierkegaard's *Edifying Discourses: A Selection* (London and Glasgow: Collins, 1958), p. 250. *Pace* Edward John Carnell, we should neither hesitate over Kierkegaard's sense of terror nor play down the concluding sense of God's love in this famous sermon. *The Burden of Søren Kierkegaard* (Grand Rapids: Eerdmans, 1965), p. 171.

is light and in him there is no darkness at all. Election and predestination belong to the light, though we now see darkly, as in a mirror.[30]

Assurance?

"Whenever the doctrine of election is discussed, it is followed by the question regarding the certainty of salvation."[31] In refusing to make an exception to the rule as Berkouwer describes it, I am mindful of the objection that, in conforming to it, we again remain within the orbit of traditional dogmatic concerns and sustain a failure to widen out the discussion of election in accordance with OT themes taken up in the NT. Yet, it is hard to avoid treading briefly on the familiar path of assurance. Moreover, we might be reconciled to doing so because, in the course of treating assurance, we are bound to find ourselves addressing a theological question in relation to election which demands attention in its own directly biblical right, namely, the question of perseverance.

Historically, the questions of election and assurance have often been bound up, the connection between them conceived in more ways than one. On the one hand, election has been taken not only to provide but even to ground assurance. How can I know that my profession of and commitment to Jesus Christ is no feeble effort of my frail, mutable, vulnerable, and fallible will, except by an assurance that it is the strong, immutable, conquering, and infallible will of the electing God which is my stronghold? On the other hand, the boot may be on the other foot and election identified as the enemy of or, at least, an obstacle to assurance. In such cases, what is in doubt is not necessarily God's mercy toward all whom he calls. We may be confident that his revelation of himself to us in Jesus Christ appears in and with a universal summons to repentance and that revelation and summons, indissolubly connected, demonstrate that God desires to show mercy. There may be no problem there. Further, it is not that God's justice is necessarily in doubt. We may abide content in the belief that, when history has run its present course, we shall learn how God's mercy and justice are related to those who do not heed his call. There may be no problem there, either. Nonetheless, existential uncertainty in connection with election may remain, not on account of any avowed, or even tacit, doubt

30. Admittedly, this is not the optimal translation of 1 Cor. 13:12.

31. G. C. Berkouwer, *Divine Election* (Grand Rapids: Eerdmans, 1960), p. 8.

about God's character, but on account of the straightforward and inevitable implications of the sheer fact that not all are elect. Existential uncertainty generated by this fact may cast no shadow over God, but it does cast a shadow over me, because I do not know whether I am amongst the elect. Thus the question of assurance validly arises in connection with election. Cognate questions have been posed in terms that lack any explicit reference to election. We should not be dissuaded from referring to them just because they are familiar in some circles and cause weary dismay in other circles precisely because they are so enduringly familiar. Customary related forms of the question include: "Am I sure that I am a Christian?" "Am I sure that Christ died for me?" "Am I sure that I shall be kept to the end?" The good pastor will both discriminate between the questions that people ask and probe below their surface. This involves relating the question to the life situation in which it is asked, learning and discerning what the questioner is enduring, has endured, is doing, or has done when not voicing the question.[32] To address it aright, age and stage, physical and spiritual, mental and emotional factors are all to be taken into account. All this entails a severe constraint on the following treatment, compelling it to proceed at all too general a level, keeping the election problematic in mind. Indeed, it may be presumptuous or very risky to treat assurance at such a general level as I am proposing to do. If we read, for example, Jonathan Edwards's *Treatise concerning the Religious Affections,* we shall see what depth and detail any proper treatment of assurance requires. Reading Edwards's volume is especially instructive, whether or not we agree with its main contentions and conclusions, for it inclines us to cry out even more for the grace of consecrated discipleship than for the right doctrine of assurance. Still, a question about assurance remains as long as election remains. Does the fact that some, but not all, are predestined to life rob the believer of well-grounded assurance and security in salvation? To pose the question and focus narrowly on it is to take the risk of failing to get Christian life and service into proper perspective and its constituents in proper proportion. Yet, if we take the exegetical line taken in this volume and bind our theology to our exegesis, it is unavoidable and not symptomatic of a morbid introversion.

If the general question of assurance can take many particular forms, the Puritans were capable of proposing as many — and more — distinc-

32. "We must learn to regard people less in the light of what they do or omit to do, and more in the light of what they suffer," said Dietrich Bonhoeffer. "After Ten Years," in *Letters and Papers from Prison,* ed. E. Bethge (London: SCM, 1971), pp. 1-17, here p. 10.

tions in answering it. Surveying the corpus of literature on grace and predestination in sixteenth- and seventeenth-century Protestant theology, Dewey Wallace observed that "[t]he piety of predestinarian grace as an experience was particularly focused on providing assurance and certainty."[33] Whatever our judgment on the predestinarian theologies of these centuries, we cannot gainsay the fact that Pauline and, more widely, NT talk of predestination is meant to promote assurance and certainty. However, the Reformed emphasis on the decree of reprobation, accompanying its emphasis on predestination to life, often turned assurance into a particularly acute problem rather than a particularly sweet comfort. This ensured that Luther's struggle in the late-medieval context was not entirely a thing of the past. "How can I find a gracious God?" is impossible to distinguish successfully from: "How can I be assured that God is gracious *to me?*" if the "I" is accented.[34] In his attempt to persuade hearers and readers that God's election grounds assurance, rather than threatening it, Calvin was capable of strong language. He commented on 2 Corinthians 13:5: "Do you not realize that Christ is in you — unless, of course you are *adokimoi,*" which Calvin renders "reprobate."[35] He proceeded to say that Paul "declares that those who doubt their possession of Christ and their membership in His Body are reprobates." A worried Charles Hodge protested that Calvin, bent on opposing Catholic denial of the possibility of assurance, got things precisely the wrong way round — that this passage properly teaches us that assurance is *not* essential to faith — although Hodge was swift to point out that Calvin did not always speak as though lack of assurance were consistently viewed in the Bible as proof of lack of faith.[36] Calvin turned in

33. Dewey D. Wallace, *Puritans and Predestination: Grace in English Protestant Theology, 1525-1695* (Eugene, Ore.: Wipf and Stock, 1982), p. 195.

34. In any case, the early Luther struggled with predestination. Troeltsch's discussion of the cultural-historical significance of the question of assurance in the Reformation remains worth pondering: *Protestantism and Progress* (London: Williams and Norgate, 1912). See especially pp. 59-64 and 191-203 in the context of the overall argument. Troeltsch early declared his conviction that "every metaphysic has its roots, and must find its test, in practical life" (p. ix).

35. Calvin, *The Second Epistle of Paul to the Corinthians and the Epistles to Timothy, Titus, and Philemon* (Edinburgh: St. Andrews, 1964), p. 173. The word really means "failing the test."

36. Charles Hodge, *2 Corinthians* (Nottingham: Crossway, 1995), p. 234. We can see how problems in translation arise when the Latin is also kept in view, for, in verse 3 Paul says: "since you are demanding a proof" *(epei dokimēn zētei),* and the Latin *reprobatus* is rooted in *probare,* "to prove."

more than one theological direction in order to show how election was conducive to assurance, principally connecting it with Christ, so that we look to Christ for evidence of our election and consequent assurance, but sometimes connecting it to the witness of the Spirit within us, a witness that we are elect in Christ.

Even if we should not fix a broad gulf between Calvinism and Calvin at this point, the Calvinist tradition certainly saw fit to develop aspects of Calvin's theology further. Within the terms of the developing tradition, it is perfectly understandable that this should take the form of emphasizing our sanctification as a demonstration of our election. Beza wrote: "Seeing that good works are for us the certain evidences of faith, they also bring to us afterwards the certainty of our eternal election."[37] As he puts it in *A Little Book of Christian Questions:*

> But in the perilous temptation of particular election, where should I flee for succor?
>
> To the effects whereby the spiritual life is rightly discerned, and likewise our election, just as the life of the body is perceived from its feeling and moving . . . that I am elect is first perceived from sanctification begun in me, that is by my hating of sin and by my loving of righteousness. To this I will add the testimony of the Spirit comforting my conscience. . . . From this sanctification and comfort of the Spirit, we gather faith. And we rise to Christ, to whom whosoever is given, is necessarily elect from all eternity in Him.[38]

Beza did not believe that sanctification was the sole ground of assurance, and he is clear that it is not the ground of salvation.[39] With regard to assurance, his concern and counsel were that we begin in reflection at

37. Quoted by Joel R. Beeke, *The Quest for Full Assurance: The Legacy of Calvin and His Successors* (Edinburgh: Banner of Truth, 1999), p. 79.

38. Theodore Beza, *A Little Book of Christian Questions in Which the Principal Headings of the Christian Religion Are Briefly Set Forth* (Allison Park, Pa.: Pickwick, 1986), pp. 96-97 (question 209). Note Beza's comment that good works are so called because, *inter alia,* "they are testimonies to us of our faith, and consequently our election" (p. 65; question 165). From question 167 (p. 65) onward, Beza devotes a lot of space to providence and predestination.

39. In his *Little Book,* he can nevertheless make this statement: "If faith is necessary for salvation, and works necessarily flow out of true faith . . . certainly also it follows, that good works are necessary for salvation, yet not as the cause of salvation . . . but as something necessarily attached to true faith" (pp. 60-61 [question 154]).

the point to which God has brought us in life, namely, our developing, progressing sanctification, in order to ascend in thought to the grand beginning, from God's standpoint, in his eternal election.[40]

The place here accorded to sanctification is a perfectly understandable development within the framework of Calvinist thought. It is not hard to see why both the contemplation of God's electing decree and the contemplation of Christ himself might not safely bring assurance within this framework.[41] As for the first, the decree of election is hidden. As for the second, while Jesus Christ is God revealed, he cannot, in himself, be the sign of God's will toward *me* if we adopt a rigorously predestinarian Calvinistic theology. We may incur rebuke for lack of proper piety in not looking to Jesus Christ, but is it right to ask the heart to sense my election when the mind is bound to the conclusion that Jesus Christ, in the objectivity of his person and work, does not, in himself, signify *my* election? In his challenge to the Reformed tradition, Barth had a particularly strong point here. As for the testimony of the Spirit within — the testimony that I am one of the elect — how am I to discern it? "Experience shows," says Calvin, "that the reprobate are sometimes affected by almost the same feeling as the elect," for the Lord "steals into" their "minds to the extent that his goodness may be tasted without the Spirit of adoption."[42] Why does he do that? In order "to render them [the reprobate] more convicted and inexcusable."[43] We do not pause here to assess these words in their own right. What they surely do is to confirm the claim that it is not only understandable, but close to inevitable, that Calvinist theology should produce pressure in the direction of grounding assurance in something about me as a unique individual and grounding it in something as tangible as I can find, namely, the fruit of the Spirit in my life — sanctification.

40. Of course, Beza was not alone in seeing it this way; it became common enough. We could proceed to such a figure as William Perkins, bearing in mind that he often positioned the inward testimony of God's Spirit before external sanctification in connection with assurance. "If the testimony of God's Spirit be not powerful enough in the elect, then may they judge of their election by the other effect of the Holy Ghost namely sanctification, like as we use to judge by heat that there is a fire, when we cannot see the flame." *Golden chaine; or, the description of theologie containing the order of the causes of salvation and damnation, according to God's worde,* trans. Robert Hill (Cambridge, 1592), p. 425.

41. Although I refer to the Calvinist tradition, note Zwingli's view of works as a sign of election: W. P. Stephens, *The Theology of Huldrych Zwingli* (Oxford: Clarendon, 1986), pp. 158-59.

42. Calvin, *Institutes* 3.2.11.

43. Both this and the following section of the *Institutes,* 3.2.12, are germane.

If it is understandable that sanctification be regarded as a ground of assurance within a Calvinistic framework, it is also understandable that this be thought problematic within that same (not to mention, another) framework. What degree or kind of sanctification breeds or permits well-founded assurance? If sanctification is the principal source of assurance, is it not all too liable to overbalance into a de facto attempt to justify myself by works and so lead to either despair or presumption? Is christocentric spirituality now forfeited? What of Luther's point: "A Christian is even hidden from himself; he does not see his holiness and virtue, but sees in himself nothing but unholiness and vice"?[44]

We may believe that these questions can be sufficiently answered, but the question we must face is whether they do not expose a difficulty in Augustinianism. A non-Augustinian, agreeing with those Augustinians who demur from making sanctification a ground of assurance, will urge that anyone who has conceded to Augustine what I have conceded, even in its minimal form, has brought his troubles on his own head here. We are stuck with no option but to make sanctification the logical ground of assurance, however theologically reluctant we are to do so. Attempts to avoid the antecedent decree of reprobation, however valiant and well meaning, do not deliver single predestinarians from the clutches of the awkward truth that it is hard to place assurance on a well-founded basis. We are in trouble trying to have even our half-baked Augustinian cake and our penny. There is no escape from the anxious quagmire in which predestination lands us, and sanctification, the only logical place to go, is no safe refuge. The sanctification problematic in connection with election, taken up in the celebrated *syllogismus practicus,* exposes the problem attending any broadly Augustinian theology of predestination.[45]

Is this criticism justified? I doubt it. Suppose that I maintain that assurance is a desideratum, even a requirement, for the life of faith to flourish, but that I also reject any Augustinian form of predestination. Suppose, also, that I am a non-Augustinian dogmatic nonuniversalist or, at least, a non-Augustinian who rejects dogmatic universalism. Is the logical pressure felt within the Augustinian/Reformed tradition to ground assurance in sanctification really much relieved for those who stand outside it? Will

44. "Preface to the Revelation of St. John [II]," in Luther, *Works,* vol. 35 (Philadelphia: Muhlenberg, 1960), p. 411.

45. For a good account of the *syllogismus practicus,* roughly the deduction of our spiritual standing from the evidence of our lives, see Berkouwer, *Divine Election,* pp. 278-306.

any nonuniversalist theology which prizes assurance succeed much better than does Augustinianism in avoiding relevant scrutiny of the course of our lives? Our religious sensibility and theologically tutored piety may bid us look to Jesus Christ, and we shall not demean that requirement. Still, how does Jesus Christ stand before me as the guarantor of *my* salvation if he does not do so as the guarantor of the salvation of *all?* How does the non-Augustinian avoid the weight that must be placed on my persevering will, as opposed to predestination, as I strive mightily to get to the end of salvation's road, even in the grace and strength of God? Is that not the same as emphasizing sanctification, a sanctification now evidenced in the fact that I have deployed my will properly and well?[46]

Theologically, we may wish either to affirm the strong and positive role sanctification must play in relation to assurance or to protest against any theology which does so. If our subject were assurance per se, we should want to pursue this, but then we would have started the whole discussion in a different place (not with election and predestination) and ordered its course in a different way. However, assurance per se is not our subject. We are concerned only with assurance in connection with election. Let it be clear that I am not arguing that an Augustinian interpretation of election delivers a stronger assurance than other schemes do. Obviously, it does not deliver a stronger assurance than would a belief in universalism which did not flinch from affirming that universal election entails universal salvation. It is beyond my remit to offer analysis of the comparative kinds, degrees, or strengths of assurance provided by different theologies. All that is claimed here is that Augustinianism in the form in which I have espoused it escapes solitary confinement in the sphere of the problematic.[47]

A comprehensive investigation would have to take into account the suggestion that the difficulty with Augustinianism, in relation to assurance, has to be located at a point on which we have not touched at all: the connection between discriminate predestination and the particularity of

46. "Sanctification" is used throughout this discussion to refer to growth in the Christian life. Biblically, however, it is a setting aside for God and his service as well as (and before) a personal growth.

47. On the surface, the strength of universalism lies far more in its theological insistence that universal salvation coheres better than do other notions with the power and love of God than in its exegesis. However, evil and suffering are the last phenomena we should expect to be compatible with the existence of a God of love and power. This seriously stymies attempts to deduce anything with great confidence from divine perfections in relation to the scope of salvation. Quite generally, the fact of evil tends to mock system.

atonement.[48] It can be argued that, if the atonement is not universal in scope or intent, the grounds for assurance will always be constitutionally unsteady if we are willing to grasp the theological nettle, notwithstanding the best efforts of an Augustinian believer to provide a theological rationale for the psychological practice of ratcheting up a sense of personal security. The axiomatic status of the universality of the atonement in part governs Barth's belief in the universality of election, and there is no gainsaying the importance of exploring the interrelationship of the concepts "atonement" and "election."

As with the earlier remarks on providence, only a little can be said here on this score. If we assign particularity to the atonement *simpliciter,* the objection in relation to the difficulties of assurance might have to be sustained; but if we conceive of the relationship between predestination and genuine summons and opportunity as I have, the language of universality applied to atonement in the NT may be retained and upheld alongside the language of particularity.[49] The genuineness of summons and opportunity for those who reject it implies a provision of God in the atonement of Jesus Christ wider than its provision for the elect. From the perspective of historic Protestant theology, we are here stepping onto the territory occupied by such debates as those which featured Amyraldism in the seventeenth century. All that can be mooted here is that, if the theological riddle of the connection between particular predestination and general call awaits eschatological resolution, it is plausible to assume that then only will we understand the nature and scope of the atonement in their interconnection, if God is pleased to disclose such things to us on the new earth.[50] Meanwhile, in connection with assurance, we must

48. This was a question raised in relation to Augustinianism both long before the Reformation and, within Catholicism, after the Reformation, although accusations of crypto-Calvinism were leveled against the Jansenists who pondered this. Blaise Pascal, who was closely associated with them, was continuing a medieval debate on this point in his *Provincial Letters* (Harmondsworth: Penguin, 1967). See particularly letter 17. Jansen came under judicial fire on the grounds that he claimed that to affirm "that Christ died and shed his blood for all mankind" was semi-Pelagian; see M. O'Connell, *Blaise Pascal: Reasons of the Heart* (Grand Rapids: Eerdmans, 1997), p. 125.

49. Defenders of particular atonement usually retain the language of universality anyway, though what is meant by it is not identical with what is meant by those who oppose particular atonement.

50. Debate over the scope of the atonement is largely debate over its nature; this emerged clearly in the very title of his work when John McLeod Campbell published *The Nature of the Atonement* (London: Macmillan, 1869).

say that the banquet has been prepared and is provided for those who are summoned to it but will not come. It is accomplished. And not a morsel will be wasted.

The Problem of Perseverance

In the Reformed tradition within which the connection between election and assurance has seemed particularly problematic, the connection between election and atonement has frequently been adumbrated so that the immutable determination which applies to the former applies to the latter as well. Election and atonement, in their nature, secure the salvation of particular persons or the church. Barth's refusal to convert universal atonement into a dogmatic universalism was nothing new; his refusal to convert universal election into dogmatic universalism was quite distinctive.[51] It raises a question which may be raised on other grounds as well, namely, whether election or predestination constitutes a determination of destiny. It is a question which extends back to the NT, independently of Barth's theological interpretation. There is scarcely a book in the NT which does not either explicitly or implicitly warn believers against failure to persevere, to all appearances assuming the real possibility of failure when addressing a people as elect or predestined. According to Augustinian theology in the form in which it was appropriated in the Protestant Reformation, those who fail to persevere to the end were never of the elect. The elect are vigorously exhorted to persevere and the warnings sound in their ears, but they strictly cannot fail to reach their goal. This is open to the charge of manifest implausibility. It is not surprising that "the doctrine of the perseverance of the saints" has been judged "likely the weakest link in the Calvinian logic, scripturally speaking."[52] If we are assuming that the biblical text prima facie should be interpreted along Augustinian lines in relation to predestination, must we not with equal, or greater, conviction insist that it also prima facie envisages that the elect can fail to reach the goal? Assurance of God's

51. See, however, the illuminating study by Matthias Gockel, *Barth and Schleiermacher on the Doctrine of Election: A Systematic-Theological Comparison* (Oxford and New York: Oxford University Press, 2006).

52. Clark Pinnock, ed., *The Grace of God and the Will of Man* (Minneapolis: Bethany House, 1995), pp. 17-18. Pinnock felt compelled to surrender Calvinist theology in light of the biblical warnings about "falling away."

promises and keeping power are given, but are not the warnings even more frequent?[53]

It may seem that the consistent thing to do here is to invoke Simeon again. He believed that we must appropriate both promise and solemn warning without attempting to interrelate doctrinal truths systematically in this connection. Within Christian life, they cohere. "Does not every man feel within himself a liableness; yea, a proneness to fall . . . that there is enough corruption within him . . . eternally to destroy his soul? On the other hand, who that is holding on in the ways of righteousness, does not daily ascribe his steadfastness to the influences of that grace, which he received from God; and look daily to God for more grace, in order that he may be kept by *his* power through faith unto salvation?"[54]

Simeon has not got it quite right at this point. What generates the paradox is not the experiential sense that grace *can* keep us, but the dogmatic assurance that we *shall* be kept. Even so, should we not simply reformulate Simeon's point and then have recourse to the principle of paradox briefly adumbrated in the last chapter? I believe not. "Paradox" was not marketed there as an all-purpose net in which to capture every intriguing and otherwise elusively net-resistant theological object that floats into sight. We must ask about election and perseverance in their own right. In relation to election, some are responsible for rejecting the summons; others receive the grace of accepting it. In this case, the relation of divine to human action is not existentially important to figure out. I know what I must do sufficiently to own my responsibility, without knowing how to conceptualize in theological detail its relationship to what God does. I can know what God does sufficiently to give him all the praise without knowing how to conceptualize in theological detail its relationship to what I must do. The situation is different where perseverance is concerned. We are not now talking of

53. Although, on the surface, perhaps they are, we cannot judge by the surface; the whole fabric of NT soteriology has to be considered in evidence without losing appropriate concentration on explicit sayings. For present purposes, it does not greatly matter how the question is answered. In assigning importance to the exact relationship between biblical exhortation and existential circumstance, D. A. Carson approaches the question in a way compatible with that component in Simeon's thought which I have sought, quite generally, to bring out. "Reflections on Assurance," in *Still Sovereign: Contemporary Perspectives on Election, Foreknowledge, and Grace,* ed. Thomas R. Schreiner and Bruce A. Ware (Grand Rapids: Baker, 2000), pp. 247-76.

54. Simeon, *Helps to Composition; or, Five Hundred Skeletons of Sermons, Several Being the Substance of Sermons Preached Before the University* (Cambridge: John Burges, 1801), p. vii.

two "groups" of people. God both promises and warns one and the same group of people — the elect — that they shall be kept and that they may be destroyed. There are existential reasons, quite apart from conceptual ones, for trying to get clear on this. Are we now coming across a further reason to wonder about the degree or even kind of assurance to which the believer is entitled? It is a pressing question if assurance, as Anthony Burgess put it, is as "wings and legs in man's service to God."[55]

In responding to this question, we must bear in mind that the New Testament is largely made up of epistolary addresses to churches. Israel gives us our pattern of interpretation. Prophets spoke in the name of the Lord to the people, a mixed group of faithful and unfaithful Israelites, characters sometimes steady in either respect, sometimes en route from one to the other, sometimes oscillating between states. Apostles follow suit. Augustine observed that those who fail to persevere, those called rather than chosen, "are called elect by those ignorant of what they shall be."[56] This way of putting it insufficiently credits the NT for using the vocabulary of election in a way continuous with the OT. It is better said that the NT determination of a visible body as "the elect" does not necessarily entail anything about the final destiny of its individual members. It is not the case that "elect," in the NT, breaks the OT mold and primarily means "personally chosen" as opposed to being "collectively called," as Augustine more or less assumes here. Rather, when Paul and his companions lovingly surveyed the churches in their charge or within the remit of their address, they saw a motley group, as had the prophets and leaders of Israel. The disobedient or those whose faith is skin deep or has never taken root in the heart coexist with the zealous, faithful, and joyous and those at all points in between, whether mobile or fixed in religious affection. They are all there in the church. Collectively, they are addressed as the elect, and, like the people of Israel, they are sanctified by virtue of their inclusion in the community. It would have been interesting, not to mention illuminating, to hear those who conveyed or read Paul's letters expounding, glossing, and applying them in detail to the congregations. Once we interpret the elect in terms of the OT, the conjunction of promise and warning sheds any paradoxical garb with which it has been clothed in the dogmatic tradition. We are back with

55. Beeke, *Quest for Full Assurance,* p. 159.

56. "On Rebuke and Grace," in *A Select Library of the Nicene and Post-Nicene Fathers of the Christian Church,* vol. 5 (reprint, Grand Rapids: Eerdmans, 1991), p. 478. In this work Augustine contrasts the predestined, who "are elected to reign with Christ," with those who, like Judas, are elected to a task (p. 477).

Simeon to the extent that the existential (homiletical and pastoral) crux of the matter is the proper application of promise and warning, but we are not embedding this within the rule of paradox. The "elect" characteristically includes both the true believers and the whole visible community.[57]

However, can promise and warning apply to one and the same *individual?* The notion of "one and the same individual" is only perspicuous as long as we stick rigidly to that vocabulary and do not lapse into talk of one and the same *person.* If we use the word "person" as a strict synonym for "individual," the perspicuity obviously remains, but once we begin independently asking what it is to be a person and begin considering whether to answer in terms of the person as "being-in-act," for example, we are deluged by the clamant demands of a theological and philosophical anthropology, Brunner, Barth, and Kierkegaard being prominent amongst those who rejoin or replace Simeon on stage.[58] Embarked, as we have been, on a tricky voyage on the waters of election, we must momentarily heed but soon shut our ears to the siren song of those who propose that we should now consider the concepts of ego, person, self, and identity to get a sophisticated hold on the question of "one and the same individual" as the recipient of promise and warning.[59]

Sticking to the prosaic, ordinary-language "one and the same individual," we simply note that she or he can be faithful or faithless. Quite generally — but the generalization is not existentially vacuous — the one who is faithful, expectant, humble, and broken is the subject and recipient of promise; the one who is faithless, not expectant, humble, or broken is the subject and recipient of warning. One and the same individual can be promised and warned at different times. At the risk of opening the philo-

57. If one were to follow a *"loci"* approach to dogmatics, "election" should appear under "Israel" or "ecclesiology," if not under "Christology."

58. Nor should we forget Immanuel Kant; see John Macmurray's impressive correction and development of core aspects of Kant's thought in *The Self as Agent* (London: Faber and Faber, 1957).

59. The kind of detail involved here is well indicated in Wolfhart Pannenberg, *Anthropology in Theological Perspective* (Edinburgh: T. & T. Clark, 1985), pp. 191-312, whose discussion includes a good deal of engagement with Kant, including in specific discussions of identity. I sympathize with J. Louis Martyn's observation that "[m]erely to reread Paul's letters while entertaining the expression 'history of the human agent' is to begin to suspect that a historical series of several images may be a central key, enabling us to bring Paul's understanding of agency into truly sharp focus." "Epilogue: An Essay in Pauline Meta-Ethics," in *Divine and Human Agency in Paul and His Cultural Environment,* ed. John Barclay and Simon Gathercole (London: T. & T. Clark, 2006), pp. 173-83, here p. 179.

sophical floodgates which we have just sailed past, we may say that humans exist in both act and potency. The individual is the *homo viator.* Some individuals take more time than others to acquire religious stability; some never acquire it. Both promise and warning need to ring in one and the same wayfaring ear, but not with invariant monotone quality. I am sometimes meant to hear the warning with a joy and gratitude that lead me to seek God to the accompaniment of peaceful assurance, and I am sometimes meant to hear it as a summons to examine with due trepidation what my life is like.

We do not make shipwreck of particular predestination by viewing the scene from the standpoint of human mutability and implying that "one and the same person" is not even a simple matter in God's sight. Eschatological distinctions will emerge when what appears as earthly potency becomes manifested as new earthly actuality; when the faithful and faithless, the weak, the immature, and the vacillating in the church visible are no longer in any outward or inward state of flux. In all this, the Lord knows all along who are his (2 Tim. 2:19), knowing when and how they become his in the course of historical time, the time given to individuals to hear and heed both promises and warnings. Without proper exegetical examination, it cannot be shown that the vocabulary of "predestination," as of "election," covers more than one possibility and that the requirement of attending to context should not be overridden by a supposed linguistic imperative.[60] However, it can be plausibly proposed. Context seems to leave open the possibility that predestination, like election, is not always the determination of the destiny of all individuals in the collective addressed as "predestined." Those whom God has predestined, called, justified, and even glorified might be cut off (Rom. 8:30; 11:22), so we must make our calling and election sure (2 Pet. 1:10). The whole of 2 Peter testifies eloquently to the fact that election is not necessarily the determination of destiny. The NT materials, with all they say about the postmortem destiny of humans and the pretemporal counsel of God, must keep in view the pattern of election outlined in the OT with respect to Israel. If election comprises both those who are members of the visible community eternally secured by God and those who are members but not eschatologically secured, there is no reason why predestination should be semantically sealed off against the possibility of the same variation. When we consider statements about predestination in the light of the whole writing in which they are embedded, the "elect" or the "predestined" may alike

60. A number of Greek verbs with the "pro-" prefix, not to mention words signifying "election," would have to be ranged up here for consideration.

connote security at one time and visibility without security at another, or it may embrace both possibilities when the collective is addressed.[61]

How does this affect our original question about assurance? Hearers of the word are genuinely invited, summoned, and given the opportunity to repent and believe. They are ipso facto assured of God's mercy. However, if assurance remains on that basis alone, it is closer to what John Owen termed a state of "adherence" than to the assurance of a heart which personally appropriates the fruit of what God has done for us in Christ.[62] If the question "Can I be sure that I am amongst the elect?" is pressed by a serious soul willing to submit to the Lordship of Jesus Christ, the question should be shifted back: "Have I responded to the gospel in repentance and faith?" It is with the summons to repentance and faith that I am approached by Christ, clothed with the gospel. If I have not so responded, my question about election is in vain, its religious validity annulled, for it is my responsibility to respond to the call. I have no right to inquire about election absent that response. We can only handle existential questions aright when we ask and address them in the appropriate order, way, and time granted by God. It is not a matter of shunting aside awkward questions until later. The Bible is an open book, speaking openly of election and predestination, but that does not mean that I am entitled to ask any question that I like at any time or in any place and assume a religious right to do so. We need the simplicity of the Second Helvetic Confession, the work of Heinrich Bullinger, joint architect of Swiss Protestantism and exemplar of what Cornelius Venema described as "homiletical Augustinianism."[63] "That you are elect is to be maintained beyond doubt if you believe and are in Christ."[64]

61. However, Pinnock's substitution of "an all-inclusive set of goals" for "an all-determining plan" in talk of predestination is too weak and not what I have in mind. Pinnock, *The Grace of God,* p. 21. Predestination is a divine appointment of the collective; the question is whether all the individuals in it are subjects of a predestination which secures an eternal destiny.

62. John Owen, "A Practical Exposition upon Psalm CXXX," in *The Works of John Owen,* vol. 6 (Edinburgh: Banner of Truth, 1967), p. 426. I borrow Owen's terminology without "adhering" to the whole context and set of distinctions Owen makes in this extremely rich work.

63. Cornelius P. Venema, *Heinrich Bullinger and the Doctrine of Predestination* (Grand Rapids: Baker Academic, 2002), pp. 111-17. The Second Helvetic Confession, "a dogmatic work of magnificent and impressive completeness," is a good statement of Swiss Reformed thought. The description is that of Ernst Koch, cited in Bruce Gordon, *The Swiss Reformation* (Manchester and New York: Manchester University Press, 2002), p. 182.

64. "The Second Helvetic Confession," 10.8. For reference to the Corinthian text

In response, then, to the question of how I know that I am elect, we must advocate its initial reformulation in terms of: "How do I know whether I have repented and believed?" To ask that question is not necessarily to invite or perpetuate an unhealthy subjectivity which clouds the objectivity of Christ crucified. It is a question which may be asked and answered keeping Christ and his cross at the center of our thought, but simultaneously honoring the consistent NT summons to faith. In answering the question, we must bear in mind that, while we are justified by faith alone, it is faith of a kind which has love in its very marrow, for to believe in Christ and to receive Christ is to begin to love Christ, which is impossible without beginning to love others. I am not justified by love, but the fabric of the faith which justifies is that which works through love.[65] If we love Jesus Christ, we will obey what he commands (John 14:15). If I have never understood that this is the fruit of my faith and the goal of my life, then I must ask whether I truly love and, if it is doubtful whether I love, I can have no ground to suppose that I have believed and am among those who are called to rejoice in their election.

How well must I keep the commandments of Christ to be entitled to assurance? Despite my resolution not to drift into a wider discussion of assurance which unhinges it from the context in which we are discussing it, a moment's apostrophizing seems suitable. I am under grace and not under law. Mathematically measurable degrees of attainment do not apply, but I must ask whether I am growing at all. If I have begun to love Jesus Christ, I shall grieve when I willfully disobey and my aim will be first to obey, not first to receive assurance. Where there is a desire to keep Christ's commandments, rooted in love for him, there need necessarily be some power to do so in one that is born of the Spirit, a power accompanied by grief, for the sake of Christ, at failure to do so. Yet, perhaps it is more dangerous to work with broad brushstrokes, as I do here, than to say nothing at all. Richard Baxter taught his people "to be sure that the first, and far greater part of your time, pains and care, and inquiries, be for the getting and increasing of your grace, than for the discerning it. . . . See that you

---

whose interpretation by Calvin troubled Hodge (2 Cor. 12:5), see 10.2. The text of the Confession may be found in Philip Schaff, *Creeds of the Evangelical Protestant Churches* (London: Hodder and Stoughton, n.d.), pp. 233-306.

65. As John Owen formulates it: "We are justified by faith *alone;* but we are not justified by that faith which *can be alone.*" "The Doctrine of Justification by Faith through the Imputation of the Righteousness of Christ; Explained, Confirmed, and Vindicated," in *The Works of John Owen,* vol. 5 (Edinburgh: Banner of Truth, 1965), p. 73.

ask ten times at least, How should I get or increase my faith, my love to Christ and to his people? for once that you ask, How shall I know that I believe or love?"[66]

It was in attending to assurance in the context of election that we came upon sanctification. As the Christian life progresses, the active desire to keep Christ's commandments, rooted in our love for him, is by no means to be dismissed as a ground of assurance. On the contrary, developments in early Reformed thought at that point pick out something important in the NT, whatever we make of the basic and surrounding convictions of Reformed theology. The person who asks about assurance in *this* context, wondering whether she or he is numbered amongst those whom the Lord knows are his, is the person committed to perseverance in the strength of the Lord. With perseverance comes the realization that I can look to Christ and Christ alone for my assurance.[67] Precisely on the path of perseverance do I learn that there is only one in whom I can place faith or turn to for assurance: Jesus Christ himself. Perseverance is a subordinate ground of assurance because it is the context in which I can embrace its principal ground, Jesus Christ. Precisely on the path of perseverance do I learn of my sinfulness, unworthiness, and proneness to fall. Precisely here do I learn that the whole of my life must be lived under the sign of forgiveness of sin.

It is the logic of our particular inquiry that has led us to draw out this point, but we do not suggest for a moment that assurance can and should take form only after progress has been made in the Christian life and not from its beginning. If we make clear to those who come to Jesus Christ that they are privileged with a call to "a long obedience in the same direction" in the company of all the saints, it must not be with the overwhelming demand of a new law of perseverance which demoralizes the person who, in crushed condition, has turned to Jesus Christ for rescue.[68] The "how" and "when" of our talk of perseverance depend on person and circumstance. The "what" must always place at the center him who keeps, not what I must keep in order that I may keep persevering. It is in him and only in him that I am elect, and in him and only in him that I perseveringly live.

66. Quoted in Beeke, *Quest for Full Assurance,* p. 140.

67. This is fundamentally consistent with the weighty conclusion drawn by Jonathan Edwards in his analysis of the *Religious Affections,* in *The Works of Jonathan Edwards,* vol. 2 (New Haven: Yale University Press, 1959).

68. In this connection, I have some sympathy with William Abraham's criticism of Jonathan Edwards, in "Predestination and Assurance," in *The Grace of God and the Will of Man,* pp. 231-42, here pp. 235-39.

Conclusion

Since the second chapter of this volume, I have operated on the assumption, for which snap, prima facie reasons were given, that Augustine was justified and correct in maintaining that the NT taught a positive predestination to life which is not a universal predestination, not conditional on foreseen faith, and not the predestination of a collective or group of unspecified membership. The Augustinian inheritance has given to the doctrine of election the formal profile which it has had in Western thought. A number of efforts were made in the medieval period to modify or mitigate Augustine's conclusions during a stretch of theological time that has been characterized as "a 'series of footnotes' to Augustine and at the same time a series of efforts to amplify and correct the Augustinian legacy."[69] These efforts got under way early with a figure like Prosper of Aquitaine in the first half of the fifth century and the Second Council of Orange in 529, but it seems that the theological structure of the debate was basically established by the time we get to the bitter exchanges between Gottschalk and Hincmar in the ninth century in the course of the bitterest of that century's theological controversies. Thereafter, the way in which theology, treated as a *scientia,* shaped up in the Middle Ages seems to have prevented the problematic from escaping from the framework in which Augustine's developed thought had placed it. *Scientia,* even when Scotus and his like insisted on *scientia practica,* methodologically preserved the structure of Augustinianism at this point.

Luther and Calvin did not significantly move beyond Augustine in their perception of the way in which the problem should be structured, whatever christological or soteriological innovation we find in their thought. In Luther, there may be seeds of that modification of Augustine's mature position which emerged in sixteenth-century Lutheranism, at least in the form of an inchoate principle which moved Lutheranism into a different position from the Calvinistic or Zwinglian positions on predestination. One of the greatest theologians to arise in the Reformed tradition remarked of the Lutheran/Reformed contrast:

> The difference seems to be conveyed best by saying that the Reformed Christian thinks theologically, the Lutheran anthropologically. The Re-

69. Jaroslav Pelikan, *The Growth of Medieval Theology (600-1300)* (Chicago: University of Chicago Press, 1978), p. 3.

> formed person is not content with an exclusively historical stance but raises his sights to the idea, the eternal decree of God. By contrast the Lutheran takes his position in the midst of the history of redemption and feels no need to enter more deeply into the counsel of God. For the Reformed, therefore, election is the heart of the church; for Lutherans, justification is the article by which the church stands or falls. Among the former the primary question is: How is the glory of God advanced? Among the latter it is: How does a human get saved?[70]

Election should certainly not be of less interest to the church than is justification; yet, I believe that the judgment that we fulfill our theological responsibilities by tracking down divine decrees is mistaken. The Lutheran way of maintaining what we might want to call "paradox" in relation to election surely accords more closely than does the Calvinistic with God's revelation in Scripture, even where Calvinism embraces paradox. However, the partisanship which the designations "Lutheran" and "Calvinist" invite is regrettable, even when their respective positions are accurately described. Bavinck here speaks of the "Reformed," but we strictly need to distinguish between the Calvinistic and Zurich streams of the Reformed tradition so that we factor Bullinger, in particular, into this discussion.[71]

The designation "Augustinian" itself risks promoting partisanship, but I have tried not to make positive use of it in that spirit. To remain (without undue partisanship!) within Protestantism, it is possible to sympathize with much in the guiding spirit of Arminius or Wesley, for example, while disagreeing with them on single predestination. "A theme, no less than a face, wears an expression," but we shall not be able to take the full measure of the face of God as he revealed it to us by depicting the expression worn

70. Herman Bavinck, *Reformed Dogmatics,* vol. 1 (Grand Rapids: Baker Academic, 2003), p. 177.

71. Bullinger's treatment of predestination in *Decades,* which is a little thin, does not tell the whole tale and does not indicate his reservations about Calvinistic thought. See *The Decades of Heinrich Bullinger,* ed. Thomas Harding, vol. 4 (Cambridge: Cambridge University Press, 1851), pp. 173-94. For brief introductions which provide us with the general context within which to read Bullinger on this question, see, e.g., Edward Dowey, "Heinrich Bullinger as Theologian: Thematic, Comprehensive and Schematic," in *Architect of Reformation: An Introduction to Heinrich Bullinger, 1504-1575,* ed. Bruce Gordon and Emidio Campi (Grand Rapids: Baker, 2004), pp. 35-66; C. S. McCoy and J. W. Baker, *Fountainhead of Federalism: Heinrich Bullinger and the Covenantal Tradition* (Lousville: Westminster John Knox, 1991).

by the theme of election.[72] How we see the face of God is all-important, and all honor to Karl Barth for a christologically consistent and sustained consciousness of this. In refusing to follow his lead on election, we shall be found to demur not from the christocentric instinct, but from the way in which he orders exegesis, biblical theology, and theological deduction in relation to the christological center of believing thought. If we momentarily pedal back to Augustine and Wesley, using them as examples to make a general point, it would be possible, in principle, to agree with Augustine on election, but to judge Wesley's understanding of God as he is revealed in Christ closer to the mark than that of Augustine. If we did so, we should be saying that Augustine's understanding of predestination is somewhat marred by its enclosure within an Augustinian understanding of God and that Wesley's understanding of God is somewhat marred by the understanding of election which it encloses. I am neither adopting nor rejecting these judgments here, described, as they are, in terms that are not very conducive to theological peace and edification. Of course, doctrines of God and election are inevitably intertwined in the thought of a given theologian, but their set logical connections are not inevitable and invariant, predictable and uniform. While fundamental intuitions may drive a theology considered as a whole, it will not narrowly entail what is maintained in its various dogmatically specific and controversial parts. Our doctrine of election is an important element in our theology, but it is not the whole of it. It may drive or be driven, play a dominant role or a subordinate role or not be susceptible to any such easy characterizations or alternatives.

Simeon has guided us up to a point, and he has one more theological card up his sleeve or, lest he be shocked at this metaphor, one more hint concerning the direction of theological advance. I quote at length from Simeon's preface to the *Helps to Composition.*[73]

> A young Minister, about three or four years after he was ordained, had an opportunity of conversing familiarly with the great and venerable leader of the Arminians in this kingdom; and, wishing to improve the occasion to the uttermost, he addressed him nearly in the following words: "Sir, I understand that you are called an Arminian; and I have sometimes been called a Calvinist; and therefore I suppose we are to

72. Wittgenstein, *Culture and Value,* ed. G. H. von Wright (Oxford: Blackwell, 1980), p. 52.

73. Simeon, *Helps,* pp. vii-viii.

> draw daggers. But before I consent to begin the combat, with your permission I will ask you a few questions, not from impertinent curiosity, but for real instruction." Permission being very readily and kindly granted, the young Minister proceeded to ask. "Pray, Sir, do you feel yourself a depraved creature, so depraved, that you would never have thought of turning to God, if God had not first put it into your heart?" "Yes," says the veteran, "I do indeed." "And do you utterly despair of recommending yourself to God by any thing that you can do; and look for salvation solely through the blood and righteousness of Christ?" — "Yes, solely through Christ" — "But, Sir, supposing you were at first saved by Christ, are you not somehow or other to save yourself afterwards by your own works?" — "No; I must be saved by Christ from first to last" — "Allowing then that you were first turned by the grace of God, are you not in some way or other to keep yourself by your own power?" — "No" — "What then, are you to be upheld every hour and every moment by God, as much as an infant in its mother's arms?" — "Yes; altogether" — "And is all your hope in the grace and mercy of God to preserve you unto his heavenly kingdom?" — "Yes; I have no hope, but in him." — "Then, Sir, with your leave, I will put up my dagger again; for this is all my Calvinism; this is my election, my justification by faith, my final perseverance: it is, in substance, all that I hold, and as I hold it: and therefore, if you please, instead of searching out terms and phrases to be a ground of contention between us, we will cordially unite in those things wherein we agree."[74]

Simeon's characteristic humility forbade him from identifying himself as the young minister; John Wesley, more obviously, was the aged Arminian. His account at this point suggests that we might view Christian doctrine in terms of the distinction between rules and moves. In games there are rules and, within the rules, a variety of possible moves. Simeon's conversation with Wesley impels us to ask whether, in addressing doctrinally divisive issues such as election, we should proceed along the following lines. Let us (a) agree on the rules, (b) learn the distinction between rules and moves, and (c) not allow different moves to obscure

74. Simeon adds that "[t]he Arminian leader was so pleased with the conversation, that he made particular mention of it in his journals; and notwithstanding there never afterwards was any connection between the parties, he retained an unfeigned regard for his young inquirer to the hour of his death."

unity while (d) making the best moves. Presumably, many of us proceed theologically in that way, whether or not consciously under that description.

However, it is extremely difficult to formalize this procedure successfully so as to organize doctrinal debate more satisfactorily. This is for three reasons. Firstly, we would disagree on the doctrinal rules almost as much as we now do on doctrinal substance. Secondly, we would disagree, in a given case, on when something should be counted as a rule or as a move. Thirdly, we would disagree on when a move is or is not in accordance with the rule. By the time we embark on detailed discussion of moves, we would conclude that we have accomplished nothing more than to get to where we have so often been in theology, except by a more complicated and circuitous route prescribed by an admirable irenic ambition, steps along which route have tried our admirably irenic patience. The distinction between rules and moves has theological mileage, but, in practice, it works better ad hoc, as (some of us will judge) it did with Simeon and Wesley, than when elevated into a formal structure in dogmatics. Yet, Simeon's ad hoc achievement in the case of election or predestination is significant. Achievement and attitude are conjoined, and we have a lot to learn from the sixteenth-century Bucers, the seventeenth-century Baxters, the eighteenth-century Doddridges, and the eighteenth-to-nineteenth-century Simeons.[75]

While Simeon's thought does not undermine the need for us to attend to conceptual schemes, it does compel us to ponder whether a shift in these schemes, which may pay significant dividends when it comes to conceptual layout, will yield rather less than we may expect and hope for, as far as theological resolution goes. While I must leave this as a question posed at a stratospheric level of generalization, I am in considerable sympathy with Michael Horton here: "It may be chiefly a time requiring fresh witness and confession of Christ, not a time chiefly of systematiza-

75. It will risk alienating what friends I have left by the time they have finished reading this volume if I pick a twentieth-century figure, and our own century is yet young. I am not subscribing here to George Lindbeck's celebrated regulative theory of doctrine and stand by the criticism of it in Stephen Williams, "Lindbeck's Regulative Christology," *Modern Theology* 4, no. 2 (January 1988): 173-86. Note Luke Johnson's comment that the "most vibrant forms of interpretation in antiquity occur when Scripture is *used* to explicate the Christian life," cited by Daniel J. Treier, *Introducing Theological Interpretation of Scripture: Recovering a Christian Practice* (Nottingham: IVP, 2008), p. 26. Our last word on Simeon is that he intuitively sensed that.

tion and new scholastic enterprise."[76] If theology needs either a broad or election-specific revision in any wholesale respect, it will take the form of acknowledging its need to be increasingly guided and remolded by what we may loosely call Hebraic thought-forms and for dogmatics to absorb thoroughly the insights of recent decades into the Jewish roots of NT theology.[77] It is not clear that the whole root of the problem of election, as it has been identified in Western theology, will be removed or transplanted into completely unfamiliar soil by our execution of this task; complete deracination is one operation too many for us to expect confidently. However, the possibility must be left open.[78]

Reference to "Hebraic thought-forms" guides us to our penultimate word, which goes to Ludwig Wittgenstein. "My thoughts are one hundred percent Hebraic."[79] The question of election as I have treated it may seem to cry out for a Wittgensteinian approach. It was he who insisted that the meaning of our language resides in its use and that we understand concepts by seeing how they shape a form of life.[80] Our third chapter was gesturing

76. Michael Horton, *Covenant and Eschatology: The Divine Drama* (Louisville: Westminster John Knox, 2003), p. 251.

77. It has been over thirty years since Moltmann remarked that "[w]e stand today in a remarkable period of transition. On the one side the hellenistically structured form of the Christian faith is ebbing. . . . On the other side the Christian faith is experiencing what I would like to call a 'hebraic wave.'" This is quoted in Marvin R. Wilson, *Our Father Abraham: Jewish Roots of the Christian Faith* (Grand Rapids: Eerdmans, 1989), p. 125. Note Philip Alexander's observation that "[s]ystematic, propositional exposition was not . . . alien to the 'Hebrew' mentality." "Predestination and Free Will in the Theology of the Dead Sea Scrolls," in *Divine and Human Agency in Paul and His Cultural Environment,* pp. 27-49, here p. 27 n. 2.

78. Wilson's work, *Our Father Abraham,* offers us a quick way into "Block Logic" in the Hebrew Scriptures, pp. 150-53. Despite Barr's celebrated and effective warnings in *The Semantics of Biblical Language* (London: Oxford University Press, 1961), we should not deny that attending to the characteristics of Hebrew language may disclose something of Hebrew thought (and Barr was careful enough to emphasize that he was subjecting certain particular arguments to scrutiny, not attempting comprehensive denials or affirmations). See also Preuss, *Old Testament Theology,* 1:135-40.

79. See Rush Rhees, ed., *Ludwig Wittgenstein: Personal Recollections* (Oxford: Blackwell, 1981), p. 175. The context of this remark was Wittgenstein's response to the rejection of Origen's restitutionism. "Of course it was rejected. It would make nonsense of everything else. If what we do is to make no difference in the end, then all the seriousness of life is done away with." We have to take note of the form of Drury's notes on his conversations with Wittgenstein on which some of Rhees' material is based (p. ix) and of Drury's own admission that he did not always get Wittgenstein's words right (p. 169).

80. "And to imagine a language is to imagine a form of life." Wittgenstein, *Philosophical Investigations* (London: Macmillan, 1958), paragraph 19, p. 8.

in that direction. If Simeon already has Kant for company and Kierkegaard too, how can he possibly decline to shelter his fellow Cantabrigian, Ludwig Wittgenstein, under his roof, albeit not with full room and board? What has Simeon to do with Wittgenstein? Much, in every way. Wittgenstein would have been less interested in the conceptual help that he could give to theology than in the religious help that theology could give to him, or, rather, which that great center of theology, who is no conceptual object, could give to him.[81] It is to highlight this that Wittgenstein has been crowded into the end of my account and has surfaced only subliminally sooner. While the substance of Wittgenstein's philosophy edifies, his perspective on philosophy edifies us even more. "If I were told anything that was a *theory,* I would say, No no! That does not interest me — it would not be the exact thing I was looking for."[82] What exactly was Wittgenstein looking for? Here is his answer: "But if I am to be REALLY saved, — what I need is *certainty* — not wisdom, dreams or speculation — and this certainty is faith. And faith is faith in what is needed by my *heart, my soul,* not my speculative intelligence. For it is my soul with its passions, as it were with its flesh and blood, that has to be saved, not my abstract mind. . . . What combats doubt is, as it were, *redemption.*"[83]

81. Note the context in which Wittgenstein sought out a "nonphilosophical" priest. Ray Monk, *Ludwig Wittgenstein: The Duty of Genius* (London: Cape, 1990), p. 573.

82. Quoted in Monk, *Ludwig Wittgenstein,* p. 305. I have taken liberties with the context of Wittgenstein's remark, as a reader of Monk's source for this quotation, Brian McGuinness, ed., *Wittgenstein and the Vienna Circle: Conversations Recorded by Friedrich Waismann* (Oxford: Blackwell, 1979), will observe. See Tim Labron's comment: "The question then becomes, 'Do we have the *will* to let Wittgenstein remove the theory, or do we prefer to continually replace one theory with another theory?' " *Wittgenstein and Theology* (New York and London: T. & T. Clark, 2009), p. 5.

83. Wittgenstein, *Culture and Value,* p. 33. "The Christian religion is only for the man who needs infinite help, solely, that is, for the man who experiences infinite torment" (p. 46). In this volume, Wittgenstein underscores the fact that what appears to be an intellectual difficulty in philosophy often concerns the will and not the intellect (p. 17). For Wittgenstein's admiration for Kierkegaard, though it was no greater than his admiration for Tolstoy, see Rhees, *Ludwig Wittgenstein,* pp. 101-2. Even comments on Barth are recorded in Rhees' volume (pp. 134 and 160). Wittgenstein came to regard the feeling of being "absolutely safe" as the paradigm of religious experience (Monk, *Ludwig Wittgenstein,* p. 51). On the one hand, it is only fair to remember that Wittgenstein observed: "I am not happy, and not because my rottenness troubles me, but within my rottenness," quoted in Allan Janik and Stephen Toulmin, *Wittgenstein's Vienna* (New York: Simon and Schuster, 1973), p. 236. On the other hand, it is only right to add that because Wittgenstein once said this does not mean that his rottenness never troubled him. Cf. David Edwards and John Eddinow, *Wittgenstein's Poker:*

We should heed Wittgenstein not because he has the mesmeric right to set an agenda for theology, but because we have evangelical reason for thinking along his lines.[84] His word to us is, however, penultimate and not ultimate. It is Luther who steps in at the last. In his 1522 *Preface to the Epistle to the Romans,* Luther gave almost all his attention to the first eight chapters. Then, turning briefly to predestination, Luther made this statement: "For in the absence of suffering and the cross and the perils of death, one cannot deal with predestination without harm and without secret anger against God."[85] Perhaps Luther's reference to anger reflects his own (albeit widely shared) experience, but he specifies the context in which we shall best learn the truth of Christian doctrine, including that of predestination. That context is suffering and the cross. Probably no NT epistle makes this point more effectively than 1 Peter, which opens with the author's greeting to "God's elect" (1:1).[86] In the Western world, we are coming to the point of relearning properly, after many long centuries, that we cannot think about election in the absence of suffering and the cross without taking the risk of consigning much of what we regard as our proudly paraded theological achievements, if not to the sphere of existential near-futility, at least to the

---

The Story of a Ten-Minute Argument between Two Great Philosophers (London: Faber and Faber, 2001): "If the *Tractatus* [Wittgenstein's *Tractatus Logico-Philosophicus*] smelled of anything it was of death and decay" (p. 69).

84. Yet, I agree with what Janik and Toulmin wrote over forty years ago: "A greater familiarity with the life and times of men like [Karl] Kraus and Wittgenstein can help us to see our own situation more clearly." *Wittgenstein's Vienna,* p. 269. For a brief survey of Wittgenstein's influence on theology, see Bruce Ashford, "Wittgenstein's Theologians? A Survey of Ludwig Wittgenstein's Impact on Theology," *Journal of the Evangelical Theological Society* 50, no. 2 (June 2007): 357-75.

85. Luther, *Works,* 35:378. Here we must put clear water between Wittgenstein and Christianity, when, speaking of Christian use of the vocabulary of predestination, Wittgenstein said that it was "only permissible to write like this out of the most dreadful suffering — and then it means something quite different. . . . It is not permissible for someone to assert it as a truth, unless he himself says it in torment. . . . It's less a theory than a sigh, or a cry." *Culture and Value,* p. 30. Yet, Wittgenstein came to understand the NT better than many have done. "At one time," he said, "I thought that the epistles of St. Paul were a different religion to that of the Gospels. But now I see clearly that I was wrong. It is one and the same religion in both the Gospels and the Epistles." Rhees, *Ludwig Wittgenstein,* p. 178.

86. A study of 1 Peter will show just how much in the NT has simply been ignored in my account of election. Jesus Christ was "chosen before the creation of the world" (1:20); we are chosen "through the sanctifying work of the Spirit" according to God's foreknowledge and for Jesus Christ (1:2). My study has not touched on the conceptual dimensions, let alone taken the spiritual measure, of these words.

class of the manifestly secondary. When we learn that, we shall also learn how to appropriate election existentially.

Suffering creates new alignments. Theological friends part company. Those with theological differences find what they really have, that is, who they really have, in common. Suffering also strengthens our sense of identity, if we are talking about the suffering which comes from being a Christian rather than the suffering Christians have in common with all others.[87] The doctrine of election informs me about my identity because God's act of election gives me my identity. It takes me back even beyond Jesus Christ himself to father Abraham, into whose covenant family I am adopted in the election of grace. Despite indicating its potential theological importance, I have given disproportionately little attention to the fact that election is election to reign and have only been tentative to what that may involve. There is nothing tentative about what Paul tells Timothy. "I endure everything for the sake of the elect. . . . If we endure, we will also reign with him" (2 Tim. 2:10-12).

87. I am grateful to Paul Negrut for making this observation to me in conversation many years ago, explaining the contrast between what common human bereavement and specific Christian suffering does to our sense of identity.

APPENDIX

Karl Barth on Election

"I distrust folks who have ugly things to say about Karl Barth. I like old Barth. He throws the furniture around."[1] From a literary point of view, it is a real shame to add anything to Flannery O'Connor's words, for the prospect of such a one-sentence appendix holds an eccentric appeal. However, the tug of conscience, bad master as it is reputed to be, along with more solid considerations, obliges us to go on. In 1962 Thomas Torrance wrote that "it will take many generations, if not centuries, to evaluate his [Barth's] service adequately."[2] One of the most able and rigorous Barth interpreters of our day, George Hunsinger, granted that "it would be hard to deny all truth to this remark" and, proceeding beyond the question of evaluation to the question of interpretation, observed that "we are still in the early stages of even understanding what it was that Barth had to say."[3] How much we have moved on since these statements I do not know, but anyone disposed to treat these judgments seriously, while not being disposed to gear a life's work to essaying an interpretative and evaluative breakthrough, would do well to entertain modest expository ambitions and aim to describe Barth not *an sich,* but as he appears. Even that ambition is too high for me here, as he appears differently to different people and nowhere more so, it would seem, than in relation to the topic at hand. Better stick to any terra firma

1. Flannery O'Connor, *The Correspondence of Flannery O'Connor and the Brainerd Cheneys,* ed. C. Ralph Stephens (Jackson: University Press of Mississippi, 1986), pp 180-81. I am grateful to one of my students, Jeremy Haworth, for this reference.

2. Thomas F. Torrance, *Karl Barth: An Introduction to His Early Theology: 1910-1931* (London: SCM, 1962), p. 179.

3. George Hunsinger, *How to Read Karl Barth: The Shape of His Theology* (Oxford and New York: Oxford University Press, 1991), p. 12, where he also quotes Torrance.

that we can espy in the corpus of Barth's work, even if we end up scaling the summit of blandness, than make critical remarks on his understanding of election which are unduly hostage to controversial interpretation.

How to read Barth on election has been a particularly contentious issue in recent years. Not so long ago, scholarly skirmishes powdered the pages of the *Scottish Journal of Theology* or, if you wanted to change channels, the *International Journal of Systematic Theology,* or even to an outlet rather less wedded to traditional theological concerns, *Modern Theology.*[4] This sounds detached, if not disdainful. To detachment, I plead guilty with mildly mitigating circumstances. In part, those circumstances have to do with self-expectation in this particular volume. Beyond that, however, I am not convinced of the possibility of a well-grounded intellectual confidence in coming to detailed conclusions on some of the substantive points at theological issue, and that has a knock-on effect on the degree of interest in interpreting Barth on those points.

Bruce McCormack's essay "Grace and Being: The Role of God's Gracious Election in Karl Barth's Theological Ontology," published in *The Cambridge Companion to Karl Barth,* was a kind of opening salvo in the relevant round of engagements.[5] The very title of the essay, compared with the titles of the other essays in this volume, announced its author's intention of striking out on a definite line of interpretation. These were its opening words: "When the history of theology in the twentieth century is written from the vantage point of, let us say, one hundred years from now, I am confident that the greatest contribution of Karl Barth to the development of church doctrine will be located in his doctrine of election." According to McCormack, Barth forged a new ontology, actualistic rather than essentialist: being resides in act. He refused the classical belief that the identity of God as Trinity is constituted independently of any decision to become incarnate. On the contrary, God's very self-constitution is with a view to subsequent incarnation. The Word is who he is in eternal self-determination to become incarnate. He is incarnate for us and for our salvation. Thus, God's elevation of humankind in the Word is not a contingency, but is involved in God's eternal self-constitution. McCormack

4. I shall not list the literature here; ample guidance is given in Michael T. Dempsey, ed., *Trinity and Election in Contemporary Theology* (Grand Rapids: Eerdmans, 2011).

5. Bruce McCormack, "Grace and Being: The Role of God's Gracious Election in Karl Barth's Theological Ontology," in *The Cambridge Companion to Karl Barth,* ed. John Webster (Cambridge: Cambridge University Press, 2000). Note also the reference to McCormack's earlier work, Dempsey, *Trinity and Election,* p. 2.

doubted whether Barth was consistent here, opining that his treatment of the Trinity in *Church Dogmatics* I/1, before he arrived at election in II/2, needed revision to be brought into line with this developing and developed actualism. The novelty and heart of Barth's doctrine of election are indicated by the fact that "election is the event in God's life in which he assigns to himself the being he will have for all eternity."[6] This is the God made known to us in Jesus Christ. "Knowing God in this way, we can trust that the love and mercy toward the whole human race demonstrated in Jesus' subjection of himself to death on a cross is 'essential' to God and that election is universal in scope."[7]

A substantial response was provided in a full-length study by Paul Molnar.[8] Molnar both interpreted Barth's doctrine of God along more classical lines than did McCormack and rejected the claim that there was some disparity between volumes I/1 and II/2. On this account, McCormack was guilty of overlooking or misinterpreting the place of the *Logos asarkos* (the discarnate Word) in Barth's theology and was "misled into believing that God became the triune God by virtue of his self-determination to be our God."[9] Thereafter, a number of contributors entered the interpretative contest, McCormack himself rejoining it in due course.

Those who have read the exchanges in this debate will realize that little or nothing can be accomplished by offering only brief exegesis of Barth with a view to shoring up a particular reading.[10] The hermeneutical

6. McCormack, "Grace and Being," p. 98.

7. McCormack, "Grace and Being," p. 99.

8. Paul Molnar, *Divine Freedom and the Doctrine of the Immanent Trinity: In Dialogue with Karl Barth and Contemporary Theology* (Edinburgh: T. & T. Clark, 2002).

9. Molnar, *Divine Freedom,* p. 64.

10. There is undoubtedly a strong streak of inchoate, if not blossomed, actualism in *Church Dogmatics* from the beginning, although some will make more than do others of those statements which appear to modify — or, perhaps contextualize — it. "God Himself is not just Himself. He is also His self-revealing. . . . He Himself is not just Himself but also what He creates and achieves in man" are statements from *Church Dogmatics* I/1 (Edinburgh: T. & T. Clark, 1975), pp. 298-99, in which volume Barth also alludes to "the essence or act in which God is God" (p. 364). (From here on, references to *Church Dogmatics* [*CD*], 14 vols. [Edinburgh: T. & T. Clark, 1956-1975] will be placed in the text.) Later talk of God as "event" has to be read bearing in mind the wider application of this language before the doctrine of God is formally treated: "My neighbour is an event which takes place in the existence of a definite man definitely marked off from all other men" (I/2, p. 420). For what it is worth, I am inclined to agree with Hunsinger (see chap. 4 of Dempsey, *Trinity and Election*) and Molnar (see also his essays in chaps. 2 and 3 of Dempsey's volume) in their interpretations of Barth; I find it hard to believe that Barth traveled as far away by II/2 as he did, on McCor-

task in relation to Barth has to be undertaken with a steady, unblinking eye on the nature of his rhetoric. Rhetoric is an enduring and dominating feature of the communicative, homiletic style of *CD,* suffused with the fervor of perlocutionary ambition, but Barth is also rhetorical in the narrower sense of the word, as when we speak of striking or brazen rhetoric in relation to the use of a particular word or phrase. While an example of what we are up against here is bound to be rather arbitrary, perhaps it is not useless. As election and ethics are treated in the same volume, we might wonder whether a good way to gauge the force and so get a firmer grip on the meaning of Barth's interpretation of election is by examining its implications for ethics.[11] With this in mind, we read on in II/2, progressing to Barth's accompanying discussion of "the command of God," where we are immediately assured that God "does not exist, therefore, without the covenant with man which was made and executed in this name" (II/2, p. 509).[12] What looks like a non sequitur in the next sentence is the well-nigh-immediate reward for having plowed on trustingly into this section of *CD.* "God is not known completely — *and therefore not at all* — if He is not known as the Maker and Lord of this covenant between Himself and man" (my italics).[13] Rhetoric in the narrower sense, of negligible hermeneutical weight? Or deeply indicative of what Barth has been getting at in his treatment of election and in the preceding volumes? Two pages on from that, after we think we have been soaked for several hundred pages in the claim that all humans are elect willy-nilly, Barth tells us this: "As he [man] measures himself against God he necessarily judges himself. Unless he accepts this question — however it is answered — he obviously cannot be elect" (p. 511).

We might succumb to hermeneutical despair or we might conclude that it is worth making the effort to overcome cheap and lazy impatience

---

mack's account, from his response to Erich Przywara in I/1, p. 172. However, I am certainly not dogmatic on the matter, and this does not imply lack of sympathy with important strands in McCormack's exposition.

11. We might derive some encouragement for this strategy from I/2, pp. 792-95.

12. By simple quotation, I am not implying that the meaning of this statement is immediately perspicuous; on the contrary, our interpretation of it will depend on our interpretation of Barth's argument hitherto.

13. Although voice and mood are different in the German, this little modifies the difficulty: "Man hätte Gott nicht vollständig, mann hatte ihn darum gar nich erkannt, wenn man ihn nicht als den Stifter und Herrn dieses Bundes zwischen ihm und dem Menschen erkannt hätte." *Kirchliche Dogmatik* II/2, p. 564.

in interpretation. What we cannot reasonably attempt is to be definitive on Barth-interpretation in an appendix.[14] We can, however, comment ad hoc on what is the case if Barth is interpreted in a particular way. At no time does Barth concentrate his theological attention more powerfully than when he tries to elaborate on the meaning of "God is." In seeking to develop this statement, "we confront the hardest and at the same time the most extensive task of Church dogmatics," and behind it "also there lies concealed the hardest and at the same time the most extensive task of the whole of Christian preaching" (II/1, p. 257). Already, in 1914, Barth had said that "the little clause 'God is' signifies a revolution."[15] If Barth ended up saying what Bruce McCormack takes him to be saying, he locked himself into an impossible position. Interpreting Barth, McCormack said: "God is so much the Lord that he is Lord even over his being and essence. The only thing that is absolutely necessary for God is existence itself."[16] Now, if Barth believed this, he tumbled into theological nonsense — let alone what we might say on the philosophical score.[17] Paul Helm has rightly exposed the insuperable difficulty attending this and surrounding statements, including some made in McCormack's original essay in *The Cambridge Companion.*[18] "For is Barth positing a God who assigns himself a being, or a character? Does this mean that God does not already have a character?"[19] God, on this scenario, is choosing his own essence, including Trinitarian essence; but who on earth or in heaven is this God who chooses his own essence? Either McCormack or Barth or both have misspoken, as Hillary Clinton would put it. Be that as it may, deciding whether Barth should be

14. This author is amongst those who would prefer to go to their grave wondering whether it is they who are confused or Barth who is confused (and reckoning that the odds are roughly even) than to make sure that their CV includes a sign of confidence that they have got him right.

15. Eberhard Busch, *The Great Passion: An Introduction to Karl Barth's Theology* (Grand Rapids: Eerdmans, 2004), p. 8.

16. McCormack, "'Seek God Where He May Be Found': A Response to Edwin Chr. Van Driel," *Scottish Journal of Theology* 60, no. 1 (2007): 62-79, here p. 67.

17. The philosophical question is whether it makes sense to talk of any existing entity whose sole determination should be that it is some kind of existing entity. If the question is adjudged an un-Barthian intrusion of philosophy into theology and someone is willing to say: "So much the worse for philosophy," then we can stick with the theological point.

18. Helm, "Karl Barth and the Visibility of God," in *Engaging with Barth: Contemporary Evangelical Critiques,* ed. David Gibson and Daniel Strange (Nottingham: Apollos, 2008), pp. 273-99.

19. Helm, "Karl Barth," p. 284.

so interpreted will distract us from the task of assessing elements in Barth's understanding of election which are susceptible of critical evaluation on any interpretation of Barth's ontological actualism.

Generally speaking, the debate over how to interpret Barth, conducted by theologians committed not just to interpreting Barth but to the importance of the substantive theological issues at stake, is in danger of propelling us speculatively into a transcendent, immanently-Trinitarian realm where we simply do not know, where we are not meant to tread and where it can be impossible even to figure out easily whether we are making sense or not. Throw an object high enough into space and it will never come down, at least in this world, since it has exited the earth's gravitational sphere. So it seems to be with a great deal of theological debate on the question of God's Trinitarian being. The only spectacle worse than theologians kicking up the dust and complaining that they cannot see is theologians kicking up the dust and insisting that they do see.

I do not say this in desolate continuity with the self-pity I expressed in the preface with respect to the plight of systematic theologians, thus lumbering this volume with a kind of grumpy *inclusio.* The point can be made in connection with discussion of Barth by noting that theologians have often simply sailed past Brunner's warning about speculation in dogmatics. Although Brunner's position was set out in the "Prolegomena" to the first volume of his *Dogmatics,* his chapter on the Trinity in that volume, including his following brief excursus on historical theology and on Barth, aptly sounds the particular warning note that we need to hear.[20] Brunner has sometimes been suspected of denying the Trinity, but the suspicion cannot be well sustained with respect to this chapter. What he lamented was the fact that belief in God the Father, Son, and Spirit who are one and coequally divine, was all too often, from the patristic period onward, a starting point for speculation (even if mounted on biblical truth and doxological practice) instead of a terminus, a confessional declaration of limits. Brunner was rather prone to exaggeration, and while Berkouwer himself may have exaggerated a little when he accused Brunner of a tendency to play "fast and loose with many scriptural data without attempting any thoroughgoing and serious exegesis," Brunner did sometimes take what looks like exegetical shortcuts, in the sense that he could be exegetically negligent, and perhaps Berkouwer's sentiment should earn our qualified

20. Brunner, *The Christian Doctrine of God: Dogmatics,* vol. 1 (London: Lutterworth, 1949), pp. 205-40.

approval in that light.[21] Nonetheless, we should not sail past the warning cries even of a man who takes shortcuts on exegetical land; if we do, we should not complain if we hit rough speculative seas which break up our craft or if we end up navigating an ocean whose longitude and latitude are impossible to pinpoint precisely on any reliable theological map.[22]

Is the accusation of being speculative directed to Barth, as well as to some protagonists in active combat over the interpretation of Barth on election?[23] There is a lot to ponder here, including the somewhat gnomic and pretentious averment (even if we are on the lookout for Barthian irony) that "[f]ear of scholasticism is the mark of the false prophet" (I/1, p. 179).[24] However, it may not require the judgment of charity, and simply be a matter of fairness, if our first word be one of exoneration in respect of Barth, to the extent that "speculation" is viewed pejoratively. We might, with more or less justification, judge something that he says to be a matter of ontological speculation, but it is not hard to see that, if this is so, it is driven by nonspeculative theological motives. The reasoning goes like this: that God should be known as the God of grace is the greatest knowledge possible for

21. Berkouwer, *The Triumph of Grace in the Theology of Karl Barth* (London: Paternoster, 1956), p. 388. The qualification is that some of this may be accounted for by lack of space when he had to write rather than lack of interest when he had to think.

22. I suspect that one reason for the widespread neglect of Brunner's work is that he is not (or not any longer?) a theologian's theologian. This is surely a badge of merit. It should go without saying that to complain about neglect does not require adherence to the body of a neglected author's theology.

23. The very first essay in Dempsey's collection, written by Kevin Hector, highlights at its beginning that parties in the dispute affirm, in line with Barth, that theology must be nonspeculative. *Trinity and Election,* p. 30. Not long after that, Hector quotes Bruce McCormack: "What Barth is suggesting is that election is the event in God's life in which he [God] assigns himself the being he will have for all eternity" (p. 35). If this is not being speculative, it is hard to know what is. On the one hand, we need terminological exactitude: McCormack regards as nonmetaphysical what many of us regard as a blatantly metaphysical matter; see, e.g., his response to Hunsinger in Dempsey's volume, pp. 122-23. If Paul Dafydd Jones is right to describe a theological suggestion by Barth as "metaphysically dizzying" ("Obedience, Trinity, and Election: Thinking with and beyond the *Church Dogmatics,*" in *Trinity and Election,* pp. 138-61, here p. 149), does anyone think that elaborating it will not be engaging in metaphysics? On the other hand, theologians should just come clean and admit that they enjoy speculation and metaphysics. We might add that Barth's first and early reference to Brunner in *CD* briefly alludes to the changing contexts of dogmatics which have an impact on what is discussed therein (I/1, p. 26).

24. Note his remarks on metaphysics on the next page, p. 180. In the preface to this, the opening volume of *CD,* Barth refers to both speculation and scholasticism (p. xiv).

humankind, for it is knowledge of the greatest truth. It is in and through Jesus Christ that he is known. If election is not universal, God is not truly known in Jesus; despite all efforts to argue the contrary, God remains hidden, because Jesus Christ can never, in his person, work, and revelation, be the pledge of God's grace toward *me.* If God's very self-constitution is for the sake of incarnation and entails universal election in Jesus Christ, who is electing God and elected man, we have the strongest possible guarantee that the God who appears is the God who is. A sound gospel doctrine of election needs to be grounded in a sound doctrine of God, of which it is a part. That is how Barth sees things, and only unappreciative arrogance could unhesitatingly pin on him the charge of unseemly speculative intent in his adumbration of this. "The reality of God which encounters us in His revelation is His reality in all the depths of eternity," said Barth, long before he came to discuss election, and who can deny the shabbiness of readily suspecting the intrusion of a speculative interest in the course of trying to discern and set forth the majesty of the triune God (I/1, p. 479)? When we remember the context in which Barth wrote, including the legacy of post-Enlightenment theology and culture, we should register our gratitude for his determined and reiterated insistence that God is truly known. Not only should we credit Barth with refusing to take an interest in the theologically arcane for its own sake; also, criticism should not be too heavy-handed if the occupational hazard of the theologian turns out to lead Barth or anyone else in a speculative direction as he or she seeks to clarify and test the proclamation of the church by producing good dogmatics. Perhaps only a prophet or mystic silence will be capable of avoiding the hazard.

Nonetheless, assume, for the sake of discussion, (a) that God has elected all and (b) that we need to know it. If Barth made an ontological move in the direction of actualism in order to secure these positions, this was unnecessary, whatever wider theological benefits and intrinsic theological justification such a move may have. As far as we humans are concerned, all that would be needed for God to elect all would be for God to will to do so. As far as we humans are concerned, all that would be needed for us to know that he had elected us all, would be for it to be clear to us in his Word. If we want to affirm that God is truly known, so that no divine hiddenness hinders our assurance and confidence, we need to climb no higher than this, even if some theologians think they are capable of doing so and are in fact capable of doing so. Neither the entertainment nor the elaboration of an actualistic ontology is essential for our security. If such an ontology is entertained or elaborated, it must be for some other reason.

If we find reasons for resisting Barth's understanding of election, perhaps we shall find them in examining his actualistic ontology, but such resistance is not at all dependent on what such an examination might yield.[25] The plain reason for disagreeing with him is that to speak of universal election in Christ is to speak of election in a way not only different from but contrary to the way Scripture speaks of it. It may be judged that to speak of Jesus Christ as electing God and elected man is also unwarranted; for myself, I am untroubled by a formulation along these lines even if it is not the way that it is biblically put, because it seems to me not to run athwart of what is said there and one might even express support in more positive, stronger terms for the possibilities of Barth's formulation.[26] However, universal election is a different matter. Election, however we interpret its detailed theological content, is always discriminate in Scripture. Israel or the church or particular individuals are elected.

What about Jesus Christ, the Elect One?[27] Does he not embody the universality which marks Barth's interpretation? It is a question of what kind of universality we ascribe to Jesus Christ in the unity of his person and

25. To my mind, the problem with Barth's treatment of the doctrine of God arises less from any speculative bent than from the failure to make proper distinctions. In his discussion "The Being of God in Act," Barth collapses "God as living" into "God is act" (II/1, p. 263). The movement of thought to the statement, on the same page, that "God's Godhead consists in the fact that it is an event" actually involves a logical leap: no rigorous reasoning leads to this statement and we have been given no logically compelling reason to subscribe to it. By the time we get to the summary claim that we should "always understand God as event, as act and as life" (p. 265: "als Ereignis, als Akt, als Leben," *KD* II/1, p. 295; Barth has already spoken of "das Wort 'Ereignis' *oder* 'Akt'" [my italics] in *KD,* p. 294), the necessary analytic work has not been done. Analytic philosophical-theological reason yields little in the way of religious insight; that is its limitation. Nonetheless, it has its place when advancing or adumbrating theological insight.

26. This is not to say that I agree with the content which Barth invests in it; his description would take us into questions of Trinity and Christology. Since remark was earlier made on Brunner's exegetical shortcomings, we might note that his objection to Barth's description of Jesus as the "eternally Elect Man" and "pre-existing God-Man" is that "the Bible contains no such doctrine" (*Christian Doctrine of God,* p. 347). (He adds that "no theory of this kind has ever been formulated by any theologian.") Notwithstanding what I have said, I take to heart Brunner's earlier warning about biblical language and the description of Jesus Christ as the electing God (pp. 313-15).

27. In the Synoptic Gospels, the Father speaks twice: at the baptism and at the transfiguration of the Son. Luke's language in 9:35 makes the connection with election. In Matthew 12:17-21, we encounter the significance of Christ as elect virtually in all its fullness. In Luke 23:35, rulers call Jesus "elect" (*ho eklektos,* following the Greek of Isa. 42:1; cf. *ho eklegmenos* in Luke 9:35).

work, being and act. As in talk of Christ as electing God, any warranted difficulty with it is not predicated on an axiom to the effect that it is theologically out of order to speak of matters spoken of in the Bible in a way different from the way the Bible speaks of them. The difficulty arises when we talk in terms that materially contradict it. If theologians have quarreled with this demurral for the last three centuries or so, at least Barth seems not to quarrel with it, certainly not when we are dealing with the gospel; and Barth thinks that is exactly what we are dealing with when we are dealing with election.

"The election of grace [is] . . . the sum of the Gospel . . . the whole of the Gospel, the Gospel *in nuce*" (II/2, pp. 13-14). Election, which "should serve at once to emphasise and explain what we have already said in the word grace" (p. 10), is part of the doctrine of God, grace having been treated in II/1.[28] It is not part of the doctrine of divine providence, for the providential ways of God are ordered to his electing purposes, as is creation, since all has been created in and through Jesus Christ, who is the electing God and God's elect for us. Whereas creation is treated in volume III, election is part of the doctrine of God in volume II because it is constitutive of God's self-determination. God does not want to be God other than as the electing God (II/2, p. 7); this is a primal decision made in God's own being (p. 50); election is, first and foremost, self-election, as the words which head up Barth's whole treatment of election boldly announce (p. 3). Election is a sovereign act, an act of God's self-determining being to be this God for us (pp. 76-77). He is this for us in Jesus Christ, and election is this, first and foremost, and not the ordination of a private relationship between God and particular individuals. "When we utter the name of Jesus Christ we really do speak the first and final word not only about the electing God but also about elected man" (p. 76).

From this point, Barth moves into the three main divisions of his exposition: "The Election of Jesus Christ," "The Election of the Community," and "The Election of the Individual." Aware of the unusual theological move that he is making, Barth concentrates his exposition of the election of Jesus Christ on an interpretation of John 1:1 and on Jesus Christ as the Word of God. "The electing consists in this Word and decree in the be-

28. In II/1, God is described as "the one who loves in freedom," and when his perfections are elaborated, grace, in its connection with holiness, is the first to be elaborated (pp. 351-68). Before that, we have read that, "whatever else He may be, God is wholly and utterly the good-pleasure of His grace and mercy" (II/1, p. 75).

ginning" (p. 100). God has from all eternity ordained himself to be Jesus Christ. The Word is also that very God who ordains his own incarnation; Jesus Christ in person is the electing God. Barth expresses puzzlement that this move has not been made before in the history of theology. Hermeneutical control rightfully ought to be in the hand of this Johannine text (1:1), for "the Word of God is the content of the Bible." "The exegesis of those passages," says Barth, alluding to those which refer explicitly to election and predestination, "depends upon whether or not we have determined that our exposition should be true to the context in which they stand and are intended to be read" (p. 152).[29] If Jesus Christ is not himself the electing God, who God is will be unknown to us; we shall have ended up with a God *behind* Jesus Christ. We must know God as God in Christ; as the electing God in Christ; ourselves as elect in Christ. "The substitution of the election of Jesus Christ for the *decretum absolutum* is . . . the decisive point in the amendment of the doctrine of predestination" (II/2, p. 161). Positively and alternatively: "The eternal will of God in the election of Jesus Christ is His will to give Himself for the sake of man as created by Him and fallen from Him" (p. 161). Christ, then, is elect and electing in the act of divine self-determining self-election.

Knowing full well that Scripture speaks particularly, rather than universally, of election, Barth gives plenty of expository space to the election of the ecclesial community and of the individual. Barth holds that election in these cases is not determination to life at the expense of those who do not bear the overt designation: "the elect." In Christ, the elect are indeed elect to life, but there is also an election to service, and here Israel and the church come into their own. "It seems to me that if we want to keep the order of the NT we must say: God has ordained and chosen them [the body and society of believers] into his temporal and eternal service and, consequently, into everlasting life."[30] The work in which Barth says this consists of talks on the first part of Calvin's 1545 catechism (Calvin's explanation of the Apostles' Creed), and it has been adjudged a work in which Barth comes especially close to Calvin.[31] Even so, in these pages Barth permits himself "a small criticism" of Calvin in relation to the doctrine of election

29. "The Word was made flesh: this is the first, original and controlling sign of all signs" (II/1, p. 199).

30. Karl Barth, *The Faith of the Christian Church: A Commentary on the Apostles' Creed according to Calvin's Catechism,* trans. Gabriel Vahanian (London and Glasgow: Collins, 1958), pp. 115-16.

31. So Vahanian, in *The Faith of the Christian Church,* p. 7.

for failing to appreciate that election is for service, leading on to eternal life, and not just election to eternal life.[32] In *CD* I/1, Barth had remarked that OT election was an "election of Israel among the nations," whereas, in the NT, individual believers were comprehended as well (p. 159). Barth foregrounds service but does not marginalize the question of eternal life. Universal election does not banish reprobation; on the contrary, atonement occurs through the judgment on the cross of the judge who is judged in our place, Jesus Christ. In bearing the curse of sin, he is the reprobate one. As all are elect in this one man, so all were reprobate in this one man. Barth thinks that we are to keep open the question of whether or not this means the eschatological salvation of all individuals.

What role does biblical exegesis play in Barth's theology, when it comes to election? This already massive question is expanded because it is layered on the deeper question of what role biblical exegesis plays in Barth's theology as a whole. At the beginning of *CD* I/1, Barth programmatically observed that "dogmatics as such does not ask what the apostles and prophets said but what we must say on the basis of the apostles and prophets" (p. 16).[33] Barth aspires to treat this "basis" as a norm. As he distinguishes between dogmatics and exegesis, so he distinguishes between dogmatics and "a biblical theology of the Old and New Testaments" (I/2, p. 821). At the same point as he does the latter, he tells us that "[w]hat is really demanded of dogmatics is that this examination, criticism and correction [by dogmatics of the proclamation of the church] should be carried out with the same biblical attitude of thought and speech to which Church proclamation is called." We note the reference to "speech" here. We note, too, that, in his preface to II/2, Barth tells us that "[t]he specific subject-matter of this half-volume made it necessary for me to set out more fully than in the previous sections the exegetical background to the dogmatic exposition" (p. ix) and that, on the first page of the exposition, he underlines the way in which what follows adheres to the self-testimony of God in Scripture (p. 3).

What follows in respect of election is surely different from what these words portend. Here, we enter familiar enough territory. To take a recent contribution, Suzanne McDonald describes as "utterly withering" James Dunn's "exegetically accurate remark that, for Paul, there can be absolutely

32. Barth, *The Faith of the Christian Church,* pp. 115-16, and Vahanian, p. 7. As Barth puts it in *CD* IV/4, "service is the characteristic feature of the Christian life" (p. 72).

33. "Nor can it ever be the real concern of dogmatics merely to assemble, repeat and define the teaching of the Bible" (I/1, p. 16).

no suggestion of 'all men and women as willy-nilly "in Christ" whether they want to be or not, whether they know or not,'" and she provides extended observations on this score.[34] There are plenty of examples throughout Barth's work of that kind of thing going on here. I deliberately select them from different parts of *CD* and from other works and deliberately select key, not marginal, statements (if there are marginal statements in *Church Dogmatics*). All participate in Christ, justified and sanctified in him.[35] Our conversion to God "took place in His death," the death of Christ (IV/1, p. 290). "The resurrection of Jesus Christ affirms that which is actual in His death, the conversion of all men to God which has taken place in Him . . . all men are in Him the One. . . . He the One is in them . . . in the midst of them" (IV/1, p. 317).[36] The Holy Spirit is promised in Christ to *all* in the following sense: "And when there comes the hour of the God who acts in Jesus Christ by the Holy Ghost, no aversion, rebellion or resistance on the part of non-Christians will be strong enough to resist the fulfillment of the promise of the Spirit which is pronounced over them too" (IV/3.1, p. 355). "We are no longer addressed and regarded by God as sinners, who must pass under judgment for their guilt," for now "it is only at this one place where God's wrath has burned as consuming fire — Golgotha," and it cannot so burn again.[37] Does not Barth here speak a foreign language, as far as the Bible is concerned?

When exegesis and dogmatics pull apart in this way, the question of principle which arises in interpreting Barth is the question about their relationship, and this is a formidable matter whose dimensions are too large to handle here. As for the treatment of election, it is the hermeneutical

34. Suzanne McDonald, *Re-Imaging Election: Divine Election as Representing God to Others and Others to God* (Grand Rapids: Eerdmans, 2010), p. 68. Her whole discussion in chapter 3 shows the extent to which Barth has gone exegetically quite astray. Along with Matthew Levering, *Predestination: Biblical and Theological Paths* (Oxford: Oxford University Press, 2011), McDonald provides a recent contribution to our theme which explores paths which I am unable to.

35. See, prior to *CD* II/2, II/1, pp. 128-78, on "The Readiness of Man."

36. Cf. the reference to Kohlbrügge in I/2, p. 709. See too IV/1, p. 250: "In this suffering and dying of God Himself in His Son, there took place the reconciliation with God, the conversion to Him, of the world." Sometimes we are concerned with Barth's use of explicitly biblical terminology, e.g., in relation to justification and sanctification; sometimes we are concerned with his use of common theological terminology, e.g., in relation to conversion.

37. Statements found respectively in *Dogmatics in Outline* (London: SCM, 1949), p. 120, and *Learning Jesus Christ through the Heidelberg Catechism* (Grand Rapids: Eerdmans, 1981), p. 45. Barth's exposition of "The Praise of God" (*CD* I/2, pp. 401-54) is instructive if we want to understand the unity and distinction between the "children of God" and the "neighbor."

role of John 1:1 that grabs our attention where the questions which cluster around dogmatics, exegesis, and biblical theology are concerned, and we shall shortly turn to this. The Word of God was, of course, the subject of *CD* I/1 and I/2, and election is often mentioned in those volumes.[38] Both these references and the initial stages of the discussion in II/2 tell us that, in some respects, we need to read Barth backward or, if that sounds plain silly, backward and forward at the same time.[39] This is the case in two ways. It is the case on the microscale: Barth often takes up theological positions prior to his detailed exegetical discussions, and we have to resist the temptation to think he has stitched up the issue before coming to Scripture, for he does eventually, at least putatively and frequently, seek to ground — and not simply to bolster — his theological convictions in biblical exegesis.[40] As it requires patience and faith to read and study Scripture aright, so it requires patience and faith to read and study Barth aright, though for different reasons. Patience, because he states his conclusions before providing his proofs; faith, because we are required to take these conclusions seriously in the trust that the proof will come.[41] It is also the case on the macroscale. Barth begins *CD* by discussing the foundation of dogmatics in the Word of God, which requires a preliminary statement of its content in order to describe theological method. The content is essentially atonement, which is "the real centre — not the systematic, but the actual centre of dogmatics and Church proclamation" (I/2, p. 882; cf. pp. 871-84). Nevertheless, he does not focus on atonement in its own right until the fourth volume of *CD.*

The force of Barth's argument for universal election stems from his belief in a universal atonement: If Christ died for all, how can Christ *not* be elect for all and all not be elect in him who represents us, indeed, incorporates our humanity in his divine humanity?[42] In connection with the

38. The "election of grace" and predestination have already been mentioned as early as I/1, pp. 21-22. No biblical book is cited more often in I/1 and I/2 than the Gospel of John, and a proportionately high number of references to it are to its first chapter.

39. Note how quickly *CD* IV comes to dominate one of the most solid expositions of Barth's theology, Busch's book *The Great Passion,* from part II, chapter 2 onward.

40. Yet, it would be a very generous reading of Barth indeed to affirm that exegesis grounds rather than bolsters a theological conclusion reached on the question of natural knowledge; note his method of treatment in "The Readiness of God," II/1, pp. 63-128.

41. It should go without saying that the language of "proof" and "conclusion" is not being used with philosophical strictness here in relation to Barth's theological procedure.

42. I mean "force" rather than logic, whatever the logical role of this belief. In terms of logic, it is the identification of Jesus Christ with the Word of God, the Word of love and

universality of reconciliation, Barth has announced in previous volumes the basic truth about election which he expounds in II/2.[43] He has assigned to election what has been characteristically assigned to atonement in the Christian tradition, namely, universality. "The doctrine of election is the last or first or central word in the whole doctrine of reconciliation. . . . But the doctrine of reconciliation is itself the first or last or central word in the whole Christian confession or the whole of Christian dogma. Dogmatics has no more exalted or profound word — essentially, indeed, it has no other word — than this: that God was in Christ reconciling the world unto Himself (2 Cor. 5:19)."[44]

Atonement is the heart of the reconciliation of which Paul speaks in 2 Corinthians and of which Barth speaks in *CD,* and must be understood as the expression of election, election made visible, and of reconciliation enacted in historical time; but it is certainly not a "work" apart from the person — "Jesus Christ is the atonement" (IV/1, p. 34) — and our first word is about Jesus Christ, the Elect One, in whom we are elect.[45] As Barth transfers into the domain of election what has standardly characterized the domain of atonement, that is, universality, so he transposes into the domain of atonement what has standardly characterized the domain of predestination, that is, the language of reprobation. Jesus Christ is the reprobate One. Barth is attempting a studiously, if revisionary, Reformed neo-universalism.

It is not difficult to concede the theological strength and to feel the religious force of Barth's argument. If Jesus Christ died for all and, as God, is the revelation of God's being and will, he is the electing God; and how can election be other than universal if God's will is the expression of his being and is both revealed and executed in the death of Jesus Christ for all

grace because God is love and grace and Jesus Christ is God, that holds the commanding place. A logical connection had been made early in Protestant theology. William Perkins, in his *Golden Chaine; or, the description of theologie: containing the order of the causes of salvation and damnation, according to God's worde,* trans. Robert Hill (Cambridge, 1592), combated a new doctrine of election or predestination whereby all are elect, the universality of election being inferred from the universality of divine love and atonement (pp. 402-8).

43. E.g., I/2, pp. 348-52. Also predestination, e.g., pp. 372-73.

44. II/2, p. 88. The doctrine of election is the "decisive word," the "mystery of the doctrine of reconciliation" (p. 89). Reconciliation is the fulfillment of election (IV/3.1, p. 3). In II/2, p. 633, Barth allows God's eternal decision for reconciliation and his act of reconciliation in time to overshadow to the point of misrepresenting Paul's teaching on the judgment of human works in 2 Cor. 5:10.

45. On the question of a distinction between person and work, see IV/1, pp. 127-28.

humankind? How can we *not* say that all are elect in Jesus Christ? Must we not say that, even if it is not formulated in this way in the NT, it is manifestly an expression of its theology and that it is precisely the task of dogmatics to draw this out? The Reformed tradition has, of course, sought to formulate the belief that Christ died for all in conjunction with the conviction that he died effectively only for the elect; the thematic connection with predestination is evident in the belief in the particularism of the atonement. Predestination, in its traditional form, is one of the things that drives this conclusion about the atonement, along with the conviction that a universal atonement would logically require universalism as its entailment and, of course, along with direct exegesis of biblical texts touching on the death of Christ.

Suppose that we grant Barth two things. Firstly, Calvinism — which he treats with such respect, a model of courteous ecclesial dissent — really does have a problem with the relationship of Jesus Christ to God's decree. We have little solid ground to affirm with assurance that Jesus Christ is God *pro nobis* if he executes a decree in which some are of the *nobis* and others are most certainly not.[46] Secondly, there must be a meaningful sense in which the death of Jesus Christ is for all, and the particularity of a Calvinistic view of the atonement, riveted to its doctrine of predestination, makes it difficult to see how it is meaningful.[47] Are we, nonetheless, bound to his conclusion that all are elect in Christ?

Barth deploys the word "election" or some form of the verb "elect" in a number of ways throughout *CD*.[48] Taking a comradely step toward Barth, we might go so far as to admit that, speaking very loosely, to speak of all being elect in Jesus Christ accords with or is entailed in the universality of the atonement and the universal outreach of the grace of the God who wants all to be saved and to come to a knowledge of the truth (1 Tim. 2:4).[49] Speaking

46. Obviously, this is a brutal summary of the difficulties of traditional Calvinism; for Barth's elaboration of this point in II/2, see, e.g., pp. 106-15.

47. Barth does not explicitly concentrate on this point in the discussion of election in II/2, pp. 3-506. The plan of my discussion has occluded the fact that, speaking for myself, I am not denying a particularity for the atonement. It is particularity as it is worked out in the full-blown Calvinistic scheme of things that is in view here, not just any affirmation of the particularity of the atonement.

48. See, e.g., talk of electing Christ's "fleshness" (I/2, p. 44) and of the eternal Word choosing "human nature" (1/2, p. 122). The German has a form of *erwählen* in both cases.

49. Some will maintain that the omission of the word "men" in my citation of this text in the NIV, in the interest of inclusive language, has the prejudicial effect of eclipsing the exegetical possibility of reading "all" as (something like) "all kinds of."

very loosely has a definite (positive) point and an equally definite limitation, and my comradely step is actually not a very long one. The positive point is that we can see how talk of all being elect in Christ is analytic in the universality of atonement and of grace, as long as we give solid substance to these universalities and the language of election is used in an ordinary-language sense. However, here is the rub and here are the limits: the specifically theological sense attached by Scripture to "election" is occluded by talk of its universality, and it is not hard to imagine Barth angrily denying any true comradeship involved in a concession which robs universal election of its theological sense and allows it only in an ordinary-language sense.[50] Even if the principle that dogmatic terminology ought inflexibly to follow biblical semantics is shaky beyond support, the consequence of not doing so in this case is to mistake the biblical-theological substance of election. The price of effectively expanding the theological scope of the word in dogmatics is to land us in dogmatic thickets which are not only verbally unnecessary, but threaten the substance of Christian doctrine.[51]

The obvious point at which to tease out this claim a little is the familiar one in connection with universalism. Those of us who deny that universalism is taught in the NT and deny that it should be theologically maintained will obviously deny that election entails it. Yet, even those who maintain universalism may well deny that pressure in the direction of universalism is credibly exerted by election.[52] Barth agrees that "theological

50. In saying that Barth uses the word "election" in "counterintuitive" ways, David Gibson, in his helpful and fair-minded study, *Reading the Decree: Exegesis, Election, and Christology in Calvin and Barth* (London: T. & T. Clark, 2009), p. 42, is observing the same phenomenon as I am under a different description. Is there even a sleight of hand involved, or is it unfair to suggest it, when Barth says in II/2, p. 148, that we must always take "as a starting-point" the biblical passages "which speak expressly and directly of the divine election and predestination," but adds immediately: "But what is it that these passages speak of, and in what direction do they constrain us to look," developing this point in such a way that we wonder what exactly he means by "starting-point"? Within a short time of reading this declaration, we are told that "[i]n their own way even the reprobate and those whom God merely uses are elected" (p. 149). We have rapidly traveled away from the passages which speak expressly!

51. This does not simply apply to election. See Barth's statement, in connection with the history of Israel in the OT, that "the non-elect, indeed the rejected . . . are in their own way sanctified by and for God" (II/2, p. 420). Given the use of the phrase "in their own way" with reference to election (n. 50, above), we cannot be confident that Barth's caveat will protect his theology against distortion.

52. "The difficulties raised by Barth's denial of *apokatastasis* have their source not only in the counter-claims of God's freedom and human logic, but in the consequences of

consistency might seem to lead our thoughts and utterances most clearly in this [the universalist] direction" (IV/3.1, p. 477). He does not have in mind just "thoughts and utterances" narrowly specifying election, but these are included. Whatever a biblical account of election entails in the way of theological consistency, it is certainly not universalism, and if it is legitimate to speak of biblical "thoughts" alongside "utterances," we must conclude similarly. Barth, of course, denied a dogmatically universalist conclusion; we can be hopeful, but certainly not dogmatic, universalists.[53] However, even if someone espouses hopeful, as opposed to dogmatic, universalism, it is hard to see how and why election should put pressure in that direction as long as dogmatic language keeps in touch with biblical language.[54]

Christology lies at the heart of the matter; hermeneutical moves which determine Barth's reading of Scripture occur under the rubric of Christology or, better, in the name of Jesus Christ. "If dogmatics cannot regard itself and cause itself to be regarded as fundamentally Christology, it has assuredly succumbed to some alien sway" (I/2, p. 123).[55] The claim is that a christological or christocentric hermeneutic, to put it more crudely than Barth does (he characteristically speaks of Jesus Christ or the name

---

an overweighted election christology at the expense of pneumatology, and in a generally inconsistent account of the relationship between the two." McDonald, *Re-Imaging Election,* p. 72. Although I am not claiming that McDonald is a universalist, this illustrates my point about the pressure exerted by Barth's interpretation of election, a point that could well be made by a universalist. See Barth's attempt to relate "non-Christians" to "the promise of the Spirit" in IV/3.1, pp. 353-57.

53. Barth's language is puzzling in this conclusion to IV/3.1. He speaks of the "supremely unexpected withdrawal of that final threat of perdition" (p. 478), but, on Barth's theology, it is to be supremely expected.

54. With hindsight, we can see that Barth's first reference to election in *CD* does not augur well in this respect, when the Pauline phrase "the election of grace" is used to say that "the decision as to what is or is not true in dogmatics is always a matter of the election of grace" (I/1, p. 21).

55. On the next page, Barth expands this to "Trinity and . . . Christology" (p. 124). See too I/2, p. 123: "[I]n the basic statements of a church dogmatics, Christology must either be dominant and perceptible, or else it is not Christology." I do appreciate the force of Murray Rae's observation: "The essential element of any Christian theology is revealed, above all, by the approach it takes to Christology." *Kierkegaard and Theology* (New York and London: T. & T. Clark, 2010), p. 168. What we must guard against, however, is the temptation to derive a doctrine of election from what we suppose to be christologically necessary. One weakness of a brief dogmatic outline such as I attempt in this volume is that it cannot elaborate complementary methods of approaching a subject. See Michael Polanyi, *Knowing and Being,* ed. M. Grene (London: Routledge and Kegan Paul, 1969), pp. 124-25.

of Jesus Christ), should regulate our theology.[56] By Barth's standard, the second and third chapters of my volume have not only contained substantive mistakes, but also demonstrated extraordinary and culpable theological superficiality and infidelity. I have no doubt that both chapters would have been enriched by elaborating on the requirements of christological and christocentric thought, not just as a matter of duty, as though such thought pertained to some selected theological item that should be kept in mind, but as the form of the foundational depths of a biblical or theological account. What I (obviously) deny is that this elaboration would have modified or altered their substance. The form taken by Barth's admirable desire, so effectively executed, to think theologically in Christ and to think Christ in all our theology, is substantively determined by a material Christology which, I believe, is unbiblical and has no legitimate purchase on theology so long as that material Christology includes the belief that all are elect in Christ.

We return here to the point that John 1:1-2, rather than the vocabulary of election, steers Barth's interpretation of election. The untutored Bible reader will not be alone in supposing that this text falls short of possessing the christological meaning which Barth ascribes to it in relation to election. Barth obviously knows this is true, so he offers an interpretation of it in the context of a theological proposal that ranges far outside the immediate confines of the text. Up to a point, this may be hermeneutically defensible, but not beyond a point where the derivation of a theology of election from John 1:1-2 upsets the meaning of election as found in the explicit biblical vocabulary of election. Barth declared himself puzzled by the failure of the church throughout its history to grasp the implications of this text, although two or three — Athanasius is particularly notable — came close (II/2, pp. 108-10, 155). However, it is Barth's puzzlement that is puzzling. If, as we construct our understanding of election, he had simply declared that we should interpret election texts in their wider context and thus not give priority attention to those passages that speak of it explicitly, that might not be so puzzling. What is strange is that Barth should think that what emerges in his account, when he gives John 1:1 the role he does, has more to commend it theologically in the eyes of those who concur in

56. "The content of the New Testament is solely the name of Jesus Christ, which, of course, also and above all involves the truth of His God-manhood" (I/2, p. 15). Even if we can interpret this formulation in an acceptable way, what cannot be accepted is that beliefs about election and universalism can be deduced solely from the name of Jesus Christ.

his high view of Scripture, than a more sober synthesis of the biblical materials which stick closer to its theological language and explicit internal theological pattern.[57] By all means, let the argument be made that biblical theology is not yet dogmatic theology and that the church needs dogmatics. Yet the path from biblical exegesis to dogmatic theology needs to run more transparently or more straightforwardly through the wide grove of biblical theology so that Scripture can govern dogmatics more strictly.

"Sober synthesis" is just what Barth will not have, and here we can but declare that we part company with him in the way he relates Scripture to dogmatics.[58] The question is: How do we arrive at the theological content of Scripture? Barth's remarks on Cocceius and federal theology are amongst the most instructive here, if we have the broad area of election in view.[59] His remarks on method in this connection are illuminating, especially since we are at the heart of dogmatics (IV/1, p. 3). Barth complains that the federal theologians "were the first to read the Bible as a divinely inspired source-book, by the study of which the attentive and faithful reader can gain an insight and perspective into the whole drama of the relationship between God and man, act by act, as by the help of some other source-book he might do in any other historical field." This is to "historicise," says Barth — to go "beyond Scripture . . . missing its real content." The Bible is "testimony," not "sourcebook." This reveals what lies at the heart of my disagreement with Barth's view of election. I am not necessarily defending everything in the view of Scripture that Barth is attacking, but his "sourcebook" language is meant in a needlessly and, I should say, baselessly pejorative way. We should not theologically diminish the way in which Scripture presents its matter to us just because it may share some characteristics found in sourcebooks or other historical fields.[60]

57. John 1:1 should not be highlighted at the expense of John 1:14, as far as Barth's theology is concerned. The latter is truly pivotal; see the connection between the "collapse of church dogmatics in modern times" and inattention to John 1:14 (I/2, p. 123). "To say revelation is to say 'The Word became flesh'" (I/1, p. 119), and to say "revelation" is to say "reconciliation."

58. Neither synthesis nor system is in Scripture: I/2, p. 509.

59. In what follows, I am quoting from IV/1, pp. 55-56.

60. Barth's attitude toward Cocceius in *CD* is far from negative. He is certainly criticized at this important juncture in IV/1, as he is on divine Lordship and system or providence (III/3, pp. 31 and 70). If he came to a sticky end, he got off to a good start in *CD,* surviving all dangers in I/1 (pp. 3, 13, and 192); coming out well in I/2 (pp. 284 and 287), despite the criticism of IV/1 being lightly foreshadowed (p. 94), and occupying an interesting and relatively honorable place in the midst of Barth's discussion "The Election of Jesus Christ"

On a wider front, in identifying the problem involved here, James Barr refers to Barth's discussion of biblical theology in I/2 (pp. 483-84). Backing up Nicholas Wolterstorff's account of what Barth is *not* doing, Barr is only reproducing what Barth himself says when he observes that "there is and was in Barth's theology no place for the importance of a separate subject of biblical theology which could bring together the biblical material in a holistic synthesis"; Barth "clearly forbade" an attempt "to make a dogmatic out of the totality of the biblical text."[61] Barth refers to the seventeenth-century theologians in these pages; they mistake the relation of revelation to the biblical witness, which, in the form of recollection and expectation, cannot be systematized as they do so as to produce a biblical-theological foundation for dogmatics, without losing revelation itself. On Barth's account, the trap into which I have fallen in this volume is to turn theology into a synthesis of the witness. As opposed to this, his own theology is *vera theologia,* because it expresses or is a witness to that to which the biblical witness bears witness.[62]

Barth on election, then, can only be satisfactorily treated if we also treat Barth on Scripture and the Word of God in dogmatics.[63] These pastures are too wide for us to enter. For myself, I confess that I find Barth's treatment of Scripture to be mired in illogicality and injustice.[64] Given his

---

in II/2, pp. 94-194. That is not the end of his positive accomplishments: e.g., he recovers in III/3 to make worthy contributions to the subject of divine accompanying (pp. 135-54) and even divine ruling (p. 159). In this respect, Ryan Glomsrud's observations are liable to mislead when he turns from discussion of Barth's *Göttingen Dogmatics* to *Church Dogmatics:* "Karl Barth as Historical Theologian: The Recovery of Reformed Theology in Barth's Early Dogmatics," in *Engaging with Barth,* p. 104.

61. James Barr, *The Concept of Biblical Theology: An Old Testament Perspective* (London: SCM, 1999), pp. 244-45.

62. The content of Christian utterance is determined by dogmatic theology, not by biblical theology; biblical theology gives us its basis (I/1, pp. 4-5). Barth appears to use the terms "exegetical" and "biblical" interchangeably in this context: "Exegetical theology investigates biblical teaching as the basis of our talk about God," something dogmatics must "keep . . . in view" (I/1, p. 16).

63. Barth's treatment is focused in the discussion in I/2, pp. 457-537. It would be possible to pursue criticism here along lines that reconnect us with the question of actualism. Thus, out of fear of system, Barth makes the completely wrongheaded statement that "[p]ure doctrine is an event" (I/2, p. 768).

64. To say that people who wish to identify the Word of God with Scripture are on the path to wanting to "gain control over His Word, to fit it in with our own designs, and thus to shut up ourselves against Him to our own ruin" (I/1, p. 139) is a completely absurd prejudice, as even those who do not wish to make that identification, and who agree that

reiterated ambition to produce a dogmatics that is bound to Scripture, he owes us something more than what he gives us. In the second chapter, I focused on Acts 13:48. Nowhere in *CD,* as far as I can tell, does Barth do anything with this text, although he picks up the passage in which it is embedded (II/2, p. 279). Of itself, that may be no criticism, as he cannot be expected to refer to every verse in Scripture, and he does cover a massive amount of biblical material, exegetically and theologically, in *CD.* However, when Barth announces that "all men are ordained to eternal life" (IV/2, p. 702), does he not owe us something on Acts? Given the stated ambition of *CD,* does he not owe it to us to square theological statements with theological statements in the NT account when the discrepancy appears stark and appears to portend theological, not just verbal, collision? At least, does he not owe it to us to inform us that there is a clear collision, rather than attempting a coherent theological interpretation of Scripture that skips over texts that say something different from what he says in his own constructive theology? After all, Luke's statement is a theological description. Does Barth not owe it to us in his capacity as champion of election as the biblical Word? Instead of giving what he owes, he expresses surprise when he upsets the balance of biblical vocabulary and, with it, upsets concepts in biblical theology and when, subsequently, others cannot

---

this often happens as a matter of fact, should see. The logic in these pages (pp. 137-39) is askew: to say (a) that *x* is a revealed proposition is not to say (b) that Scripture is a fixed sum of revealed propositions; to say (b) is not to say (c) that Scripture can be systematized, and to say (c) is not to say that it can be systematized "like the sections of a corpus of law." When Barth unfolds his exposition of the Word of God as the ground of dogmatics in I/1, he does not trouble to study comprehensively the biblical use of this phrase, majoring, rather, on its christological identification. Barth, apparently a bit disingenuously, announces that "[t]he direct identification between revelation and the Bible which is in fact at issue is not one that we can presuppose or anticipate" (I/1, p. 213). The apparently disingenuous element creeps in because Barth actually does anticipate the negative, i.e., that they should not be identified, before coming on, much later, in I/2, p. 514, to a discussion of such a passage as 2 Tim. 3:16. By then, at the point that we have been told that we cannot anticipate a direct identification, we are also told that "the doctrine of mechanical inspiration" is an expression of the Renaissance man's desire to control. "The Bible is revelation"; "the Bible is inspired"; "the Bible is mechanically inspired": Barth does not make distinctions here. I am not supporting (and not abjuring) the position Barth opposes, but he gives no reason for us to have confidence that exegetical theology does lie at the basis of his dogmatics or that a disciplined conceptual analysis attends his theological exposition. In I/1, p. 119, what the Bible means by the word "revelation" suddenly seems to become important (cf. I/2, p. 56), but we have had no indication that what it means by the phrase "word of God" might also be important beyond the uses to which Barth attends.

see it his way. What is the theological gain of Barth's assurance that he will give special attention to exegesis when discussing election (II/2, p. ix)? The least that can be said is that Barth fails to protect himself effectively against the accusation that his kind of substitution of dogmatic language for biblical theological language amounts to a material alteration of the content of Christian doctrine as it is grounded in Scripture, which it is his stated intention to promote.[65]

If a room is in darkness and we are allowed a single powerful overhead light to illuminate the whole as evenly as possible, it has to be angled very precisely. If it is not, it casts a bright light on some areas but leaves the rest in comparative darkness and the whole is not as well served as it could be. It appears to me that Barth's thought can be conceived along some such lines. Jesus Christ, the light of the world, is the light of Barth's dogmatics, and who can praise him enough and be grateful enough for that? Barth wants the name of Jesus Christ, not our theological conceptions of him, to be the regulative principle of dogmatics. In the course of his work, Barth invests that name with divine, saving, and theological power, with confidence, humility, and joy. A profound consistency pervades *Church Dogmatics:* what we learn is central in volume I, we hear with much the same accent in volume IV and at all points in between. Above all — and this is a high commendation of any theologian — his work is suffused with a persistent, sustained sense of the majesty, glory, sovereign greatness, and goodness of God, whose transcendence is never forgotten or eclipsed even when Christ, in the depths of his humiliation, is also kept in mind, as he constantly is, center picture. Yet, the product is a theology which recasts the biblical witness to that divine and saving power in a way that effectively undoes concepts which lie at its heart.

Jesus Christ as the electing God and Jesus Christ as the elect man do not add up to universal election in Christ. They do not add up, either, to the belief that only the church is elect in Christ. If nothing else is factored in, they actually do not add up to anything with respect to election. If they do add up to anything, it can only be when the limitation which election biblically involves is factored into the sum *from the beginning* in a way that Barth does not. As I have indicated, the argument of this volume has proceeded without reference to Jesus Christ as electing God and elect

65. Barth is capable of proceeding differently; see, e.g., the prominence of his appeal to "the linguistic usage of the Bible" in connection with grace (II/1, p. 353) and the unobtrusive announcement of where to begin our thinking about "vocation" (IV/3.2, p. 515).

man not because this would not have enriched the account, but because it would not have altered it. This is not the scandalous marginalization of him who is Lord of church and world; he is presupposed, and in his light and grace alone have we spoken of anyone's election or predestination. My way of criticizing Barth makes it sound as though his universal election is a deduction from general principles, ascribing to him a theological method which he would abjure. It is worth asking whether, as a matter of fact, he is guilty precisely of a version of this — "reading off" from Jesus Christ what cannot be read off.[66] Perhaps we should admit that he is not or is not quite guilty of this; but, if we do admit that, then universal election is simply presupposed by Barth as the content of revelation, and I find no reason to suppose, presuppose, or conclude that.

Barth moves along skillfully joined conceptual planks in theological construction leaving exegetical awkwardness on the ground, vindicated in his own eyes when theology amounts to the adumbration of exegetical conclusion, untroubled when others protest against the dissonance between his own language and biblical theological language.[67] Theological construction apparently takes dogmatic priority over a (dare I say?) more humble synthesis of biblical data. Why? Why, particularly, in relation to election? The answer has a lot to do with natural theology. It goes without saying that natural knowledge of God contains no knowledge of election,

66. See Berkouwer, *The Triumph of Grace,* p. 198, on abstract principle and theological motif.

67. However we conceive continuity or discontinuity between Barth's early work on Romans and his later *CD,* considered overall, the problem that some of us find in Barth's approach to exegesis in the former remains in the latter. On the one hand, particularly from the preface to the second edition onward, Barth insists that his commentary is a work of exegesis and he attends to exegetical fine points. *The Epistle to the Romans,* trans. E. Hoskyns (London: Oxford University Press, 1933), pp. 2-15. On the other hand, he can expound a text in terms of its theological *res* with little attention to Paul's form of thought; for an example of this, see his commentary on the fifth chapter of Romans, in *Epistle to the Romans,* pp. 149-87. At the level of principle, it might be possible to get away with that. However, we are taken to a new level when Barth's language in what we might call his theological exegesis of a passage actually clashes with the relevant biblical language, and it is arguable that we have a pertinent example of this in Barth's commentary on Romans when he starts talking in language which he will keep up during the exposition of Rom. 9, referring to "the Church of Esau" and its speech (pp. 341-42). Obviously, that is contrary to Pauline usage. Barth combines this with an attempt to be meticulous on exegetical detail when expounding Romans on election, something which is also a feature of *CD* where, for instance, he corrects his earlier reading of the Greek of Rom. 9:5 (II/2, p. 205) and interests himself in the designation of Rufus as "elect" in Rom. 16:13 (p. 429).

and, if God is truly known, Barth insists that he is known as the electing God. Reading Barth's discussion of election, we are constantly alerted to the connection between his defense of universal election in Jesus Christ and the question of knowing God. He confirms his aversion to natural theology early in II/2: a theology which "allows itself on any pretext to be jostled away" from the name of Jesus Christ "is inevitably crowded out by a hypostasised image of man" (p. 4). The unity of revelation and reconciliation is axiomatic for Barth, if we may use the word "axiom" without any necessary technical connotation in relation to theological method. At the beginning of *CD* I/1, we read of this unity (p. 4), and toward its end "we understand God's action in Jesus Christ materially as reconciliation . . . formally as revelation" (p. 434). This will continue throughout *CD.*

Prior to his hefty, explicit treatment of the doctrine of election in II/2, Barth described his position on the knowledge of God from I/1 onward, and nowhere more passionately than in the bitterest of all polemics in *CD,* the polemic against natural theology. Barth fears and fights nothing like natural theology. As an object of distaste, traditional Calvinistic double predestination has nothing on it, and the traditional Catholic *analogia entis* is given hostile treatment on account of what it cedes to natural theology.[68] As far as I can tell, Barth does not systematically distinguish between the claim to a natural knowledge of God and the construction of a natural theology. If there is an implicit distinction, presumably his attitude to it is fairly represented in terms of: "Claim the one and you are headed for the other; the one is the other *in nuce.*" For Barth, to declare that there is a natural knowledge of God is to resist grace (II/1, pp. 25-56). As one commentator has put it, at one point in II/1, "Barth's abrasive tactics are clear: he wants to discredit natural theology by holding it responsible for the crucifixion."[69] The battle against natural knowledge has to be fought constantly, and "every decision to which we are summoned will always be

68. Barth's celebrated remark in the preface of *CD* I/1 comes to mind about the need to be liberated from the "secular misery" of a traditional Roman Catholic view of the natural knowledge of God. "I regard the *analogia entis* as the invention of Antichrist, and I believe that because of it it is impossible ever to become a Roman Catholic, all other reasons for not doing so being to my mind short-sighted and trivial" (p. xiii). My *Doktorvater,* Hans Frei, no friend at all to natural theology (or to Brunner in particular), referred to this in tutorial conversation, with a tinge of uncharacteristic exasperation toward Barth, as an "ill-considered blast of cold air."

69. Robert B. Price, *Letters of the Divine Word: The Perfections of God in Karl Barth's "Church Dogmatics"* (London and New York: T. & T. Clark, 2011), p. 111.

in the last resort a decision on this point," the point being "that we know God in Jesus Christ alone" (II/1, pp. 318-19). According to Barth, devotees of natural knowledge believe that "what the Bible calls death is only sickness. What it calls darkness is simply twilight. What it calls incapability is merely weakness. What it calls ignorance is only confusion. The grace of God which comes to man [according to an outlook which claims natural knowledge] does not really come to lost sinners" (II/1, p. 105).

This turns out to parallel the accusation Brunner made against Barth on election. Barth cites Brunner on natural theology as early as the first section of the second paragraph of the introduction to *CD,* where he sets his face and the course of dogmatics in an opposite direction (I/1, p. 27).[70] Brunner, for his part, offering his judgment on the potential universalism which arises out of Barth's doctrine of election, remarks that Barth's humans "are like people who seem to be perishing in a stormy sea. But in reality they are not in a sea where one can drown, but in shallow water, where it is impossible to drown. Only they do not know it."[71] Who plays down the human plight — Brunner or Barth, the one who affirms natural knowledge or the one who affirms universal election? The counteraccusations have something of a mirror-image quality. From Barth's point of view, universal election and natural knowledge are in grim combat, at grisly odds; from Brunner's, universal election and saving need are in that position.[72]

In opposing natural theology in the corpus of his work, Barth cites a case more significant than that of Brunner and less well known, the case of the Swiss Lutheran late-seventeenth- and early-eighteenth-century theologian Johann Franz Buddeus. Barth was worried that Brunner's program was a repristination of Buddeus's, and according to Barth's *Protestant Theology in the Nineteenth Century,* you could not keep worse theological company (even if he was a nice man).[73] It was Buddeus who steered Prot-

70. Barth is back with Brunner just two pages later, on pp. 29-30.

71. Brunner, *Christian Doctrine of God,* p. 351. Whatever meaning death now has for humanity, it is "[c]ertainly not our condemnation, perdition and negation" (Barth, *CD* III/2, p. 604). Nothingness "can therefore injure but no longer kill or destroy" us (III/3, p. 293). I leave aside the question of whether the fact that Barth does not always speak in this way modifies or confuses his stance.

72. Yet, Brunner has considerably weakened his position with respect to Barth — not to mention any weaknesses that are intrinsic to his argument on this point — by the way he had already set forth his own openness to universal salvation. *Christian Doctrine of God,* pp. 334-36.

73. Barth, *Protestant Theology in the Nineteenth Century: Its Background and History* (London: SCM, 1972), pp. 141-73. Buddeus also appears in the role of villain in *CD,* but

estant theology to the fatal point of launching a "dogmatics" with a positive discussion of the natural knowledge of God. This means that Jesus Christ "is no longer accepted as our One and All and we are secretly dissatisfied with His lordship and consolation" (I/2, pp. 29-30). Barth certainly gets his revenge on Buddeus in his own *Church Dogmatics.* If Buddeus wrecks dogmatics by beginning with the natural knowledge of God, Barth will make quite sure that we will repel all thought of it before we even get to Scripture. Faced with the need to exegete Scripture *after* he has already ruled out natural knowledge on theological grounds, Barth observes that "it is *a priori* extremely improbable" that a witness to God independent of his own revelation will be taught in Scripture (II/1, p. 102). The a priori actually takes us to the heart of the conflict, and it bears similarities to what we have encountered with respect to election. Barth indicts Buddeus for the massive theological a priori that is natural theology, skewing dogmatics to fatal effect, as shown by the advent of Schleiermacher, inheritor of the authentic Buddean legacy.[74] Buddeus would have calmly replied that anyone who, in dogmatic exposition, has stitched up the question of natural knowledge before even considering the biblical data which Buddeus invokes in its favor had better consider whether there is an a priori mote in his own eye or (for Buddeus was irenic) a speck of at least equal size to the one Barth detects in Buddeus's theological eye.

For Barth, natural knowledge is not an authentic correlate to a form of revelation, not even a general revelation. It is the ominously realized dream of human reason. It comes up with another God, "one whose action is not essential to him."[75] It is the product of "intrinsically godless reason" (I/1, p. 28). In his sustained, uncompromising, shrill, and bitter assault on natural knowledge of God and natural theology in II/1, Barth cannot conceive of this claim or enterprise as anything except the work of god-

---

here he shares the honors with Salomon van Til (I/2, pp. 288-89). Cf. Barth's reference at the beginning of *CD* to what happened in the last half of the eighteenth century (I/1, p. 28). Barth is effectively making substantially the same connection here between Brunner and the eighteenth century as he makes between Brunner and Buddeus in John Baillie, ed., *Natural Theology* (London: Bles, 1946), p. 110. (Buddeus actually puts in a very early appearance in I/1 in connection with theology as a *scientia* [p. 7].)

74. Barth's account of the history of nineteenth-century Protestant theology begins with Schleiermacher (pp. 425-73), but considerably more time has been spent on the background than is subsequently spent on the theology. Buddeus is the éminence grise silhouetted against that background which he helped to shape.

75. Busch, *The Great Passion,* p. 69.

less humanity exalting itself against God and grace.[76] The possibility of a humble, submissive attitude toward general revelation is apparently not on Barth's radar. No volume in *CD* better reveals what is driving and shaping Barth's theology. Assaults on natural theology also feature in the middle of Barth's discussion of election.[77] Natural theology conjures up a God other than the God of Jesus Christ, other than Jesus Christ himself. That is the threat of threats in dogmatics, preaching, church, and life. It is a vast presumption. More than a *consequence,* moralistic works-righteousness is the *root* of natural theology, which is never the product of well-meaning spiritual innocence.

In the principle of his opposition to works-righteousness, Barth appears to join the Protestant Reformers wholeheartedly. At first glance, he adheres to the Reformation *sola gratia* and *sola fide* for good Reformation reasons.[78] At second glance, there seems to be a difference of emphasis. The Reformers combated the self-righteousness of pride in justification by works, but also — as the Lutheran confessions and writings evidence especially well — the problem of seeking justification by works is that it generates incessant torment of conscience and despair.[79] In his corpus as a whole, Barth seems to differ a bit here in his emphasis: where Luther pits grace and faith against *self-doubt* (though he does so against pride as well),

76. See especially pp. 63-178.

77. See particularly the excursus in II/2, pp. 127-45 and 158-61.

78. Yet, Brevard Childs found something lacking in Barth's treatment of faith compared to the power of Calvin's discussion; Barth's seems "almost listless in comparison, say, to his chapter on election." *Biblical Theology of the Old and New Testaments: Theological Reflection on the Christian Bible* (London: SCM, 1992), p. 621. He has in mind discussions in I/1 and IV/1.

79. Luther observed that "it is necessary either to despair when one understands the law, but is ignorant of the grace of God, or, one must trust in one's self, not understanding the law and despising the wrath of God." "Theses concerning Faith and Law," in *Works,* vol. 34 (Philadelphia: Muhlenberg, 1960), pp. 116-17 (thesis 42 on "Law"). Despite the apparent differences between Melanchthon's and Luther's experience of life, it is the connection of justification to conscience and its terrors which strikes us on reading Melanchthon's introduction to his commentary on Romans, where he follows up some of the concerns developed in his *Loci Communes.* Philipp Melanchthon, *Commentary on Romans,* trans. Fred Kramer (St. Louis: Concordia, 1992), pp. 11-58. (This is the 1540 edition.) See, too, the impressive Martin Chemnitz, who begins his examination of Tridentine teaching on justification with the words: "This is the chief topic in the Christian doctrine. For anxious and terrified minds which wrestle with sin and with the wrath of God seek this one haven, how they can have a reconciled and gracious God." *Examination of the Council of Trent: Part 1,* trans. Fred Kramer (St. Louis: Concordia, 1971), p. 461.

Barth pits them against *self-confidence,* if we may lamentably modernize and thus domesticate the issue in these formulations. However, against third glances there is no law, and, after working through Barth's uncompromising denunciations of natural theology through II/1, we are surely bound to wonder if his problem is existentially related to Luther's, after all. Exactly how closely is a moot point; but they are both asking: How can I find a gracious God? At the risk of indulging in unhealthy and presumptuous psychoanalysis in bad taste, the virulence of Barth's attack on natural theology invites the question of whether existential fear is a driver. Natural theology will not yield a gracious God, and *nothing* must cloud our discovery of him in Jesus Christ. The question on which we touched earlier comes round: Does a kind of fear drive Barth's ontological Trinitarian exploration beyond what is really intellectually safe in order to find spiritual safety?[80]

In the social and political circumstances attending Barth's clash with Brunner, it should certainly be possible to sympathize with anyone who, like Barth, experienced a prolonged shudder of horror at learning that now, of all times in the history of the church and of theology, there might be "another task" of theology alongside dogmatics, a task which embraced natural theology. However, Barth believed that we cannot tolerate theological differences on this point at any place and time, not just in his own place and time, and aspired to "a purifying of the Church not only from the concretely new point at issue but from all natural theology" (II/1, p. 175). How did Barth get himself (if that is not too tendentious a way of putting it) into the opposite situation to that of Brunner — Brunner fearing the potential of universalism much more than natural theology, Barth fearing natural theology much more than the possibility of universalism?[81]

Barth described theology as *eine fröhliche Wissenschaft,* a "joyous science."[82] This replicates the title of Nietzsche's book of that title.[83] *CD*

80. See III/2, pp. 597-98; pp. 612-24. A lot of anxiety creeps into IV/4, pp. 136 and 142.

81. While I am not interested in defending a position here on the natural knowledge of God and can sympathize with some of Barth's difficulties with natural theology, I believe that theological reason deserts him in the course of great stretches of his attack and that he loads onto the natural knowledge of God and natural theology the sins of some of its forms which may well deserve opprobrium, but not at the cost of wholesale dogmatic prejudice.

82. Karl Barth, *Fragments Grave and Gay* (London and Glasgow: Collins, 1971), p. 125, quoted by Martin Rumscheidt. Cf. Paul Ricoeur's description of his own philosophy as "a style of 'yes' and not a style of 'no,' and perhaps even a style characterized by joy and not by anguish," quoted by Kevin J. Vanhoozer, *Biblical Narrative in the Philosophy of Paul Ricoeur: A Study in Hermeneutics and Theology* (Cambridge: Cambridge University Press, 1990), p. 6.

83. Except that *Die* replaces *Eine* in Nietzsche's title. Nietzsche taught Barth's father

is a song of joy — although Barth might scowl at the echo of Beethoven in that description — and, in that respect, its mood presents a suggestive contrast to the relative turbulence of Calvin's *Institutes.* The brief Barthian work which best acquaints us with this aspect of Barth's theological mood is probably his *Evangelical Theology.*[84] Martin Rumscheidt's address at the memorial service for Karl Barth in the University of Toronto is worth consulting not only for his general emphasis on the point under consideration but also for his particular identification of Barth's humor as characteristically Basel humor.[85] Humor and joy are not the same thing, but Rumscheidt justifiably associates them in Barth's theological enterprise.

In Barthian perspective, natural theology robs authentic church theology of joy. Yet, is Barth's own joy properly proportionate and modulated, from a theological point of view? Does Barth not connive at the eclipse of biblical tragedy, and does this connivance not account for both his dismay at claims that God is naturally known, which means not known in grace, and his insistence on indiscriminate election? Barth loved Mozart, and there is just a dash of seriousness when, in his preface to III/4, he castigated his Dutch neo-Calvinist critics for disparaging Mozart, calling them "men of stupid, cold and stony hearts to whom we need not listen" (p. xiii).[86] Mozart is the musician of joy. He did not ignore suffering and thought about death every day, but, absorbing it into his music, he simply let creation sing as it should.[87] Contrast Beethoven and Brahms — somber.[88]

What Barth says about Mozart brightly illuminates his theology.

---

in the Swiss equivalent of high school, according to Eberhard Busch, *Karl Barth: His Life from Letters and Autobiographical Texts* (London: SCM, 1976), p. 3.

84. Karl Barth, *Evangelical Theology* (London and Glasgow: Collins, 1963), is required reading if we want to get a feel for Barth's conviction that dogmatics trades in the currency of joyous knowledge.

85. Published as an epilogue in *Fragments Grave and Gay,* pp. 123-27. Note Barth's reference to Basel in his preface to *CD* II/2 (p. ix). Cf. Busch, *The Great Passion,* p. 4.

86. However, Barth exonerates Berkouwer from this criticism in the preface of IV/2, playfully returning to Mozart at the same time (p. xii). See IV/3.1, pp. 173-74 on Berkouwer, but also what actually amounts to quite a high commendation in IV/2, p. 501. Much earlier, Barth had said: "I betray no secret in alluding to the fundamental (and, if I may say so, mutual) aversion which exists between the 'historical' Calvinism that follows in the footsteps of A. Kuyper and the Reformed theology represented here" (I/2, p. 83).

87. Barth's whole exposition should be read in *Wolfgang Amadeus Mozart* (Grand Rapids: Eerdmans, 1986), but for Barth's approbation of Mozart's explicit or implicit sentiments on death, titanism, or the unity of heaven and earth, joy and weeping, see especially pp. 32-54.

88. Barth, *The Humanity of God* (London and Glasgow: Collins, 1961), p. 87.

After grazing for a while in the pastures of *CD,* it is impossible to read Barth's account of Mozart without realizing that Barth seeks to emulate in dogmatics what Mozart achieved in music. Whether we can press this as far as a comparison of structure between Mozart's music and *CD,* I am not sure. Our question at this point is whether it is possible to avoid tragedy even at the apex of biblical eschatology, when God is publicly victorious. Reading the climax of the book of Revelation, it seems not. The eschatological climax is not bathed in unclouded light. Barth's theological trajectory in the direction of universalism appears to me to marginalize the reality of the shadow and tragedy in Revelation in order to have no truck with "infinite melancholy" (III/3, p. 298). Barth abjures "titanic" infinite melancholy. Hans Frei remarked that tragic imagination was the one form of imagination for which Barth had little sympathy: " 'Titanism,' he used to call it depreciatingly and wince whenever he saw it raising its classical or romanticized head."[89] "Biblical head" too, it seems to me. Biblical "tragedy," to apply ordinary-language usage to biblical materials, is not classical or romanticized tragedy, but, in this case, Barth's resistance to the latter forms seems to me to signal resistance to an element in Scripture.[90] Barth's combat on behalf of election and against natural theology apparently takes place against the background of his resistance to this assortment of literary and theological tragedies. In an essay on Schleiermacher and Barth, Alan Torrance interpreted the connection between Barth's remarks on music and his theological optimism in terms of Barth's personal experience of life as one that was certainly not free of family tragedies, but was free of the experience of "guilt, or national shame, or the humiliation of his cause."[91] Torrance prescribed as a remedy some Beethoven and Brahms, and threw some Rachmaninov into the bargain.[92]

89. Frei, "Karl Barth: Theologian," in *Theology and Narrative: Selected Essays* (Oxford: Oxford University Press, 1993), p. 175.

90. It is certainly risky to use the word "tragedy" to cover all these cases, but my argument does not hinge on the precise term to use to refer to the end of the biblical drama. We have to be precise on terminology before deciding whether to go along with Wittgenstein here and inquire into its implications for Christianity. "Tragedy is something non-Jewish. Mendelssohn is, I suppose, the most untragic of composers." *Culture and Value,* p. 1.

91. Torrance, "Christian Experience and Divine Revelation in the Theologies of Friedrich Schleiermacher and Karl Barth," in *Christian Experience in Theology and Life,* ed. I. Howard Marshall (Edinburgh: Rutherford House, 1988), pp. 83-113, here p. 111.

92. For an instructive contrast, see Gabriel Marcel, whom I named alongside Barth in the preface to this volume. In *Awakenings* (Milwaukee: Marquette University Press, 2002), Marcel speaks of the conjunction of sorrow and joy in Beethoven (p. 111); in *Being and*

In *Fragments Grave and Gay,* Barth professed admiration for Kierkegaard, professing also the desire to go beyond him and go beyond him into joy.[93] Kierkegaard's work *The Sickness unto Death,* I believe, shows that Kierkegaard understood far better than did Barth the ultimate seriousness of sin as Scripture portrays it. Kierkegaard understood the human plight better than did Barth. After talking about the relation of sin to atonement in terms diametrically contrary to those of Barth, Kierkegaard says: " 'Now I have spoken,' declares God in heaven, 'we shall discuss it again in eternity. In the meantime, you can do what you want, but judgment is at hand.' "[94] We do not have to endorse this formulation *tout court* to judge it a truer word than the putative word of a universal "Yes" in election where that "Yes" generates the programmatic, perilous, and completely unbiblical declaration by Barth that the choice of "godless man" against God "is void" (II/2, p. 306).

Having, of what he learned through a phrase in Brahms (p. 136). In *CD* Barth claims that, for Mozart, "trouble cannot degenerate into tragedy" (III/3, p. 298). The general question of Barth's attitude toward dogmatics arises here. In IV/3.2, Barth reminds us of what he said in II/1 about theology as a "singularly beautiful and joyous science," adding "so that it is only willingly and cheerfully or not at all that we can be theologians" (p. 881). This deserves careful pondering. Barth's reference to Anselm in II/1 certainly disposes me to concur in his judgment on the beauty of theology there (p. 656). Yet, in a world of sin and suffering, is it only possible to allude to "the most relevant and beautiful problems in dogmatics" (in the preface to I/1, p. xiv) because one maintains a hopeful universalism? Can dogmatic problems be beautiful when universal salvation is not the human destiny?

93. Barth, *Fragments Grave and Gay,* pp. 95-104.

94. Kierkegaard, *The Sickness unto Death: A Christian Psychological Exposition for Upbuilding and Awakening,* trans. H. Hong and E. Hong (Princeton: Princeton University Press, 1980), p. 122.

Index